LEARNING CHINESE, TURNING CHINESE

In this book Edward McDonald takes a fresh look at issues of language in Chinese studies. He takes the viewpoint of the university student of Chinese with the ultimate goal of becoming 'sinophone': that is, developing a fluency and facility at operating in Chinese-language contexts comparable to their own mother tongue. While the entry point for most potential sinophones is the Chinese language classroom, the kinds of 'language' and 'culture' on offer there are rarely questioned, and the links between the forms of the language and the situations in which they may be used are rarely drawn. The author's explorations of Chinese studies illustrate the crucial link between becoming sinophone and developing a sinophone identity – learning Chinese *and* turning Chinese.

Including chapters on:

- relating text to context in learning Chinese;
- the social and political contexts of language learning;
- myths about Chinese characters;
- language reform and nationalism in modern China;
- critical discourse analysis of popular culture;
- ethnicity and identity in language learning.

This book will be invaluable for all Chinese language students and teachers, and those with an interest in Chinese linguistics, linguistic anthropology, critical discourse analysis and language education.

Edward McDonald is currently Lecturer in Chinese at the University of Auckland, and has taught Chinese language, music, linguistics and semiotics at universities in Australia, China, and Singapore.

ASIA'S TRANSFORMATIONS
Edited by Mark Selden
Cornell University, USA

The books in this series explore the political, social, economic and cultural consequences of Asia's transformations in the twentieth and twenty-first centuries. The series emphasizes the tumultuous interplay of local, national, regional and global forces as Asia bids to become the hub of the world economy. While focusing on the contemporary, it also looks back to analyse the antecedents of Asia's contested rise.

This series comprises several strands:

Asia's Transformations
Titles include:

Debating Human Rights*
Critical essays from the United States and Asia
Edited by Peter Van Ness

Hong Kong's History*
State and society under colonial rule
Edited by Tak-Wing Ngo

Japan's Comfort Women*
Sexual slavery and prostitution during World War II and the US occupation
Yuki Tanaka

Opium, Empire and the Global Political Economy*
Carl A. Trocki

Chinese Society*
Change, conflict and resistance
Edited by Elizabeth J. Perry and Mark Selden

Mao's Children in the New China*
Voices from the Red Guard generation
Yarong Jiang and David Ashley

Remaking the Chinese State*
Strategies, society and security
Edited by Chien-min Chao and Bruce J. Dickson

Korean Society*
Civil society, democracy and the state
Edited by Charles K. Armstrong

The Making of Modern Korea*
Adrian Buzo

The Resurgence of East Asia*
500, 150 and 50 year perspectives
Edited by Giovanni Arrighi, Takeshi Hamashita and Mark Selden

Chinese Society (second edition)*
Change, conflict and resistance
Edited by Elizabeth J. Perry and Mark Selden

Ethnicity in Asia*
Edited by Colin Mackerras

The Battle for Asia*
From decolonization to globalization
Mark T. Berger

State and Society in Modern Rangoon
Donald M. Seekins

Learning Chinese, Turning Chinese
Challenges to becoming sinophone in a globalised world
Edward McDonald

Asia's Great Cities

Each volume aims to capture the heartbeat of the contemporary city from multiple perspectives emblematic of the authors own deep familiarity with the distinctive faces of the city, its history, society, culture, politics and economics, and its evolving position in national, regional and global frameworks. While most volumes emphasize urban developments since the Second World War, some pay close attention to the legacy of the longue durée in shaping the contemporary. Thematic and comparative volumes address such themes as urbanization, economic and financial linkages, architecture and space, wealth and power, gendered relationships, planning and anarchy, and ethnographies in national and regional perspective. Titles include:

Bangkok*
Place, practice and representation
Marc Askew

The City in South Asia
James Heitzman

Representing Calcutta*
Modernity, nationalism and the colonial uncanny
Swati Chattopadhyay

Global Shanghai, 1850–2010*
A history in fragments
Jeffrey N. Wasserstrom

Hong Kong*
Becoming a global city
Stephen Chiu and Tai-Lok Lui

Singapore*
Wealth, power and the culture of control
Carl A. Trocki

Asia.com

Asia.com is a series which focuses on the ways in which new information and communication technologies are influencing politics, society and culture in Asia. Titles include:

Japanese Cybercultures*
Edited by Mark McLelland and Nanette Gottlieb

The Internet in Indonesia's New Democracy*
David T. Hill and Krishna Sen

Asia.com*
Asia encounters the Internet
Edited by K. C. Ho, Randolph Kluver and Kenneth C. C. Yang

Chinese Cyberspaces*
Technological changes and political effects
Edited by Jens Damm and Simona Thomas

Mobile Media in the Asia-Pacific
Gender and the art of being mobile
Larissa Hjorth

Literature and Society
Literature and Society is a series that seeks to demonstrate the ways in which
Asian literature is influenced by the politics, society and culture in which it is
produced. Titles include:

The Body in Postwar Japanese
Fiction
Douglas N. Slaymaker

Chinese Women Writers and the
Feminist Imagination, 1905–1948*
Haiping Yan

Routledge Studies in Asia's Transformations
Routledge Studies in Asia's Transformations is a forum for innovative new
research intended for a high-level specialist readership. Titles include:

The American Occupation of Japan
and Okinawa*
Literature and memory
Michael Molasky

Koreans in Japan*
Critical voices from the margin
Edited by Sonia Ryang

Internationalizing the Pacific
The United States, Japan and the
Institute of Pacific Relations in war
and peace, 1919–1945
Tomoko Akami

Imperialism in South East Asia*
'A fleeting, passing phase'
Nicholas Tarling

Chinese Media, Global Contexts*
Edited by Chin-Chuan Lee

Remaking Citizenship in Hong
Kong*
Community, nation and the global city
Edited by Agnes S. Ku and Ngai Pun

Japanese Industrial Governance
Protectionism and the licensing state
Yul Sohn

Developmental Dilemmas*
Land reform and institutional change
in China
Edited by Peter Ho

Genders, Transgenders and
Sexualities in Japan*
Edited by Mark McLelland and Romit
Dasgupta

Fertility, Family Planning
and Population Policy in
China*
Edited by Dudley L. Poston,
Che-Fu Lee, Chiung-Fang Chang,
Sherry L. McKibben and
Carol S. Walther

Japanese Diasporas*
Unsung pasts, conflicting presents and
uncertain futures
Edited by Nobuko Adachi

Pirate Modernity
Delhi's media urbanism
Ravi Sundaram

China on Video
Smaller screen realities
Paola Voci

The World Bank and the post-Washington Consensus in Vietnam and Indonesia
Inheritance of loss
Susan Engel

Overseas Chinese, Ethnic Minorities and Nationalism
De-centering China
Elena Barabantseva

Critical Asian Scholarship

Critical Asian Scholarship is a series intended to showcase the most important individual contributions to scholarship in Asian Studies. Each of the volumes presents a leading Asian scholar addressing themes that are central to his or her most significant and lasting contribution to Asian studies. The series is committed to the rich variety of research and writing on Asia, and is not restricted to any particular discipline, theoretical approach or geographical expertise. Titles include:

Southeast Asia*
A testament
George McT. Kahin

Women and the Family in Chinese History*
Patricia Buckley Ebrey

China Unbound*
Evolving perspectives on the Chinese past
Paul A. Cohen

China's Past, China's Future*
Energy, food, environment
Vaclav Smil

The Chinese State in Ming Society*
Timothy Brook

China, East Asia and the Global Economy*
Regional and historical perspectives
Takeshi Hamashita
Edited by Mark Selden and Linda Grove

The Global and Regional in China's Nation-Formation*
Prasenjit Duara

* Available in paperback

LEARNING CHINESE, TURNING CHINESE

Challenges to becoming sinophone in a globalised world

Edward McDonald

Routledge
Taylor & Francis Group

LONDON AND NEW YORK

First published 2011
by Routledge
2 Park Square, Milton Park, Abingdon, Oxon OX14 4RN

Simultaneously published in the USA and Canada
by Routledge
270 Madison Avenue, New York, NY 10016

Routledge is an imprint of the Taylor & Francis Group, an informa business

© 2011 Edward McDonald
The right of Edward McDonald to be identified as author of this work
has been asserted by him in accordance with sections 77 and 78 of the
Copyright, Designs and Patents Act 1988.

Typeset in Times New Roman by
Book Now Ltd, London
Printed and bound in Great Britain by CPI Antony Rowe Ltd.

British Library Cataloguing in Publication Data
A catalogue record for this book is available from the British Library

Library of Congress Cataloging in Publication Data
McDonald, Edward.
Learning Chinese, Turning Chinese: Challenges to becoming Sinophone in a globalised
world / Edward McDonald.
    p. cm. — (Asia's transformations)
1. Chinese language—Study and teaching. 2. Second language acquisition. 3. Chinese
language—Globalization. I. Title.
PL1065.M43 2010
495.1'80071—dc22
2010018999

ISBN 978–0–415–55941–6 (hbk)
ISBN 978–0–415–55942–3 (pbk)
ISBN 978–0–203–83980–5 (ebk)

To my 'teacher-parents' M.L. and M.A.K.H.
and to my 'student-siblings'
J.B., J.X.K., G.Y.H., L.K.K. and J.O.
who helped me make sense of China and Chinese

承蒙多位学术前辈指引和指正
帮助我理解中国语文与文化
深为感激
谨将此书献给
师长陈老师、韩老师
学长老金、季大哥、老高、陆大姐、老欧

CONTENTS

PART C
Getting over the Walls of Discourse 153

ACKNOWLEDGEMENTS

I first set out on the sinophone path almost 30 years ago with very little if any idea where the journey was to take me. The practical, intellectual and emotional debts incurred during this period of living and working in and on China would require another whole book to do them justice, one containing much anecdote and personal history. What I will attempt here is the more modest task of mentioning the teachers, friends and colleagues who have accompanied me on this journey, from and with whom I have learned most of what I know about China; and then thanking those who contributed directly to the writing of this book.

Then Department of Oriental Studies at the University of Sydney was my Chinese alma mater. Founder and Head of that department, the late Professor A.R. Davis, was sadly taken from us in only my second year in the department, but his influence and personality were palpable throughout my undergraduate years. His loyal lieutenants, the late Dr Agnes Stefanowska and the very much still with us Dr Mabel Lee, carried forward the legacy of his classical approach; Mabel and Dr Lily Lee ensured that we were equipped with knowledge and skills for the contemporary Chinese world as well; and the late Professor Liu Wei-ping, the late Dr Raymond Hsu, Dr Tony Prince, and Mr Toshihiko Kobayashi rounded out our repertoire of 文史哲. My 同学们 Harriet Parsons, Michael Paton, Glen Wines, Debbie Goh, Kyung-sook Langley, Debbie Kong, John Varga, Lindsay Lee, Cathy Duloy, Sally Baird and the late Bronwyn Thomas explored the sinophone path with me, while my 学长们 Ben Penny, Sally Sussman, Sarah Biddulph and Steven Brent showed me in advance some of the ways I might explore.

When I graduated to the other side of the classroom, first with a Summer School course in Elementary Chinese at the University of Sydney, and then with Elementary Grammar and Intermediate Conversation in the undergraduate program at Macquarie University, the students in my first year of teaching must have wondered exactly what qualified me to teach them (about) Chinese, but they proved very indulgent to a raw novice, and I remain grateful to them and all my students since for keeping me up to the mark despite my many and manifest inadequacies. Colleagues who have provided support and encouragement in my Chinese teaching career include: at the University of Sydney, Michael Halliday, John Keenan, Lily Lee, Mabel Lee, Michael Paton, Jane Simpson, Linda Tsung, Maghiel van Crevel, Wang Yiyan; at Macquarie University, Jean Brick, Shirley Chan, Lance Eccles, Jennifer Grant, David Holm, Danny Kane, Qian Yan; at the University of New South Wales; Philip Lee, Michael Schenzer, Wai Ling Yeung, Zhong Yong; at the University of Western Sydney, Madeleine Cincotta.

The Chinese Department at Macquarie University became my second alma mater. Lance Eccles was a patient and reliable support there, a regular correspondent during my years at Beida, the constant recipient of my half-baked ideas on the teaching of Chinese grammar, and always generous with advice and practical help. David Holm supported several teaching grants and proved open to exploring new and unorthodox paths for the teaching of Chinese; Jean Brick, Li Jingbing, and Bian Xiaoxia, alongside Lance as a constant guiding hand, helped map out those paths with me. I would like to extend a particularly warm expression of gratitude to the current Head of Chinese, Danny Kane, a regular intellectual 'sparring partner' over many years, both face to face and via email. Two hundred years ago our exchanges may well have been published in a series of 'learned correspondence', and Danny has been a constant source of ideas and references. Although he would no doubt disagree with many of the claims put forward particularly in Chapters 4 and 5 of this book, they could not have been written without his input.

The Peking University English Department was my first institutional home in China and to its then Dean, Professor Hu Zhuanglin, I owe an enormous debt of gratitude, not simply for organising a joint academic program for me with the Chinese Department under the late and sorely missed Professor Ye Feisheng, but also for introducing me to then PhD candidate, now Professor Gao Yihong. The Linguistics Salon which she founded along with He Wei, Liu Feng, Liu Shisheng, Qian Jun, Wang Ling, Zhang Hua and myself was a stimulating and friendly forum for the exchange of ideas and is still going strong 20 years on. Most recently Lao Gao convened an extraordinary session of the 小沙龙 along with Lin Mengxi, Liu Honggang, Song Chengfang, and Xu Nanxiao, for much good talk on 'sinophone' and 中国通 and some timely suggestions for modifications to the book's subtitle. In the Chinese Department, I learned much from Lu Jianming, Ma Zhen, and the late Xu Tongqiang, while Guo Rui and Wang Jing helped me negotiate the interpersonal as well as intellectual demands of 中国语言学.

Lao Gao also introduced me to the work of Shen Xiaolong, with whom I entered on a more than decade long intellectual exchange which will hopefully come to fruition sooner than later in the form of a final draft of our much promised 'East-West dialogue on language and culture'. More recently Andy Kirkpatrick of the Hong Kong Institute of Education brought me on to the

Linguistics Node of the Creation of Modern Academic Disciplines in China project, a multidisciplinary endeavour launched and coordinated by John Makeham from the Australian National University, which has broadened my understanding of the history of linguistics in China as part of the general intellectual ferment of the late nineteenth and early twentieth centuries, and Andy and K.K. Luke of Nanyang Technological University have been patient and supportive companions in the herding-cat-like activity of assembling contributors for an ever-changing edited volume.

My first year in China was funded by a Rotary International Understanding Award, and I am grateful to the members of the St Ives (Sydney) branch of Rotary, especially Michael Hook and Neville Chambers, for their welcome and support; Mr Kaydn Griffin capably managed the finances from Sydney. The Australia-China Council funded my second year and I am grateful to the Council and its then Chair, the Hon. E.G. Whitlam, AC QC, as well as the Chair during my recent stay in China, Dr John Yu, AC. My first weeks in Beijing were immeasurably helped by Thelma Chow, Tom Christensen, Li Hu, Wang Qiang, and Yin Hui. My 勺园同学 navigated the cross-cultural shoals with me, especially the 'United Colours of Shaoyuan' – Christina Boukouka, Tom Christensen, Kyllikki Kivijarvi, Josh Klenbort, Obess, Wang Da and Wang Xiaolong – and the 'reading group' fronted by Emily Purser with Mary Hirsch, Karin Myhre and Gin Simpson; as well as an international smorgasboard including Suzanne Bassett, Helen Calle, Leo S. Chang, Paul Connolly, Benedikta Dorer, Michel Hockx, Itami Tadashi, Nouredine Kassé, Maria Lo Guidice, Laurent Malvesin, Rod McDonald, Paula Nichols, Sermsak Sanvanitphattana (Por), Czesek Tubilewicz, and Naris Wasinanon.

In Beijing, Dr Bruce Doar has been a figure of wonder to me from my early days in the Northern Capital, which I first experienced in his company. His strongly Aussie-accented Chinese belies an enormous vocabulary and voracious command of written Chinese ancient and modern, not to mention being an unparalleled source of gossip; the late Sue Dewar was the perfect foil to him and continues to be sorely missed. Brian Wallace, in creating the first private gallery for contemporary Chinese art in Beijing, to which process I was lucky enough to be a witness, has immeasurably broadened my visual horizons as well as uncomplainingly putting me up – not to mention putting up with me – on frequent visits to Beijing. Other companions of my first Beijing adventure include Paul Crook, Eugene Chang, Bobbie Lees, Jeff Turner, Henry Wang, Zhen Li, and all the interesting and varied people I met at the great meeting place that was Zhen Li's apartment near the Xiyuan Hotel.

In more recent times in Beijing, through and around 'Bulang' and the Red Gate Gallery – and facilitated always by the 'Guo Dynasty' of Xiao Guo and Shao Qi, and Xiao Guo and Xiao Han – I have benefited also from linguistic and cultural interactions with John Brennan, 'Neo' Chen Hongjie, Chen Xin, Chi Peng, Kate Croll, Jayne Dyer, Reg Dyer, Judy Farquhar, Guan Wei, Guo Jian, Guo Wei, Li Liang, Eric Ling Yuhui, Liu Ding, Liu Ping, Madeleine O'Dea, Yusuf Osman,

Tony Scott, Wang Zhiyuan, Wang Zongbo, Xu Ming, George Yeo, Liyu Yeo, Zhang Tao and Jack Zhao Zhiwei. Dave and Philippa Kelly have provided beds, keyboards and much good talk and hospitality. Alex Pearson through her 'house concerts' provided a focus for much musicking and general good times shared with the other members of 'Hoar M'Horrie' – Jo Lusby, Matt Forney, Meilan Frame and Luna Peng – as well as with Bob Blanch, Anne Burraston, Gillian Cull, Paul Eldon, Nancy Fraser, Martina Goecke, Tjy Yingliu, Jack Li, Kaye Marshall, Suzie Michaelis, Dan Sanderson and Nick Smith; while The Bookworm which Alex founded continues to provide a space for the civilised activities of reading and eating and drinking and meeting. Klemens Affandy and Rob Delaney provided a focus and more often than not a venue for the 哥们儿 to get together, along with Cameron Bai, M. Le Baron, Chang Yuping, Fred Chen, Park Yong Chua, Deng Zong, Luis Espino, Fu Hao, Gustavo Infante, Jason Leow, Alex Ng, Eithan Plasse, Qiao Lüshi, Olivier Rousselet, Andrew Ryan, Ek Soltong Sitthimet, Stone Shen, Sun Daifu, Darren Thng, Craig Watts, Tars Wong and Zhou Daifu; other venues of a late night nature often found gathered Scott Aurong, Cao Shengyu, Daniel Feng, Wing Ho, Huang Jiankun, Daniel Hui, Jet Liu, Liu Ka, Sun Jun, Val Thompson, AJ Wang, Reds Wang, Sandy Wang Jin, Allon Wong, Jim Xu Jun, Zhang Yi and Zhu Wenchang.

From my time at the National University of Singapore, Desmond Allison, Umberto Ansaldo, Bao Zhiming, Madalena Cruz-Ferreira, Mark Donahue, Ho Chee Lick, Lee Cher Leng, Laurence Leong, Lisa Lim, Daisy Ng, Ni Yibin, Kay O'Halloran, Srilata Ravi, Chitra Sankaran, Jim St André, Chris Stroud, Ismail Talib and Lionel Wee have been drinking buddies, supportive colleagues and firm friends, Linda Thompson has been a confidant and mentor, and Ruth Bereson has been all these and more. In my year at Tsinghua University, Lisa Buckley, Anna Coyle, Adam Geisler, Andy Godfrey, Fang Yan, Feng Zongxian, He Honghua, Liu Shisheng and John Thomson helped make my time there productive and enjoyable. During my two year 'out' from the academic round as a language consultant at CCTV, I enjoyed working with and learned much from Zoe Allsebrook, Bi Bingbin, Chang Yiru, James Chau, Dang Bing, Duan Rong, Han Bin, Michael Harrold, He Yujie, He Yuan, Ramy Inocencio, Ji Xiaojun, Jiang Heping, Jiang Rui, John Jirik, Sam Kierath, Laurie Lew, Liu Yang, Liu Ying, Ma Jing, Ma Shuo, Edwin Maher, the late Sue McTaggett, David Rathbun, Song Dongmeng, Wang Ping, Wang Wei, Xiao Wang, Wang Xi, Wang Xian, Xu Fujin, Yang Jing, Yang Fuqing, Zhu Bing and Zhu Jun, not to mention the (often twice) daily discussions with Zhao Hongjun.

During the time this book was in the planning and/or writing, I benefited from the hearts and minds of: in Sydney, Xiao An, Patrick Bao Hongwei, Rob Booker, Jean Brick, Gilbert Caluya, Geemeng Chew, Jhasi Delei, Dorothy Economou, Trevor Johnston, Nick Jose, Scott Morris, Guenter Plum, Claire Roberts, Adam Schembri, Neil Thompson, Jo Ye, Seva Vlaskine, Canzhong Wu, Licheng Zeng; in Melbourne, Cate Burns, Andrew Deane, Rhondda Fahey, Jane Orton, Budiadi Sudarto, Katsuhiko Suganuma, Elizabeth Thomson; in Armidale, Kristal Yee; in Hong Kong, Gilles Guiheux, Kelvin Law, Andrew Leung, Graham Lock, Shirley

Chan, Lawrence Ku, Linck Tsang, Sam Wu, Graeme Young; in Auckland, Chako Amano, Mark Amsler, Quentin Allen, Don Barron, Tim Berend, Albert Chan, Chan Fui Loong, Helen Charters, Chen Laoshi, Stephen Chu, Hilary Chung, Paul Clark, Liz Eastmond, Jennifer Devlin, Uwe Grodd, Lucille Holmes, Hsichen Hsieh, Huang Laoshi, Ross Jenner, Joce Jesson, Reiko Kondo, Christine Kim, Jane Kostanich, Alistair Kwun, Sunny Jin, Wayne Lawrence, Seng Poh Lee, Younghee Lee, Raymond Leung, Nina Mamnani, Gary Martin, Harumi Minagawa, Ellen Nakamura, Patrick Pang, Pearl Picardo, Krys Pulley, Lynette Read, Rumi Sakamoto, Shi Laoshi, Richard Smith, Changzoo Song, Sun Nan, Todd Warner, Peter Wills, Daniel Wang, Kaye Wong, Inshil Yoon and Perry Zhang.

At the Australian National University, Geremie Barmé has been a regular inspiration and delight to spark ideas off: sinophone *par excellence* and a polymath who wears his enormous learning very lightly, he has shown great welcome and encouragement to me over the years. Current Head of Chinese, John Minford, has also been a source of inspiration through his writings and for demonstrating the potential of a broad and inclusive Chinese program. Originally my Honours supervisor at the University of Sydney, Michael Halliday set me on the path of Chinese linguistics, and has always been available to discuss my work with me, just as much to worry over detailed analyses as to debate broad theoretical points. His breadth of understanding and feeling for connections between seemingly disparate phenomena are awe-inspiring, but his unfailing modesty and tolerance of dissent ensure that he remains always approachable and inclusive. Originally my supervisor on an uncompleted Masters at Macquarie University, Ruqaiya Hasan is an incredibly broad and generous thinker who continues to prove a firm supporter of this academic outlier. In Beijing, magazine editors Wang Yipeng, Yang Lin, Tang Xiaosong and Zeng Xiaoliang provided indispensable insights into the workings of Chinese men's magazines in interviews and conversations, as well as providing much needed copies of the magazines.

Matt Allen sparked the idea for the book on a trip between Babinda and Cairns, looked at a couple of developing lists of contents and pressured me to find a 'hook' to hang the collection on (this 'hook', it may be of interest to note, eventually developed into the opening paragraph of the introduction). Matt then passed me onto that doyen of academic editors Mark Selden, who quite apart from his scarily quick turn-around time has a sharp sense of what will work and what won't: he was particularly hard but fair on Chapter 9, which took some seriously pulling to get it into shape. Mark continually challenged me to deliver the book he could see in me: that it is not even better is due only to my own limitations. Once I'd completed a proposal to Mark's satisfaction he put me in the hands of the people at Routledge. Leanne Hinves managed the project in its initial stages, then handed me over to Ed Needle who helped with the complex process of permissions and many other matters, ably advised by Stephanie Rogers. Maureen Allen at Book Now edited with brisk efficiency and helped clear up all sorts of stray threads. Margaret Binns produced a clear and elegant index.

Academic colleagues who read or discussed the work in progress at varying stages of disorder and saved me from errors of fact or judgment and general infelicities include: Ben Archer, Jean Brick, Katherine Cao, Helen Charters, Chris Cléirigh, Bruce Doar, Rhondda Fahey, Judy Farqhuar, John Keenan, Andy Kirkpatrick, Rachel Lee, Gao Yihong, Graham Lock, Ahmar Maboob, Victor Mair, Jane Orton, and Sophie Reissner.

A note on the texts

The sources of all texts cited are given under Primary Sources. Translations of Chinese texts are my own.

Permission to reproduce texts here is gratefully acknowledged as follows:

Chapter 1: Dark Horse (2005) *Saddam, SARS, Sex*《250演播室》黑马著, reproduced by permission of the author.

Chapter 4: an earlier version appeared as 'Getting over the Walls of Discourse: "Character Fetishization" in Chinese Studies', by Edward James McDonald, *The Journal of Asian Studies*, Vol. 68 (November 2009) pp. 1189–1213 Copyright © 2009 The Association for Asian Studies, Inc. Reprinted with the permission of Cambridge University Press.

Chapter 5: an earlier version appeared as (2002) 'Humanistic spirit or scientism?: Conflicting ideologies in modern Chinese language reform', by Edward McDonald, *Histoire, épistémologie, langage*, (2002) 24.2. 51–74. Reprinted by permission of Société d'Histoire et d'Epistémologie des Sciences du Langage.

A note on the images

In his definition of 'sinophone', Geremie Barmé refers to 'sinophone texts *and* images' (my emphasis), both of which would be regarded as types of 'text' in the terms of this book. Although the main focus here is on linguistic texts, and only a small proportion of the visual texts supplied have been explicitly analysed, they are of course equally important, along with other kinds of semiotic texts not dealt with at all here – embodied, musical, artistic – in understanding the cultures of the sinophone sphere. The images on the cover and at the beginning of each chapter can be thought of as providing an alternative take on the issues dealt with in each chapter: they have been chosen to open up possibilities and to spark thought and discussion. I should pay special tribute here to my youngest sister, Margaret, who provided many of the images on a trip around China in 2005. The particular image which fronts the introduction was beautifully described by Ben Archer, Senior Lecturer in Imaging and Communication Design at De Monfort University Leicester, as follows:

Your sister's image is a one-off. A tailor-made piece of imagery. It contains a perfect visual metaphor for the subject, i.e. a wall (or land-scape, or even a wave) of Chinese characters that is now an unavoidable feature of nearly all global urban scenery. We also understand and appreciate the irony of this image; the only piece of English in it is the nonsensical (and presumably arbitrary) car name just visible in the extreme foreground. To use my favourite food analogy, your sister's image is like a proper piece of home-made cooking with fresh produce and good seasoning; it 'satisfies' and has the 'appropriate values for flavour and nutrition'.

Permission to reproduce images here is gratefully acknowledged:

For cover, Samantha Kierath
For Introduction 'Kunming Street' and Chapters 1 'Beijing Traffic', 2 'Gate Lion', 4 'Multilingual polity', 5 'Iconolatry', and 6 'Old Stuff Shop', Margaret Lucy McDonald
For Chapter 3, 'Language Ambassador', Ms Chong Yin Fong and Singapore Press Holdings- *My Paper*
For Chapter 7, 'The Metrosexuals are here!', Editor Xiang Wei and *Men's Style*; 'Usual suspects' and 'Unusual suspect', Editor Zhou Song and *Trends Health*; 'Magazine proper' and 'Magazine improper', *MENBOX*
For Chapter 8, 'Mafioso Metrosexual', Adam Gordon and LG New Zealand; 'Cyborg Metrosexual', Rick Waiariki and Motorola Australia Pty Ltd
For Chapter 9, 'Dr McHorse Does Discourse' Emilia Mendes

Kunming Street

INTRODUCTION: LANGUAGE IN CHINESE STUDIES

That which stirs up action in the world resides in words.

(Yijing/The Book of Changes c.200 BCE)

Learning Chinese

Why learn Chinese? What is the point of training university students in the language and culture of the Chinese sphere? What sorts of skills and knowledge do they acquire in the process to inform their future careers and contribute to their respective societies? And how is Chinese studies as a field facing up to the challenges of its role in an inextricably globalised world? The current book puts itself in the shoes of (prospective) students of Chinese to ask the crucial question, one not often raised: how well does the field measure up to their needs? The paradoxical answer would be that, although university Chinese teaching as currently constituted aims to give students access to Chinese language and culture, too often its effective outcome is to *prevent* foreigners from learning to use the language properly.

Although obviously not an intended outcome, and never stated as an explicit objective, there are a number of barriers to foreign students becoming functional users of Chinese, barriers that are unconsciously created by Chinese language teachers, incorporated into the design of Chinese language textbooks, and reflected in many of the academic and popular understandings of the nature of the Chinese language itself. A series of what Haun Saussy has dubbed 'Great Walls of Discourse' has over the years been erected between 'the Chinese' – rightful possessors of the priceless piece of cultural capital that is 'Chinese' – and 'the Foreigners', who with the best will in the world will never succeed in bridging the awful gap of their inherent foreignness.

This observation is of course not only paradoxical but highly controversial, and would be strongly resisted by most of those professionally or institutionally involved in the teaching of Chinese language and Chinese culture. Nevertheless, in the troubled chronicle of China–foreign relations, this kind of cultural 'exceptionalism' – a strongly held ideological position that China cannot be treated on a par with other countries and cultures – has often gone hand in hand with political exclusionism – the felt need to keep foreigners from penetrating the inner circles of the Chinese sphere. From the beginnings of China's contact with the West in the modern era, the existence of an irreducible difference between 'the Chinese' and 'the Foreign' has commonly been taken on both sides as a fundamental and unchallengeable presupposition. As applied to the language learning process, this presumed 'essential' difference means that Chinese is regarded by its very nature as a 'difficult' language, and so the sorts of linguistic and cultural strategies which would allow students to operate comfortably in Chinese-speaking culture are never explicitly taught; more damagingly, the type of language that *is* taught always marks the learner out as a foreigner.

It is a basic tenet of Chinese studies that linguistic and cultural fluency is a prerequisite for any meaningful engagement with the phenomenon of contemporary China and its roots. But if such fluency, through an insidious kind of self-fulfilling prophecy, is widely felt to be unattainable – if Chinese is felt to be 'too difficult' for non-Chinese ever to master – what then is the purpose of Chinese studies, and what is the value for educational institutions and governments investing in it? Why train students to become, in Geremie Barmé's term, 'sinophone': in other words, able to operate fluently in the languages and societies of the Chinese cultural sphere?

The short answer to this question is that the goal of a university Chinese studies program should be to turn students into linguistic and cultural *hybrids*: in other words, that *learning Chinese* should inevitably involve, to a greater or lesser degree, a process of *turning Chinese*.

The increasingly close relations between China and the rest of the world that have developed over the last thirty years have seen more and more traffic between the sinophone sphere and the rest of the world, and more and more individuals who operate effectively and comfortably across these linguistic and cultural boundaries. But the academy, I would argue, has still not adjusted itself to this multi-dimensional reality. While it claims to have long moved beyond its previous paradigm of that relic of colonialism, 'sinology', and to be in the process of moving beyond the current paradigm of that product of the Cold War, 'Area studies', the understandings and practices of language teaching and 'culture teaching' – if the latter even exists in any systematic form – remain trapped in pre-modern misconceptions about the nature of Chinese language(s) and culture(s). Such misconceptions fit easily into a contemporary model of a 'Great Power' struggle between the two cultural poles of sinophone China and anglophone America, where it is in the ideological interests of both sides to stress separateness and incommensurability. The perspective taken here goes beyond this dichotomy, arguing instead that belonging to more than one linguistic-cultural sphere, and taking on multiple simultaneous identities across personal and professional contexts, is becoming the norm in a globalised world.

Aims and methods of this book

This book is an attempt by a participant observer in both the learning and teaching of Chinese at university level to critique the current state of the field, and to reveal how barriers to engagement have been created and maintained. As not simply a learner and teacher of Chinese in foreign contexts, but also a long-term user of the language in Chinese-language contexts, I am able to draw on my own sustained and continuing experience negotiating linguistic and cultural boundaries to evaluate the success or otherwise of current paradigms for teaching Chinese. My disciplinary background in socially and contextually grounded linguistics also enables me to carry out close analyses of the language and culture of the sinophone sphere and of Chinese studies itself.

The sorts of evidence drawn on in making this case are those seemingly mundane but omnipresent phenomena of cultural life: *discourses*. This term as used here refers not simply to the traditional notion of 'ways of speaking and writing', as realised in the form of spoken or written *texts*; but also to Foucault's extension of that term to include the 'ways of framing' that reflect power relations lying behind and beyond linguistic expressions, as realised in implicit or explicit *ideologies*. The complex relations between discourses in the traditional and the Foucauldian senses exist at various levels of cultural awareness but there is almost always an implicit gap between the two, a gap that the current book attempts to make explicit. The challenge here, to quote the conclusion of Chapter 4, is 'to see cultural China as "distinctive" rather than "unique", as "interpretable" rather than "inscrutable"', and to acknowledge the continuing legacy of both *orientalism* – in the form of misperceptions of China from Euro-American viewpoints, and *occidentalism* – misperceptions of the West from Chinese viewpoints, across the cultural divide.

This challenge is approached here from three different disciplinary points of view, as reflected in the three parts into which the book is divided: from the respective viewpoints of *language pedagogy*, *linguistics*, and the inter-disciplinary field known as *social semiotics*. All three of these fields, I believe, struggle with the problem of 'Chinese exceptionalism' but at the same time have the potential to make a positive contribution towards combating it. The arena chosen to explore these issues is that in which texts and ideologies are, at least in theory, deliberately brought together: the *university Chinese studies program*. While most such programs claim to integrate the 'language' and 'studies' sides of their teaching, in my experience it is all too rare that the links between the two are positively drawn. More commonly, the two sides very much keep out of each other's way, even when the same people are engaged in both kinds of teaching. (For this reason, the current book does not consider the situation of Chinese language teaching at secondary or primary level, where, although many of the same ideologies operate, there is much less formal attention paid to the 'studies' side.)

While this book looks at Chinese studies from a number of different disciplinary viewpoints, it does nevertheless have a number of common threads that link it together. First, from the angle of the reader, normally referred to in the text as 'you', it attempts to take the point of view of the *potential sinophone*: that is, the university student who is currently studying Chinese or intending to do so. This, of course, is a rhetorical strategy: most current students are more concerned with getting their assignments in on time, and earning enough money to pay their fees and keep themselves alive, than they are with philosophical reflections on the nature of the field in which they are studying. Nevertheless, I believe the student's point of view is a very important, and commonly neglected one. It forces us to think in terms of the purpose and utility of the field of Chinese studies as a whole. If we claim, as many scholars of Chinese do, that the languages and cultures of the sinophone sphere are worth studying, then we need to explain why, and what are the key factors involved in that process.

As explained above, there are currently a number of significant barriers to non-Chinese speakers becoming functioning sinophones, so it is even more important for the nature of these barriers to be understood, and for you as potential sinophone to be fully aware of the challenges you face. For the sorts of people who *will* be reading this book, who will include: students, most likely at advanced undergraduate or postgraduate level; teachers of Chinese at both tertiary and pre-tertiary levels; academics in cross-cultural communication, linguistic anthropology, Chinese language education, and Chinese linguistics; educational policy makers; and even those involved in trade and diplomatic relations with China, it is crucial for you to understand what 'engaging with China' really means on the nuts and bolts level, and what sort of long-term investment is needed to equip those who will be in the front line of that engagement.

Second, from the writer's point of view, referred to as 'we', this is not the loftily omniscient 'editorial we', but in the words of the influential linguist of Chinese, Yuen Ren Chao, in the preface to his seminal *Grammar of Spoken Chinese*, the 'we' of 'author and reader jointly exploring questions of mutual interest'. Again, this is a rhetorical strategy, but I believe a very useful one, because it emphasises the interaction between author and reader. As author, I create a virtual conversation with my intended readers – of all the types listed above and more – 'I' talk to 'you', and even though unlike a real conversation you have no opportunity to talk back directly, your own background and beliefs, and your developing understanding of the ideas put forward in this book, are part of what I as author must take into account in managing that conversation. Hence the use of 'we': I try, as far as possible, to identify myself as author with the 'you(s)' who are the readers of this book. If, on occasion, I express a personal opinion, I will use 'I'.

Third, from the point of view of the text itself, this is organised around a series of what these days would be called 'critical discourse analyses', but which would have been familiar for millennia to scholars in both the Chinese and European cultural spheres as 'textual commentaries'. As the quotation from the *Yijing* used as epigraph above puts it: 'that which stirs up action in the world resides in words'; and it has long been recognised that as human beings, we live not just in the *material* world of immediate experience like other animals, but in a *semiotic* world created through our own potential for meaning-making. Hence, if we take language as one aspect of our human semiotic repertoire, the basic stuff of linguistic interaction, *texts*, can tell us a lot about how we understand and act on our world. Of course, a book like the current one that focuses on language should need to make no apology for making texts the ground and centre of its arguments. Each text, usually an extract from a longer exchange or discussion, is analysed in terms of the particular concerns of the chapter in which it appears. Such analyses are not intended to be either exhaustive or definitive: there may well be aspects of the text not covered in a particular analysis; and there is no implication that the current analysis is the only possible one. On the contrary: as a potential sinophone, you as reader will no doubt have your own ideas about interpreting these texts, and will have a knowledge of similar texts that have formed part of your own developing sinophone repertoire.

What this book can be seen as setting up are complex relations of *intertextuality* between these different texts, with the contemporary field of Chinese studies and the kinds of views held within it, and with the history of the field as contacts have evolved between China and the rest of the world, particularly the European cultural sphere, over the last five hundred years. In this book I stress the historical roots of the current situation, not only because we cannot hope to understand 'our' present without knowing at least something about 'their' past – as the opening of the novel *The Go Between* puts it 'The past is a foreign country: they do things differently there' – but also to give our current situation a much needed dose of relativity. We might liken the current situation to the surface of the sea in which we are swimming, familiar and reassuring; but not far below the surface into the recent past, things begin to look a little different; and when we don diving gear and plunge into the depths of the more distant past, we come across a completely different world. Just because we do things in this way now doesn't mean they were always done this way, or will always be done this way in the future.

Turning Chinese

The English word *Chinese* is multiply ambiguous, corresponding to *Zhōngguó* (*de*) 'related to China', or *Huárén* (*de*) 'related to Chinese ethnicity' or *Zhōngwén* (*de*) 'related to Chinese language'. It was no doubt for this reason that in recent years within Chinese studies the third of these meanings has received a new English coinage, *sinophone*. In this book, however, rather than using sinophone to refer just to 'Chinese language', I have chosen to give it a broader connotation, playing on its etymological meaning of 'Chinese voice'. This book works not just by establishing a network of different texts, but by creating a dialogue between different *voices*. As a potential sinophone, you yourself must develop your own Chinese 'voice', quite literally in terms of mastering the sounds and wordings of the language, but also in the sense of finding an identity for yourself, of establishing a reference point for yourself in the sinophone world. In the course of this process, you will obviously talk with and learn from others, in the first instance your teachers and fellow students, and then the widening circle of Chinese speakers with whom you come into contact. After a while you will begin to assert yourself as a sinophone, to intervene in the dialogue, to put forward your own point of view, and to take issue with others' points of view.

The term 'sinophone' has already received the ultimate contemporary accolade – being included in Wikipedia – which, in line with my broader usage given above, defines it not only as an adjective, i.e. descriptively, but as a noun, as a kind of role or identity.

> *Adjective*
>
> *sinophone* Speaking one or more Sinitic languages
>
> *Noun*
>
> *sinophone* (plural *sinophones*) A person who speaks one or more of the Sinitic languages either natively or by adoption.

This book takes up the second part of the latter definition 'a person who speaks one or more of the Sinitic languages … *by adoption*' and explores how that process of 'adoption' might actually work. The French version of Wikipedia goes into more detail on specifically this point, giving a list of criteria to be attained in both spoken and written Chinese and then commenting that 'becoming sinophone' requires: 'a number of years of learning and/or a stay in China. The period of study could begin with a prolonged stay in China but that can't by itself replace the requisite time for study.' It then goes on to comment, in terms very similar to those given in Chapter 1 of this book (first written in 2005): 'The terms "sinophone" is ambiguous, but it suggests a high degree of cultural familiarity with China, which implies having had extensive time there or with Chinese communities overseas …'.

This process of becoming sinophone and developing a sinophone identity – learning Chinese *and* turning Chinese – should allow you to operate in Chinese language environments with a comparable degree of familiarity and comfort to those of your own native language. This is a complex challenge, but it is an achievable aim, and gives you the best chance of being able to make use of Chinese professionally and personally.

What you will find here

This book starts its exploration of contemporary Chinese studies and its roots by way of *language pedagogy*, with Part A exploring the notion of 'The Great Wall of Chinese language teaching' which to a great extent interposes itself between learners and the language.

- Chapter 1, 'Arguing semantics with a Beijing taxi-driver', demonstrates that the reference point for teachers and learners of Chinese should be, not the language classroom itself, but rather real-life interactions in a Chinese language environment. This shifted pedagogical focus opens up new concerns as to how the learner becomes inculcated into that environment, not just linguistically, but also socially and culturally. For students to appreciate how learning Chinese inevitably involves themselves becoming part of sinophone culture, the aims of teaching broaden from simply learning the sounds and wordings of the language, to *relating* instances of language use – *texts* – to their *contexts*.
- Chapter 2, 'Gateways to becoming sinophone', examines some of the common textbooks currently used at university level and the different *traditions of language learning* that lie behind them. These traditions, deriving from both Chinese and Western sources, each carry their own historical baggage and are not necessarily suited to the needs of contemporary students. The discourse of a number of currently used textbooks is subjected to a critical analysis to show how they are not always coherent or consistent about what they claim to be doing, and a recent official mainland publication 'Chinese for the Olympics' is clearly shown to be putting forward a type of Chinese that the Chinese don't actually speak! – but presumably foreigners are supposed to.
- Chapter 3, 'Learning Chinese the Lee Kuan Yew way', examines a particularly influential 'model student', the former Prime Minister of Singapore, whose account of his own Mandarin learning experiences provides an invaluable test case for examining the wider social and political contexts of Chinese language learning. The Singaporean perspective also sheds light on the challenges of mastering a *standard language* in a multilingual setting, as well as on the status and function of different kinds of 'Chinese' in the sinophone sphere.

Part B moves on to the *linguistics* of Chinese both within and beyond cultural China to critique the different understandings – and misunderstandings – of Chinese that lie behind its teaching traditions, examining how the language and its writing system have provided fodder for 'Drawing battlelines over language'. Chapters 4 and 5 look at the place of language in the traditions of *sinology* or *Chinese studies*, in other words, those scholarly enterprises looking at China from Western points of view.

- Chapter 4 identifies the notion of 'Character fetishisation', defined as 'an inordinate emphasis given to Chinese characters in the interpretation of Chinese language and culture', as central to understanding the distortions and confusions focused on and stemming from the Chinese writing system.

These confusions turn up not just within the linguistics and language pedagogy of Chinese but in wider intellectual contexts: the case of French philosopher Jacques Derrida basing a whole new view of the relationship between spoken and written language, 'grammatology', on a misunderstanding of the Chinese writing system being only the most prominent example.

- Chapter 5, 'Ideolatry versus phonolatry?', goes back to the late 1930s to a famous dispute between two American sinologists over whether Chinese characters are best understood as representing 'ideas' or 'sounds', as well as another debate that took place in the early 1960s as sinological approaches were giving way to an Area studies paradigm. It shows how arguments over the *role of Chinese language in the study of China* not only tend to get trapped on either side of a scientific versus humanistic divide, but also depend on the global-political context in which the study of China is regarded as relevant.

- Chapter 6, 'Keeping Chinese for the Chinese', shifts the focus from Western scholarship to the interaction between the Chinese and foreign intellectual worlds that started with the official Westernisation policies of the late Qing dynasty, revisited in the May Fourth era under the new Republic. This chapter traces the process by which misunderstandings stemming from Western orientalism about the nature of Chinese, particularly in relation to the writing system and the grammar, became nativised among Chinese scholars and then put to political work arguing for the uniqueness of the Chinese situation. Paradoxically, of course, this kind of *reactive relativism* – 'Chinese is everything Western languages are not' – ends up trapping understandings of Chinese distinctiveness within Western paradigms. This chapter thus addresses in a linguistic context the still unanswered question of modern China: *is modernisation possible without Westernisation?*

Part C broadens the discussion to the whole field of Chinese studies and the theoretical paradigms that coexist within it, in an often unidentified mixture of supposedly outmoded approaches and their equally supposed replacements. It identifies the multi-disciplinary approach known as *social semiotics* as the key to 'Getting Over the Walls of Discourse' currently separating different disciplines within the field of Chinese studies, acknowledging their equal concern with understanding both (social) contexts and (semiotic) texts, and drawing the links between them.

- Chapter 7, 'Construing "metrosexual" in Chinese', applies a jointly social and semiotic framework to the investigation of how this gendered fashion term has been adopted from 1990s Western popular media to their newly arisen counterparts in mainland China since the early 2000s. It traces the process by which the concept 'metrosexual' has been progressively adapted to Chinese conditions, both as a standard-bearer for male consumption and a kind of disguise for homosexual identity. This chapter shows that neither the multiplying renderings and connotations of this concept, nor the socio-economic conditions that made its adoption useful, can be understood in isolation from each other.

- Chapter 8, 'Reconstruction versus deconstruction', traces the historical background of *textual studies* in pre-modern East Asia and Europe, and shows how in both cultural polities techniques of textual reconstruction were developed in order to gain access to the 'original' forms of the canonical texts which underpinned their traditional world views. In the modern era attention turned to new techniques of textual *deconstruction* that reversed the relation between text and context by finding the ideological underpinnings of texts in the socio-economic context of their production. This chapter critically evaluates some attempts at social semiotic analyses of Chinese texts, and suggests that it is in these kinds of analyses that all scholars working in Chinese studies can find common ground, and that the basic commonality within the field is a complementary focus on both text and context.

Finally, the focus comes back to the question of how students position themselves amid this welter of overlapping contexts and competing discourses.

- Chapter 9, 'From "Ed McDonald" to "Ned McHorse"', returns to the learner of Chinese as *linguistic and cultural novice*, tracing this process of acculturation in relation to one particular test case – that of the author himself. From his growing up as Ed McDonald in the multi-culturalising Australia of the 1970s, through his initiation into Chinese language and society as the sinophone Ma Aide in the 1980s, to his 'rediscovery' of his Scottish family heritage as Eadairt MacDhomhnaill and his creation of the cross-ethnic critical persona of 'Ned McHorse' from the 1990s onwards, his struggles to sort out and accommodate these multiple identities offer insight into the processes of personal redefinition central to the creation of the successful 'sinophone'.

If Chinese studies is to genuinely consider the needs of the potential sinophone, it needs to adopt a contingent and instrumental approach towards such cross-cultural journeys, rather than the monolithic and essentialist world view embodied in current Chinese teaching and in China–foreign relations more generally. A multi-dimensional field will be able to offer a more realistic understanding of the value of becoming sinophone, as well as providing better tools for dealing with the personal and political conflicts that inevitably arise in this process.

What you will *not* find here

This can be thought of as a distinctly *antipodean* book, not only in the sense that it is based on first-hand experience with the practice of Chinese studies in Australia and New Zealand, but also that it comes at Chinese studies from a non-mainstream, non-consensus point of view. In doing so, it puts forward a number of very controversial propositions, and makes some very debatable claims – adopting the general approach recommended by eminent Chinese linguist Lü Shuxiang: 大胆提出问题，深入分析矛盾，探索解决途径 'Be bold in putting forward questions, dig deep in analysing problems, and search for ways of resolving them'. If the current book does more of the first and second than the third, it is because it deliberately sets out to raise questions which, currently at least, have no clear answers. As a practitioner within the field of Chinese studies, I believe that much of the 'commonsense' of the field, much that is currently taken for granted, needs to be problematised and critiqued, and the field needs to develop a greater clarity both about its goals and how it should set about achieving them.

This book has thus been written with the deliberate aim of sparking constructive criticism of the positions put forward in it – a result I believe I have some reason to think will be forthcoming! However, as a book with such a wide scope, it needs to be clear what it does *not* cover, and what it does *not* set out to do.

While the anglophone contexts from which this book has emerged are, in geo-political terms, on the insular periphery of the former British Empire (and arguably on the periphery of the current American Empire) – as the Chinese proverb has it 天高皇帝远 'The sky is high and the Emperor is far away' – its sinophone contexts, by contrast, have largely been experienced in the very 'centre' of the 'mainland' itself, the traditional 'Northern Capital' of the Chinese Empire, Beijing. Because the reference point for this study is my own experience as developing sinophone and as trainer of other developing sinophones, the two 'worlds' in which this has taken place are largely those of anglophone Australasia and sinophone northern China: as I've been known to joke to Chinese friends – 'speaking Chinese, I'm a northerner; speaking English, I'm a southerner'.

However, the particular contingencies of my own experience as reflected in the focus of this book should not be taken as implying that I am unaware of, let alone dismissive of the anglophone centre(s) nor indeed of the sinophone periphery. In the latter case, as Geremie Barmé has frequently pointed out, what he calls the 'Kong-Tai Ark' of Hong Kong and Taiwan, traditionally parts of the Chinese Empire but for significant periods of time incorporated into the two foreign empires of the British and the Japanese respectively, provide a very different perspective on the issues raised here, and within sinophone culture have allowed different historical trajectories to be explored and different possibilities envisaged. To use the example of Chapter 1, the fact that most of my conversations have been with Beijing taxi-drivers, does *not* mean that I haven't had equally enlightening conversations with taxi-drivers in Hong Kong, Shanghai, Taipei, and Singapore – just to mention other locales that have played a significant role in my own developing sinophone repertoire.

As mentioned above, the basis of the book's method is a type of textual criticism, where different kinds of texts are analysed in relation to their social and cultural contexts in order to reveal their ideological positions. This is similar to the approach of scholars working within the multi-disciplinary field known as *critical discourse analysis*. However, rather than seeing the current book as a critical discourse study in the usual sense, it could better be characterised as using the tools of critical discourse analysis in order to carry out a sustained reflection on and critique of the current state of Chinese studies. In doing so, it does not hesitate to draw on the experience of one who has been both a student and teacher in that field – myself. I hope such a double-pronged approach, both professional and personal, will make its arguments more accessible and relevant to you the readers. While this approach may sometimes come across as subjective, what it is really aiming for is an *inter-subjective* understanding of the challenges facing the field of Chinese studies in relation to its main targets: potential sinophones.

Furthermore, while this book draws on the disciplines or fields of language pedagogy, linguistics, and critical discourse analysis, it is not to be regarded as an academic monograph in the ordinary sense in that it is not directed solely towards academics of one or more of the disciplines which it covers. Each of its chapters could very well form the basis for a focused academic study of this kind. Much of the discussion, particularly in Part B on the linguistics of Chinese, is in fact based on detailed research in the field, to which I have myself contributed my jot. The 'suggestions for further reading' at the end of the book provide more detail of the context from which these ideas have emerged and in which particular claims are being put forward.

However, from a strictly academic point of view, the accounts of language pedagogy, of the linguistics of Chinese, and of critical discourse analysis presented here are suggestive rather than comprehensive, the main aim being to show how they are relevant to the concerns of Chinese studies. And while I can claim some expertise in the field of Chinese linguistics, in the areas of language pedagogy and critical discourse analysis, I have the status only of a reasonably well-informed practitioner. I am able to draw on my own experience of teaching and devising teaching materials, in the case of language pedagogy, and carrying out critical analyses of contemporary Chinese texts, in the case of critical discourse analysis, as well as of course reading the scholarly literature in both areas. But I venture into these areas professedly as a linguist, or more specifically as a discourse analyst: hence the textual analysis which forms the basis for the claims made in this book. It is because, as a linguist, I have long identified preoccupations and misconceptions common to all three fields that I set out to write this book in the first place: to show where those commonalities exist and to suggest some ways of understanding the problems they cause.

Having said that, while this book directs a sustained critique at the bases of current Chinese studies, on the whole it does *not* attempt, except by implication, to suggest how Chinese studies might be 'reformed' to make it more relevant to the current situation and to the needs of contemporary students. A detailed framework for Chinese language teaching from the point of view put forward in Part A of this book would be enormously valuable for the field, but that is not what this book provides. Likewise, an explicit theory of critical discourse analysis which avoided the Eurocentrism characteristic of this still emerging field would be of great benefit, not only to Chinese studies and Asian studies more broadly, but to the field of critical discourse analysis itself, in helping to expose the biases unconsciously embedded in its current configuration. Again, that is something for another book – or another author!

So if this book does make an attempt to cover these three areas – how successfully it does so is of course for you the reader to judge – hopefully it does not fall between three stools in doing so, but rather makes connections and identifies commonalities that I believe will be of use to all three fields insofar as they impinge on Chinese studies. Whatever the deficiencies of this project, it is at least based on a clear idea of what it aims to achieve, and I hope will be judged on that basis. In this connection, it would be useful to identify some other works that have examined issues in relation to Chinese studies similar to those dealt with here. Haun Saussy's *Great Walls of Discourse* (2001) is a fascinating look at the evolution of ideas about the Chinese language in the study of China by the West over the last four centuries. Its treatment of the development of myths about the Chinese language and its writing system provides an essential background to many of the ideas put forward in this book, particularly in Part B on the linguistics of Chinese. David Honey's *Incense at the Altar* (2001) examines the increasing professionalisation of the study of China over the last two centuries and, while focusing mainly on the philological traditions of the field, has implications for all study of China that goes through the language. Bob Hodge and Kam Louie's *The Politics of Chinese Language and Culture* (1998) is probably closest to the approach adopted in this book. While in my opinion their attempt to 'import the insights of Cultural Studies into Chinese Studies' is not entirely successful, and their understandings of the Chinese language and its writing system less nuanced than is needed, nevertheless, their analyses of a range of Chinese 'texts' – verbal, visual and filmic – in relation to their social and cultural contexts are exemplary, and have provided a model for many similar analyses in the current book.

How to read this book: some alternative trajectories

Cutting across its overall division into three parts, this book has other commonalities in content and style that can guide a first reading. For an overall account of what 'learning Chinese, turning Chinese' involves, Chapter 9 explores this process in relation to my own experience; and this can be usefully contrasted with the more traditional view of learning Chinese put forward in Lee Kuan Yew's account in Chapter 3. Those interested in the current state of Chinese language teaching and learning will find Chapter 2 most immediately relevant to their concerns; while Chapter 1 discusses teaching and learning from the alternative viewpoint put forward in this book. For those focused primarily on Chinese studies, Chapters 7 and 8 give a good introduction to the sorts of analyses of what Geremie Barmé has called 'sinophone texts and images' that are commonly done in the field, as well as to the scholarly traditions of both Europe and China according to which such analyses are carried out. For those interested in Chinese linguistics, and in how ideas about language have influenced the field of Chinese studies as a whole, Part B, Chapters 4 to 6, gives a good introduction to these concerns: because of their subject matter, they may come across as more technical than the discussions in Parts A and C; however, they have deliberately been written in such a way as to be accessible to non-linguists – with what degree of success is of course up to the reader to judge.

PART A

The Great Wall of Chinese language teaching

The first part of this book looks at Chinese language teaching in relation to Chinese studies, and sets out to explore the reasons why you might want to study Chinese at university, and what are the relevant factors that will enable you to do so successfully. The first chapter of Part A addresses these questions, in the first instance, directly to you as current or prospective student, and explores the implications of those seemingly simple notions of 'learning' and 'language'. Next in Chapter 2 we examine that vital accessory for every language student – the textbook – and see how the way textbooks tend to be put together, as well as the presuppositions textbook writers bring to that process, may not be giving you as prospective sinophone exactly what you need. Finally in Chapter 3 we look at the case of one particular learner of Chinese, who has taken the trouble to put his views of that process down in black and white, and use his experiences to understand the wider context of language learning, particularly when there is more than one language, or more than one version of it, on offer. Despite the focus on language learning in Part A, the discussion as a whole is not confined within the concerns of the traditional language classroom, but goes beyond the classroom into the Chinese language environment in order to explore the nature of this environment and its relationship to the concerns of Chinese studies.

Beijing traffic

1

ARGUING SEMANTICS WITH A BEIJING TAXI-DRIVER

Relating text and context in a university Chinese language program

Introduction: discussing 'quality'

Āiyā! Běijīng de jiāotōng zěme zème zāogāo?!
'Why *is* the traffic in Beijing so dreadful?!'
Méi bànfǎ, mínzú sù.zhì tài dī le.
'Nothing you can do, people's quality is too low.'

This exchange is one I've had many a time with different taxi-drivers in Beijing, brought on by the sight of someone abruptly forcing their car across four lanes of traffic in order to get to an exit, or a pedestrian setting out into a busy road without looking to see who's coming, or a group of cyclists at the lights engaged in a battle of wills with a line of cars as to who's going to make it across the intersection first, with a traffic aide furiously waving their little flag and tooting their whistle completely disregarded on the sidelines.

Like, I suspect, many people living abroad, I've had some of my best conversations with taxi-drivers. After the inevitable *Nǎ'r lái de?* 'Where are you from?' and usually *Nǐ Zhōngwén shuō de búcuò!* 'Your Chinese is so good' – I'm waiting for the day when it's *really* so good they don't even comment on it! – we often get into discussions on everything from politics to history to social mores. But on recent trips to Beijing, it's been the notorious traffic of the capital that has forced itself on our attention, with some particularly flagrant violation giving rise to comments like the ones I've recreated above.

If it's not too late, and I'm not too tired, or too drunk, or feeling my Chinese isn't up to it, or in one of those not infrequent moods when I'd like to pull a blanket over my head and pretend the whole chaotic metropolis just doesn't exist, I attempt to probe a little deeper.

Shuō 'sù.zhì', jùtǐ shi shém.me yì.sī?
'What exactly do you mean by 'quality'?'

Talk of 'quality' in English seems to hark back to a previous age of open snobbery when the upper classes were known as 'the quality', presumably because they were thought to possess more of whatever this was than their social inferiors. 'Surely you're not saying', I press the taxi-driver, 'that Chinese are genetically *inferior* to other peoples?' Then, if I'm being particularly smart-alecky, I'll quote him the beginning of the *Sānzìjīng* 'The Three Word Classic', formerly used by Chinese children as an elementary reading primer, that sums up the traditional Confucian optimistic view of human nature:

人之初	*rén zhī chū*	'People when they're born'
性本善	*xìng běn shàn*	'their nature is basically good.'
性相近	*xìng xiāng jìn*	'By nature (people) are close to each other,'
习相远	*xí xiāng yuǎn*	'(but) habit can cause them to grow apart.'

In contemporary discourse, the term *sù.zhì* 'quality' is an interesting and rather complex concept. On the one hand, it's pretty much a synonym of that other common term of social valuation *wénhuà* 'culture', which in contemporary China tends to refer more or less directly to educational level, the higher the better – *wénhuà shuǐpíng tài dī le* 'cultural level is too low' being another common criticism. But it also has echoes of a more general term *zhì.liàng* 'quality'. So the term *sù.zhì* more or less refers to general cultivation, what people have 'made of themselves', as it were. As such the condemnation – *sù.zhì tài dī le* 'quality is too low' – is often applied by inhabitants of Beijing to *wàidìrén* 'people from outside', or by middle class to working class people, and no doubt also – though I've never been privy to any of these conversations – by Chinese to foreigners. As applied to other denizens of the roads, taxi-drivers will often pass this judgment on the 'new drivers' in ever-increasing numbers infesting the roads of which they seem to consider themselves the only users; on the bicycle riders who constitute a decreasing but still significant presence; or on the pedestrians of whom an alarming number seem to have either an obvious death wish or a touching faith in the ability of drivers to look out for them.

Language and text

What I've just told you so far might seem just like a more sophisticated version of a traveller's tale: quaint, idiosyncratic, charming, perhaps; but in the wider scheme of things pretty insignificant. And given that we're supposed to be talking about studying Chinese at university – a pretty serious undertaking, as I'm sure you'll agree – you're probably thinking to yourselves: 'when is he going to get down to the real stuff?' Well, I would argue that this is precisely the 'real stuff', and that understanding exchanges like this is in fact highly relevant to learning Chinese. But to work out why, we first need to take apart the commonsense notion of what it means to 'learn a language'.

Let's begin by defining our terms. We can start with what seems like an obvious one: what exactly is *language*? This may seem like a silly question – surely we all *know* what 'language' is? – but on closer inspection this seemingly clear concept becomes a little murky. What is the difference between 'a language', in other words, a particular language like English or Chinese, and 'language' in general? Does the latter refer merely to any sort of communication system, as in phrases like 'the language of love' – which doesn't necessarily involve speaking! – or 'the language of bees', which involves one bee dancing in the air in a particular way to show its fellows the location of a source of honey? When you and your classmates converse in English or Chinese, are you all speaking 'the same language', despite obvious differences in accent, fluency and range of vocabulary? When you started your first stumbling steps in Chinese, were you already speaking that language, or some form of translated English, or what's been called an 'inter-language' somewhere between the two?

And what about the concept of 'the Chinese language'? Confucius is commonly said to have written 'in Chinese' when he or rather his students set brush to bamboo something like two and a half thousand years ago; as is Mao Tse-Tung/ Máo Zédōng, who wrote only last century. Do the inhabitants of Peking/Běijīng and Taipei/Táiběi all 'speak Chinese', despite the many differences in pronunciation and vocabulary; let alone your Pekingese *lǎomā.zi* or 'granny' and her Cantonese counterpart, who would be hard put to understand almost anything said by each other? And how about the language of Peking Opera/Jīngjù, which is like some weird 'interdialect' where the name of the capital comes out as *Béjìng* and the port city south of it as *Tiànzìn* and the tones all sound funny? If you can speak Chinese but can't read or write, do you still 'know Chinese'? (Many Chinese speakers would say no.) How about – to get back to where we started – the language of Beijing taxi-drivers? Or comedians from the Northeast/ Dōngběi, which provides many of the professional funny people in China? Or the reader of the 7pm news on CCTV? Or a scientist from the Chinese Academy of Sciences explaining the latest discoveries in genetics to an audience of his colleagues? Do we have to be able to understand all these people in order to really 'know Chinese'?

Well, in case you're now getting seriously worried, the short answer is 'no'. From the point of view of learning Chinese, or any other language, attempting to master 'the whole language' is an impossible and unrealistic aim. For our purposes, a more manageable concept than language is that of *text*. This refers not just, in the traditional sense of that term, to 'written document', but to any coherent stretch of language, spoken or written, that functions in some sort of *context*. This related notion of context doesn't simply refer to the immediate surroundings of language use: in the conversation with the taxi-driver, the context of the exchange *was* in a sense very immediate: the appalling traffic all around us. But in an equally important sense, the context was more under the surface: the way I understood that he was in fact passing a social judgment, an evaluation of social types; and lying behind this, the sort of moralising attitudes according to which Chinese speakers evaluate, and therefore know how to treat, other members of their community, and at the same time expect certain types of behaviour towards themselves.

Text and context

Any text can yield up an enormous amount of information about the social context of its producers and receivers. We can explore this notion of context further with reference to another text, something I copied off a university notice board when I was working in Beijing in the early 2000s.

材22班刊

经过多天奋战，kill 了班上 n 位同学的 many time 和 so much money， 这份 '万众瞩目' 的班刊终于问世了，这是我们的处女作，所以当然有许多不足之处，还请各位 ggjj 不要以看待正常班刊的眼光来看待我们的 '处子秀'！切记！切记！

Materials 22 Class Magazine

After many days of struggle, and having <u>kill</u>ed n number of classmates' <u>many time</u> and <u>so much money</u>, this 'world-attracting' class magazine has finally come out. This is our maiden effort, so naturally there are many inadequacies, and we'd ask every <u>guy</u> and <u>girl</u> not to regard our 'virgin show' as they would a normal magazine. Take heed! Take heed!

This particular text is chock full of information about its social context. Let's collect some of the obvious, and perhaps less obvious clues that the text gives us. First of all, the title identifies this as the production of a particular class of students from a particular department of the University – Materials Science. As such, we would expect this kind of text to be directed very explicitly to this group of readers, a group in which there is very little difference between those who have produced the text and those who will be reading it: the text itself identifies them as *tóngxué*(.*men*) – 'fellow students' or 'classmates' – a very clearly defined social role in Chinese-speaking cultures.

Perhaps one of this text's most salient characteristics is its playfulness – a quality so closely connected with these kinds of productions that it even has its own term in English: 'undergraduate humour'. The humour comes through in the mock-military rhetoric – terms like *fènzhàn* 'struggle' being very much part of the political tradition of mainland China; the use of the slightly pompous fixed expressions known as *chéngyǔ*, often made up of four characters and in classical style, such as *wànzhòng zhǔmù*, literally '(which) the myriad masses fix their gaze (on)', whose use is singled out as facetious by the scare quotes; the purely classical exhortation at the end *qièjì* 'take heed'; and of course by the extensive employment of English words and expressions. Some of these are English phrases quoted, more or less correctly, as a whole – e.g. *many time* (for *many times* or *a lot of time*?) and *so much money*; some boldly inserted into the grammatical structure of the Chinese sentence – e.g. *kill le*, with the aspect suffix *le* simply attached to the English word, or with the mathematical symbol *n* for 'unknown quantity' inserted as a quasi-numeral into a Chinese phrase *n wèi tóngxué* 'n number of students'. The influence of English is more subtly reflected in the use of the Chinese word *xiù*, literally 'elegant' or 'beautiful', to correspond to the English word of similar pronunciation *show* in the combination *chǔzǐ xiù* 'virgin show'. An interesting in-between technique is the use of the English letters *ggjj* to stand for the Chinese terms *gē.ge jiě.jie*, literally 'big brother (and) big sister', which is used in the sense of 'guys and girls' to refer to all the members of the group of classmates, in a typically Chinese equation of professional relationships with family ones.

Learning language

So if you're comfortable now with the idea that what you're actually learning is a whole series of different 'texts' – many of them of course similar to ones you've learned or experienced before – and in that process relating them to numbers of 'contexts', we can now go on to reflect on what is involved in 'learning'. Learning a language in a formal educational context like a university is a complex process which can be broken down into three separate stages: *learning* language, learning *through* language and learning *about* language. The first of these stages should be pretty familiar in a more or less *decontextualised* way to anyone who's gone through one or two years of a Chinese studies program, getting to grips with the sounds and wordings of Chinese as well as tackling the written form. From a *contextualised* point of view, such as we've just explored above, one way of understanding the process of learning language would be to say it consists of getting a more and more detailed understanding of what kinds of texts are appropriate to what kinds of contexts. If we combine those two points of view, the decontextualised language-internal one, and the contextualised text-in-context one, we can now ask the question: what would you need to learn, or to put it another way, what level of Chinese would you need to reach, in order to be able to understand a text such as the one we've just looked at?

This probably seems like an absurd scenario: I can hear an old-fashioned sinologist – or for that matter a modern practically minded Chinese major – snorting in derision: 'Surely we're not spending all this time learning Chinese in order to be able to read student magazines?!' Well, yes and no. No: you may never in your future career need to read a Chinese student magazine and wonder what all those students obviously seem to find so entertaining. But yes: in the sense that the skills required to understand a text like this, and through it the context in which it was produced and for which it is appropriate, are highly relevant for anyone who wants to learn Chinese.

Why bother?

This of course begs the question of *why* you might want to learn Chinese in the first place. Certainly my first Chinese Professor, the late A.R. Davis, who set up the Department of Oriental Studies at Sydney University and created a program very closely based on the model of the classical studies he had followed as a youth, would have been very clear that one learned Chinese in order to gain access to the glories of Chinese literature and philosophy. In a phrase he coined for a talk he gave on this topic late in his life, 'In Search of Love and Truth' (Davis 1985), Professor Davis argued with a great deal of cogency for an informed appreciation of China and Chinese culture which did not simply adopt the attitude taken by many Westerners towards China from at least the mid-nineteenth century onwards, one summed up in the title of a study of famous late nineteenth-century Chinese translator Yen Fu to which Professor Davis's motto was a deliberate retort: 'In Search of Wealth and Power'.

Of course the 'wealth and power' aspect of learning Chinese is a recurrent attraction, and more up-to-date versions of the greedy nineteenth-century dream 'Who will light the lamps of China?' continue to motivate more or less informed forays into China – most of which end up in disaster, as chronicled by Tim Clissold in his very witty and completely frank account of how he went bust there: *Mr China* (Clissold 2004). But if that's the reason you're studying Chinese, I've got to tell you – not to beat around the bush – that you're wasting your time. If you're from a non-Chinese background, there are already more than enough Chinese-speaking people out there with the requisite linguistic, social and cultural skills – not to mention the personal and business connections – to make money out of China even before you've made it out of the university gates. And if you have a Chinese language background already, there's nothing in any university that's going to help you make money out of being Chinese. Of course having Chinese plus some other professional bag of tricks like law or economics will no doubt give you an edge in the job market, but that's not the reason you go into Chinese studies. In my (informed) opinion, and to put it in a nutshell, you come here to be turned into a *hybrid*.

The notion of 'hybrid' seems a bit creepy – conjuring up images of plastic-gloved technicians in white coats carefully attaching little sprigs of plant matter or messing around with test tubes – and seems to go directly against what many people would think is the whole aim of learning another language: to gain an authentic experience of another culture and to be able to take part in that culture indistinguishably from a native. Well, to repeat the taxi-driver's phrase, *méi bànfǎ* 'no can do'. By the time you get to university, you're already too old and too acculturated in your own culture: you're just not capable, even if you wanted to, of slicking off your mother tongue and culture in order to take on another.

What you can do, however, is to develop your language skills to the level where you take on a foreign-speaking *identity*. And once you've developed this foreign-speaking identity, you then gain the ability to switch between your own language and culture and the other language and culture: in other words, to *mediate* between English-speaking culture and Chinese-speaking culture. This mediatory role is something that works both for native English speakers who have learned to 'do Chinese', and native Chinese speakers who have learned to 'do English': to use the slang labels common in South-East Asia – it produces both 'bananas' – yellow on the outside and white on the inside, and 'eggs' – white on the outside and yellow on the inside; and it's an ability that's useful across a whole range of professional and personal contexts in an increasingly globalised world.

Learning through language

You might object that the acquisition of such knowledge does not require you to actually go to the trouble of learning the language: given the existence of a reasonably comprehensive body of up-to-date translations, surely anyone can become conversant with Chinese culture whether or not they understand the language? I believe this is a serious misconception, and we can see why by looking at the second aspect of language learning: *learning through language*. Let's do this by examining the concept of *sù.zhì* in a slightly different context, this time from a novel set at the time of the SARS epidemic of 2003. The novel focuses on a married couple who are brought back together – literally – by the enforced isolation of that period. The following extract is taken from near the beginning of the novel, before the start of the epidemic, when the wife, a doctor, is woken up by a group of people making noise underneath her window early in the morning. She launches an angry verbal attack on her disturbers and is answered in kind.

NǓDÀI.FŪ:	*Wèi, nǐ.men huàn .ge dì.fāng rāng.rāng xíng.bu.xíng?*
WOMAN DOCTOR:	'Hey, find somewhere else to make a noise, okay?'
	Hái ràng.bu.ràng rén shuì-jiào .le?
	'Can't you let people sleep?'
LÍNJŪ JIǍ:	*Yò, dōu qīdiǎn .le hái yǒu rén shuì-jiào .wa, zhēn zīchǎn-jièjí.*
NEIGHBOUR A:	'Wow, it's already seven o'clock and there are still people sleeping, so bourgeois.'
	Wǒ.men xiāng.xia qīdiǎn dōu cóng dà tián.li gē.le jǐmǔ mài.zi
	'In the country, by seven o'clock we've already cut several acres of wheat out in the fields'
	huí-jiā chī zǎofàn .le.
	'and come back home to eat breakfast.'
LÍNJŪ YǏ:	*Nǚrén.jiā chuān nè.me diǎn'r jiù gǎn kāi chuāng.hù, zhēn bú hàixiū.*
NEIGHBOUR B:	'A women wearing so little dares to open the window, quite shameless.'
LÍNJŪ BǏNG:	*Zhè guòdào .shi gōngjiā de dì'r, guǎn-zháo ma?*
NEIGHBOUR C:	'This lane's a public place, are you in charge of it?'
	Dà mǎlù biān.shang hái guò qìchē .ne, mǎlù.biān'r .de zhùjiā dōu bú shuì-jiào .le,
	'There are cars passing by the road side, if the people living there can't sleep,'
	zěn.me.zhe? Rěn.zhe diǎn'r .ba.
	'so what? Be a little more patient.'
NǓDÀI.FŪ:	*Chǎo.le biérén nǐ hái yǒu-lǐ .ya?*

WOMAN DOCTOR: 'Does that give you a reason for disturbing other people?'

Wǒ .shi yī.shēng, zhidào .ma, shàng.le yèbān, jiù-sǐ fú-shāng

'I'm a doctor, do you know, I've been on night shift, saving lives healing wounds'

wèi rénmín fúwù, xiànzài yào xiū.xì.

'serving the people, now I need to rest.'

LÍNJŪ DĪNG: *Zhè yuàn.li shéi bú.shi yī.shēng .a, wǒ ér.zi hái.shi jiào. shòu-jí .de .ne.*

NEIGHBOUR D: 'So who isn't a doctor in this compound, my son's even professor level.'

NǓDÀI.FŪ: *Nà nǐ zěn.me bú shàng jiào.shòu chuāng.hù.xia chǎo .qù .ya?*

WOMAN DOCTOR: 'Well why don't you go and make a racket under a professorial window then?'

Sù.zhì tài dī .le.

'Such low quality.'

LÍNJŪ: *Wǒ.men bù zhīdào sù.zhì, jiù zhīdào sùxiàn'r,*

NEIGHBOUR: 'We don't know anything about quality (*sù.zhì*), we only know vegetarian (*sùxiàn'r*),'

yǒu běnshì nǐ wǎng biéshù qù .ya.

'if you're so superior why don't you go and live in a villa.'

This exchange shows the class war, contemporary Chinese style, in full raucous flow. The insults traded on both sides are particularly revealing. The doctor starts, quite justifiably one would have thought, by asking why they can't choose somewhere else to make noise. To her interlocutors, however, the desire to sleep after 7 o'clock in the morning is obviously far too precious: in what until recently would have been the most damning insult, so *zīchǎn jièjí* 'bourgeois'. This big-city softness is contrasted with themselves, early-rising hard-working country people, who would already have been out in the fields for hours by this time. Attention then shifts to the fact that the woman doctor hasn't taken time to put anything over her nightdress, and she is dismissed with a classic sexist putdown: *bú hàixiū* 'shameless'. Someone else then points out that where they are is *gōngjiā .de dì'r* 'a public place', and that the doctor has no more right to complain of them making a racket than people living beside the road would have to complain of the passing cars making noise.

Although things have obviously gone far beyond the stage of reasoned argument, the doctor attempts to justify herself by saying that she's been on night duty and so needs to sleep in the daytime, but this is quickly dismissed with what we might call a 'rankist' putdown: since for many people in China housing is provided by the employer, most of the doctor's neighbours are likewise doctors, and the son of one of the noisemakers is even *jiào.shòu jí de* 'of professorial rank'. Angrily ignoring the implied threat here (one which is made good a little later in the novel when the noisemakers complain to the management), the doctor makes the snappy comeback that they should go and make noise under a *jiào.shòu chuāng.hù* 'professorial window', and then gives what for her is clearly the ultimate putdown: *sù.zhì tài dī le* 'quality is too low'. Her interlocutors are not at all abashed by this, sarcastically punning that they don't know anything about *sù.zhì* 'quality', only about *sùxiàn'r* 'vegetarian filling'(such as you would get in dumplings, etc.), contrasting her 'refined' moral standards with their own down-to-earth realism. They finish up with a final hint that she is too superior for her surroundings and should go and live in a *biéshù* 'villa', in other words, a free-standing house with a garden, likely to be way out of her financial reach, rather than the relatively cheap apartment complex she is obviously finding so unsatisfactory.

You'll note that I've been careful to provide the original Chinese for each of the insults. This is not mere pedantry on my part. Obviously a knowledge of the original language is necessary to appreciate the pun in the final retort, which strictly speaking is untranslatable as it stands, but the same principle applies to all of the other insults I've quoted. There is basically no way anyone could gain an appreciation of what these terms imply without going through the particular language in which they are expressed. Every language operates through a complex network of interlocking distinctions, most of them only implicitly understood by their users – just as very often the taxi-driver is unable to explain to you exactly what he means by *sù.zhì* – and in going from one language to another, as in translation, you are inevitably replacing the particular network provided by one language with that of another. Thus it is in principle impossible to understand the full force of the exchange between the doctor and the 'peasants' without being able to operate within the same language they are using, and through that to an understanding of the context in which that makes sense. Going through a translation, even the most 'faithful' one, inevitably leaves you looking from the outside through a more or less distorting window.

Learning about language

Which brings us to the final branch of our language learning trio: *learning about language*. To explore this concept, we can take a look at another text from a magazine, this time a professional production of a genre that has only recently arrived in China: the men's fashion magazine. In this particular magazine, called in Chinese *Shíshàng Jūnzǐ* or 'Fashionable Gentleman' which somehow ended up in English as *MENBOX* – an example of the unidiomatic English renderings very common across Asia – the editor provides a little message each month at the beginning of the issue, usually focusing on some current hot topic. An excerpted version of this is given below, just enough to give you a feel for the argument. You'll note that what I've provided here is a word-for-word rendering – what linguists call 'glossing' – rather than a proper translation: the reasons for this will become clear below.

卷首语　　　Editor's note

空也？色也？

kòng	*yě?*	*sè*	*yě?*
emptiness	EQU	colour	EQU

三藏法师在著名的《心经》中写道：

Sānzàng fǎshī　　　zài zhùmíng .de Xīnjīng zhōng xiědào:

Tripitaka Law-Teacher at famous SUB Heart Sutra in write-say

空不异色，色不异空，

kòng	*bú*	*yì*	*sè,*	*sè*	*bú*	*yì*	*kòng*
emptiness	not	differ	colour	colour	not	differ	emptiness

空即是色，色即是空。……

kòng	*jí*	*shì*	*sè,*	*sè*	*jí*	*shì*	*kòng*
emptiness	then	be	colour	colour	then	be	emptiness

孔子曰：吾未见有好色如好德者。

Kǒngzǐ　　　yuē:　wú wèi jiàn　yǒu　hào sè　rú hào dé zhě

Kong-Master say I haven't see exist love colour like love virtue NOM

这里的色指的是一切对人有诱惑力的物质因素，

Zhè.li .de sè　　zhǐ.de .shi　yíqiè duì rén yǒu yòuhuòlì .de wù.zhì yīnsù,

here SUB colour refer SUB be all to people exist tempt-power SUB matter element

当然也包括情色，而德则指的是良好的操守，

dāngrán yě bāokuò qíngsè,　ér　dé　zé zhǐ.de .shi　liánghǎo .de cāoshǒu,

of-course also contain sex whereas virtue then refer SUB be good SUB control

为整个社会或为整个群体接纳的标准。

wèi zhěnggè shèhuì huò　wèi zhěnggè qúntǐ　jiēnà .de biāozhǔn.

for whole society or for whole collective admit SUB standard

孔子很明白，人很容易被诱惑，

Kǒngzǐ　　hěn míng.bái,　rén　hěn róngyì　bèi yòuhuò,

Kong-Master very understand person very easy PASS tempt

比如金钱，比如情色，而人也总是被一些标准所束缚，

bǐrú jīnqián, bǐrú qíngsè　ér　rén　yě zǒng.shi bèi yìxiē biāozhǔn suǒ shùfù

e.g. money e.g. sex whereas person also always PASS some standard REL bind

比如道德，比如游戏规则。……

bǐrú dàodé,　bǐrú yóuxì guīzé.

e.g. virtue e.g. game rule

可惜凡人在世，往往是

Kěxī　fánrén　　　zàishì,　wǎng.wǎng .shi

be-pity ordinary-people in-world frequently be

道义放两边，利字摆中间。

dàoyì　　　fàng liǎngbiān, lìzì　　bǎi zhōngjiān.

morality-justice place two-side benefit-word put middle

The reason why I've given the text in glossed form here is that I want you to attend very closely to the actual language, which as we'll see below is actually a sort of mixed language. The glossing here, as opposed to a proper 'Englished' translation, gives you some idea of how the original Chinese works, even if it is via an abbreviated text-messagy sort of English. A gloss such as 'Confucius very understand person very easy PASS tempt' may sound like an updated version of those old 'Confucius say ...' jokes, but it does reflect fairly accurately how the Chinese is put together. In this kind of glossing, lexical or content words are matched with their closest English equivalents, while words glossed in small caps, such as PASS(IVE), are grammatical words which perform many of the functions of word endings in English: here *bèi* indicates that the following action is to be interpreted as 'be tempted' rather than 'tempt'.

In this particular issue of the magazine, which came out near the beginning of 2005, the editor discourses in philosophical vein on a concept that goes way back in Chinese thinking, that of *sè*. This translates literally as 'colour', (as in modern Chinese *yánsè* 'colour') but a more accurate equivalent would be something like 'appearance' or 'looks' (the concept comes up again in a similar context in Chapter 7). The editor quotes two ancient authorities on this term: Kǒngzǐ or Confucius himself, who contrasts it with *dé* 'virtue'; and Buddhist Master Sānzàng, literally the 'Three Scriptures', the historical basis for the Tripitaka of the classic Chinese novel *Journey to the West* and its derived *Monkey* films and television series, who contrasts it with *kòng* 'emptiness'.

But what did these two venerable gentlemen actually say? The editor quotes Confucius as follows:

孔子曰：吾未见有好色如好德者。

Kǒngzǐ   yuē: wú wèi jiàn   yǒu   hào   sè   rú   hào dé   zhě
Kong-Master say I haven't see exist love colour like love virtue NOM

'Confucius said: I haven't seen anyone who loves virtue as much as he loves appearance.'

If the language of this quotation strikes you as a bit strange, that's because it's not in modern Chinese at all, but in what's called 'classical Chinese' – in Chinese *wényán* or 'literary language' – which is based on the spoken language of Confucius's lifetime, traditionally set at 551–476 BCE. The work from which this saying is taken, *Lúnyǔ*, normally translated as *The Analects* but equally accurately translatable simply as *Sayings*, is as the name suggests a compilation of the Master's wise words taken down after his death by his disciples. It's likely to be reasonably close to how people actually talked at the time in terms of its vocabulary and grammar: the pronunciation has obviously changed drastically in the intervening two and a half thousand years, but classical Chinese is normally read according to the modern pronunciation of the characters. In this language, the grammatical word *zhě*, glossed here as NOM(INALISER), turns a preceding phrase into a description of someone who is doing something: so 'love colour [like] love virtue NOM' means something like 'appearance lovers [as much as] virtue lovers' – in Confucius's time, as at present, the former were obviously greatly in the majority!

Classical Chinese is the language in which the Chinese Classics are written, those works of literature, history, divination and philosophy created in the period between Confucius's lifetime and the beginning of the imperial period in around 200 BCE, which became the basis of education from that time up to the beginning of the twentieth century. Chinese students still learn a significant amount of classical Chinese at school, just as up till a generation or two ago Western school children studied Latin. And so like educated English speakers up till recently larding their discourse with Latin quotations, written Chinese is peppered with classical turns of phrase.

The second reverend gentleman quoted, Tripitaka, whose real name was 玄奘 Xuán Zàng (602–664 CE), was writing about a thousand years later than Confucius, near the beginning of the Tang dynasty, often taken to represent the high point of Chinese civilisation, and which was also the high point for Buddhism in China in terms of official recognition and support. Like Confucius, Xuan Zang used the colloquial language of his day, so the language of his quotation is recognisably different from that of Confucius, though still quite distinct from modern Chinese. Xuan Zang uses a series of balanced contrasts to make his paradoxical point that the physical world, *sè*, and the metaphysical or spiritual world, *kòng*, are two sides of the same coin:

空不异色，色不异空，

kòng	*bú*	*yì*	*sè*	*sè*	*bú*	*yì*	*kòng*
emptiness	not	differ	colour	colour	not	differ	emptiness

'Emptiness is no different from appearance, appearance is no different from emptiness;'

空即是色，色即是空。

kòng	*jí*	*shì*	*sè*	*sè*	*jí*	*shì*	*kòng*
emptiness	then	be	colour	colour	then	be	emptiness

'Emptiness *is* appearance, appearance *is* emptiness.'

There are a lot of things we could say about this text just from the viewpoint of what exactly the magazine editor is getting at – or perhaps more to the point *who* she is getting at – by quoting the classics. We could point out, for example, that its sophisticated literacy requirements make it a text obviously aimed at well-educated readers, at least those having finished high school, most probably university graduates. We could remark on the strangeness of a long discussion of the 'emptiness' of 'appearance' in a magazine whose very reason for existence *is* appearance: how to gain and maintain the best body, the best clothes, the best accessories, etc., etc. We could again note the marks of the moralising tradition of Chinese culture, according to which it is almost expected that every aspect of existence will be judged from a moral viewpoint – as we saw above, even the taxi-drivers do it.

But to come back to our earlier question – which you'll note I never explicitly answered – we can ask again: what you would need to *know* in order to be able to understand a text like this; and then extend that into another question: what do we need to *know about* language in order to understand a text like this? Learning how to understand a text such as the one above is not at all a simple process: it requires sustained study of the Chinese language, ideally some time living in a Chinese-speaking country, and some familiarity with the range of printed publications – newspapers, books, magazines – in which a text like the one above takes its place. In a sense, then, such fluency in Chinese language and culture is *precisely* the aim of a Chinese studies course: with all due respect to Professor Davis, understanding *MENBOX* turns out to be not so different from understanding *The Analects* after all.

Written Chinese as a mixed language

But in this case of course we *did* have to understand *The Analects*, or at least part of it, in order to understand *MENBOX*. And this reveals one of the great unspoken secrets of learning to read Chinese: you have to learn at least *two* languages, or even more confusingly, a sort of mixed language, in order to get by with anything but the simplest texts. You won't necessary always find people quoting Confucius or Xuan Zang when they write; though quoting from the classics in the original, like English writers a couple of generations ago quoting Latin, is far from unknown. But the modern Chinese written language is saturated with words and structures from classical Chinese. For example, the second half of the sentence below from a later part of the text not given here:

> wèishén.me wǒ.men zǒng.shi **zài bù jīngyì jiān** **luòrù** **máodùn?**
> why we always be at not intention between fall-into contradiction
> 'Why do we always unintentionally fall into contradiction?'

is pure classical Chinese, something which in a more colloquial style might have been put as follows:

> wèishén.me wǒ.men zǒng.shi **bú gùyì .de** **diào-jìn máodùn .qù .le?**
> why we always be not on-purpose MAN fall enter contradiction go ASP
> 'Why do we always unintentionally fall into contradiction?'

Various rhetorical forms and strategies of classical Chinese are also heavily drawn on in the modern written form: another example from the end of the extract given here uses the classic five-word line of much Chinese poetry, and the balanced antitheses that are so often a feature of that form, where the two lines match word for word lexically and grammatically (in this case they even rhyme as well!):

dào	*yì*	*fàng*	*liǎng*	*biān,*
morality	justice	place	two	side

'morality and justice are placed on either side'

lì	*zì*	*bǎi*	*zhōng*	*jiān.*
benefit	word	put	middle	between

'(and) the word "benefit" is put in the middle'

So when we're talking about Chinese, one of the first lessons in learning *about* language is to be aware that these types of mixtures are a feature of most written language; in fact, this text, coming from the mainland, is far *less* classically influenced than the sort of written Chinese coming out of Taiwan or Hong Kong. When we go from the written to the spoken language, we therefore need to be aware of the great difference between the two, greater in many cases than that between spoken and written English, so for example we can tell that the dialogue quoted later in this essay from a recent movie is much more spoken in style:

就像电影《黑客帝国2》中的对白：

jiù xiàng	*diànyǐng*	Hēikè Dìguó 2	*zhōng .de*	*duìbái:*
just like	movie	Hacker Empire 2	in SUB	dialogue

'Just like the dialogue in the movie *The Matrix Reloaded*:'

'每个人来到世界上都有他的使命，

'*Měi.ge rén*	*lái-dao shìjiè.shang*	*dōu yǒu*	*tā.de*	*shǐmìng,*
each MEAS person	come to world on	all exist	s/he SUB	mission

'"Everyone who comes into the world has their mission,'

都有他必须要做的事，

dōu yǒu	*tā*	*bìxū yào zuò .de*	*shì,* '
all exist	s/he	must have-to do SUB	matter

'has something that they absolutely must do,"'

But equally we need to be aware, as I mentioned earlier when raising the question of how exactly to define the 'Chinese language', that *spoken* Chinese will sound very different coming from the mouth of a young guy from Beijing or an old lady from Shanghai; from a Taiwanese newsreader on Phoenix Satellite TV as opposed to one of their mainland colleagues; from a university professor as opposed to a taxi-driver; from a village mayor as opposed to a national leader; and so on and so on.

None of these things should seem strange or unfamiliar to English speakers. After all we regularly deal with English accents ranging from those from New Zealand and Australia to those from the USA and the United Kingdom, and pretty much everywhere in between, without so much as turning a hair. But for some reason there seems to exist – at least in the world of Chinese teaching judging from many of the textbooks! – the myth that all Chinese people speak some perfectly standard, rather formal, and deadly serious version of the language (we'll see some examples of this in the next chapter). Well you can discard the notion of standard pronunciation for a start. As I commonly retort, with only slight exaggeration, when complemented on my 'standard accent' in speaking Chinese – 'Yes, it's only the foreigners who speak standard Chinese!' Perhaps we could add television and radio newsreaders to that list, but there wouldn't be many groups in Chinese society beyond that for whom anything like a standard accent is at all necessary in their everyday lives.

Conclusion: the importance of attending to taxi-drivers

And to get back to the importance of attending to conversations with taxi-drivers: if we remind ourselves of the centrality of language to our lives, and to the whole social and cultural world bound up with each language, we shouldn't need to be convinced that an understanding of the different world that each language provides for us, and a genuine understanding of the implications of language study in all its facets, is an essential part not just of language learning but also of the social and cultural awareness necessary for using a language successfully. So it's not so strange, or really at all trivial, that I should be 'arguing semantics' with a Beijing taxi-driver: such arguments over social, economic, political and cultural concepts are in fact the very stuff of our existence. And for those of you who have set out on the great endeavour of moving across different cultures, an endeavour which never really comes to an end, such an awareness is crucial to your ability to make sense of another culture, both to yourselves, and to your peers, anglophone and sinophone.

Afterword: becoming sinophone by way of Chinese studies

At this point, by way of reflection on the discussion you've just read, it would be useful to turn our gaze on to the aims and needs of language learning at university, understanding this as fundamentally a process of *becoming sinophone*, i.e. of learning how to operate in Chinese language environments with a comparable degree of familiarity and comfort to those of your own native language. In the typical university Chinese studies program, language learning tends to occupy a somewhat anomalous position. While it is widely acknowledged that fluency in the language is an absolute prerequisite for any serious academic work in the field of Chinese studies, language teaching itself is commonly regarded within Chinese studies and within universities more broadly as merely involving the imparting of technical skills. So not only is it not regarded as an academic subject in its own right, but the links between language learning and the content areas of a Chinese studies program are rarely explored, with the normal organisation of an undergraduate program being an uneasy compromise whereby the teaching of language skills is heavily emphasised in the first year or two, and then progressively sidelined for more 'serious' studies.

The gap between language and content in a Chinese studies program is further widened by the common if frequently unconscious expectation among teachers that the type of language taught to students needs to be a simplified decontextualised form of Chinese that no-one actually uses in real-life situations, so that the huge range of variation in spoken and written Chinese, comparable to that across the whole English-speaking world, is largely ignored in favour of a 'cleaned-up' standardised form of the language that immediately marks the user out as a foreigner. I believe that it is ultimately counterproductive to attempt to reduce the genuine complexity of the language situation, and that a continual and positive engagement with the variability of Chinese language use across different textual, social and geographical contexts is the best way to equip you as potential sinophone for a career and a life involving the use of Chinese.

In order to maximise the benefits of language learning in an academic context, we need to explicitly draw links between the learning of language and the learning of content in a Chinese studies program. It may help to explain the general approach introduced here if I borrow a distinction widely applied in foreign language teaching in China itself between 精读 *jīngdú* 'close reading' and 泛读 *fàndú* 'wide reading' (Ting 1987) and marry it to the complementarity I noted above between text (Chinese 语篇 *yǔpiān*) and context (语境 *yǔjìng*). It seems to me that the emphasis in university Chinese teaching tends to be on *jīngdú* 'close reading', in other words on gaining a detailed understanding of the words and structures of a small number of texts, at the expense of an alternative focus both on *fàndú* 'wide reading', i.e. a broader acquaintance with a variety of texts, and on the range of contexts in which such texts are used and make sense. The approach adopted here could be summed up in a quotation from the above discussion: 'learning language … consists of getting a more and more detailed understanding of what kinds of texts are appropriate to what kinds of contexts'.

In order to do this, you as language learner need to be provided with a range of linguistic and conceptual tools. The sorts of linguistic tools necessary are hinted at in the variety of approaches to 'rendering' Chinese texts into English demonstrated above, spanning a range from contextually appropriate translation without direct reference to the vocabulary and grammar of the original, whereby you can focus on the key terms under discussion; to the type of word-for-word glossing, including glossing of grammatical items, more familiar from linguistic analyses, where you are forced to make your own sense of the text; as well as the more familiar types of translation in between these two extremes.

The sorts of conceptual tools you need include ways of making sense of your own learning and of your status as language learner, and here academic notions of 'hybridity', and their popular counterparts in social types like 'bananas' and 'eggs', as well as the idea of developing a sinophone identity, are very useful (see the extended discussion of these points in Chapter 9). From a pedagogical point of view, notions like text and context, the three stages of the language learning process – learning language, learning through language, and learning about language – allow both teachers and students not just to appreciate the complexity of what is involved in language learning, but to develop ways of navigating through that complexity.

In the context of Chinese studies more broadly, these ideas about language learning are relevant to the concerns of what eminent sinologist Geremie Barmé has dubbed 'the New Sinology' (Barmé 2005). In 'relaunching' Chinese studies under this label, Barmé has argued for what he calls a 'robust engagement with contemporary China', which includes as 'a necessity' a 'rigorous textual analysis (*kaozheng*)', using the traditional term from Chinese scholarship for something very like the close reading of texts we carried out in this chapter (see Chapter 8 for a more detailed discussion). The main aims of Barmé's call for a marrying of linguistic skills and content areas can be summarised as follows:

- strong scholastic underpinnings in both modern and classical language and studies;
- an ecumenical attitude to a rich variety of approaches and disciplines;
- an abiding respect for written and spoken forms of Chinese as these have evolved over the centuries;
- an unrelenting attentiveness to sinophone ways of speaking, writing, and seeing, and the different forces that have shaped the evolution of sinophone texts and images and ways of sense-making.

I believe that university Chinese language programs *can* be designed to be sensitive to such concerns, at the same time as satisfying more focused language learning needs: in fact I see no contradiction at all between the two. First, from the point of view adopted in this book, learning language *means* learning culture – learning Chinese is inevitably, to different degrees, turning Chinese – and it makes no sense to arbitrarily confine certain learners, or certain stages of the learning process, to a decontextualised type of Chinese. Second, a closer engagement with sinophone texts and contexts can only be of benefit to you as potential sinophone in terms not only of usable skills and knowledge, but also for your own appreciation of the intellectual excitement and practical relevance of a university language course. While the approach demonstrated here is aimed at higher level students, and thus takes a certain level of language proficiency for granted, there is in principle no reason why such an approach could not be applied from the very start of a university Chinese language program.

The challenge for teachers and academics is to find and actively draw the connections between language skills and content areas in order to give you as potential sinophone a genuine appreciation of the sinophone world, not giving up the challenge before they start because the language is 'too difficult' or the culture is 'too different'. In relation to Chinese studies, I believe very strongly with Barmé, despite leaving myself open to accusations of exclusivity (see Chapter 8), that the only practical and comprehensive approach to sinophone culture is through the language. In relation to language learning, I would also contend that language and context are inextricably linked and it is not possible, without 'making up' a whole lot of language that no-one actually uses, to teach one without the other. In the next chapter, we go on to examine the different, sometimes contradictory, language teaching traditions that coexist in contemporary Chinese studies, and see to what extent they serve the needs of contemporary learners.

Gate lion

2

GATEWAYS TO BECOMING SINOPHONE

Conflicting paradigms in Chinese language textbooks

Getting into sinophone culture: the textbook shows the way

In the previous chapter, I introduced the notion of *sinophone*, defined as capable of operating fluently and comfortably in a Chinese language environment. The term 'sinophone' is modelled on terms like 'anglophone' or 'francophone' commonly used to describe citizens of former English or French colonies who still use the former colonial language for purposes of educating themselves and keeping in touch with the outside world. Many of the former French colonies in Africa and elsewhere have in fact joined themselves into a grouping defined in linguistic terms as 'La Francophonie', i.e. the 'French-speaking community', which performs some of the same functions that the British Commonwealth does for former British colonies. While this specific political context is arguably not directly applicable to the situation of non-Chinese speakers moving into a Chinese language environment, a term like sinophone is useful inasmuch as it implies that what is going on here is not simply learning a language, but getting access to a whole culture and way of life.

Most contemporary Chinese language textbooks, particularly at university level, would see at least part of their role as inculcating students into Chinese society and culture. But how exactly do they go about doing this? In terms of the language learning model put forward in the previous chapter, how do they draw links between *text* and *context* in the way the language is presented? What sorts of understandings of 'language' and of 'culture' do they incorporate? And what is the wider context in which learning Chinese – becoming sinophone, in our terms – is seen as valuable?

To provide some preliminary answers to these questions, we can take a brief look at a textbook that came out of the Australian university system in the early 1990s, and which made one of its main guiding principles the notion of 'China literacy', a concept close to our notion of 'becoming sinophone', and a specific example of the discourses of 'Asia literacy' and 'being part of Asia' that were very much in the air in Australia at the time (e.g. Fitzgerald 1997). *You Can Speak Mandarin* (Lee 1993) implies in its very title an optimistic program for Australians becoming part of Asia, while its emphasis on the spoken language places it very firmly within the communicative paradigm of language learning, one of the three paradigms relevant to Chinese studies to be examined later in this chapter.

The introduction to the textbook is worth excerpting at some length to give a flavour of the kind of language learning on offer:

1   The *dialogues* are organised according to themes (such as times and dates, family members, food and drinks). These situational dialogues incorporate about 150 *functions* and *notions* and can be freely used by students in specific *situations*.
2   The *situations* focus on Meihua, *a student from China*, and Peter, *a student who is studying Chinese at university*. The two students start their friendship by *exchanging language lessons*, and become interested in each other's lives and problems.
3   The dialogues are central to the language learning of the course. There is a *pinyin* version of each dialogue to ensure its *memorisation*. This is followed by another version written in a *mixture of characters and pinyin* to aid the recognition of the *prescribed characters* of each unit.
4   Examples incidental to the explanation of the notes are given in pinyin and students should check their character version in the two glossaries at the back of the book. Words containing characters *within the 300 character set* are given in characters or a combination of characters and pinyin.
5   Each dialogue is intended to *simulate the social context* in which the language is used. Students are encouraged to absorb what they hear on the tape in the context of the pictures they see at the opening of each unit. (Students are reminded that *these pictures are to act as prompts only*.)
6   *After the dialogue has been learned*, the functions, notions or *structures* are presented with other examples for consolidation. This practice phase is followed by the *production* phase where students are engaged in activities, in which they have to use their newly *acquired* language to complete tasks.

(*Lee 1993: xx, original numbering, emphasis added*)

This summary of teaching methodology puts forward a number of sometimes contradictory requirements. In line with widely accepted practice in communicative language teaching, the relationship between text and context is conceptualised as one between *dialogue* and *situation*, whereby a sample of spoken language is scripted as ostensibly suitable to a particular social context (although, as we will see below, the language of the particular dialogue from the textbook examined here is in fact organised around quite different principles). The dialogue is set within the socio-cultural context of a 'language exchange' between a native Chinese speaker and an English speaker learning

Chinese, a common theme in Chinese language textbooks across a range of paradigms. The relationship between text and context is further specified, in line with one influential version of the communicative model, in terms of a number of different *functions* and *notions*, explained in one account of communicative approaches as follows:

> A functional-notional approach to language learning places major emphasis on the *communicative purpose(s)* of a speech act. It focuses on what people want to do or what they want to accomplish through speech ... [i.e.] the *functions* of language which all human beings want to express at one time or another ... *functional* language must also incorporate specific *notions*; that is, the vocabulary items that ... might answer the questions *who, when, where,* and *why.*
> (*Finocchiaro and Brumfit 1983: 13–14, original emphasis*)

In *You Can Speak Mandarin*, this externally situation-focused view of language learning coexists with another internally language-focused one, whereby the language learning process is understood as the 'acquisition' of certain *words, structures,* and *characters* which are 'prescribed' within the particular unit, or for the book as a whole, and once 'acquired' can then be used in 'production' by the students to demonstrate their learning. The fact that it is these items which are the real focus of learning is underscored by the requirement that the dialogue, and so the words, structures and written characters which it contains, should be 'memorised'; and by the warning that the accompanying pictures are to be used 'as prompts only', rather than providing an alternative access to the situation not necessarily tied to the particular linguistic items incorporated in the dialogue. This narrow linguistic focus is further constrained by a requirement across the textbook as a whole to memorise a restricted set of '300 Chinese characters'. In line with this requirement, the spoken dialogues are presented not just in the standard romanised form (*Hanyu*) *pinyin* or '(Chinese) spelling' which provides a reasonably consistent representation of the spoken language, but also 'in a mixture of characters and pinyin', a written form which mixes sound-based and wording-based scripts, and which is never used outside the very restricted context of language textbooks.

We will come back to this textbook later in the chapter, and compare it with a more recent 'textbook' produced for the Beijing Olympics, which shows a similarly contradictory pull between a focus on language and a focus on situation. Before that, however, we need to get a better understanding of the traditions and models of language learning that lie behind textbooks such as these.

University Chinese teaching: the state of the art

A well-established if rather irrational tradition of academic snobbery tends to relegate textbooks to second-class status in the academic world, ignoring their fundamental contribution to inculcating students into the field. Kuhn's pioneering work on the creation of scientific knowledge (Kuhn 1962/1970) pointed out how the messiness of historical developments in a field of knowledge is often hidden from the student in the way textbooks are framed, with all predecessors unproblematically replaced by whichever framework is being put forward as the 'right' one. In contrast in Chinese language teaching, new textbooks tend to incorporate, rather than replace, the frameworks and methods used by their predecessors, and changes in academic and pedagogical fashions are reflected in the commonly mixed nature of many textbooks, where new developments are regarded as providing new tools to add to an existing toolkit.

In fairness to the textbook designers, it must first be acknowledged that university-level Chinese language teachers labour under a number of constraints not shared by their secondary colleagues, or by colleagues in European language departments. The first is the sheer time span and range covered by Chinese studies. Whereas most European language departments concentrate on the modern vernacular, say from 1500 CE to the present, the label 'Chinese' is applied equally to the language of the period beginning at least two thousand years before that, usually specified as 'classical Chinese', as to the language of the modern period. Since most official records, history, and 'serious' literature were written in classical Chinese up until the early decades of the twentieth century, it is impossible to ignore it in a Chinese studies program, but the language itself is at least as different from modern Chinese as, say, modern Italian is from Latin – neither of which are ever taught in the same course, let alone regarded as in some way being 'the same language'. Along with this long chronological scope, the thematic range of Chinese studies includes many areas such as history, philosophy, politics, etc., which would not be seen as falling within the purview of European language departments, but rather as belonging to the separate disciplines of (European) history, (European) philosophy, and so on.

Faced with this impossible *embarras de richesse*, many Chinese departments end up specialising in a particular area: traditional China, contemporary China, professional language skills, and so on. Some of these choices entail a focus on a particular form of the language: for example, courses on traditional China will necessarily stress the acquisition of classical Chinese, while courses on contemporary China will concentrate on the modern language, commonly giving only as much instruction in the classical language as is necessary for reading newspapers or works of modern literature. Nevertheless, whatever choice is made, the effective learning of language skills is vital to the successful realisation of the aims of the Chinese course as a whole.

In his comprehensive overview of Chinese language instruction in the United States two decades ago (Walton 1989), Walton argued cogently for the establishment of a field of Chinese language teaching whose practitioners hold 'a core of shared assumptions about knowledge and practice' (Walton 1989: 28). He characterised then current teaching practice as vitiated by two major tendencies. The first, which he called 'instructional diffusion', refers to the presence of conflicting paradigms, such as the 'Area Studies Paradigm', the 'Literature Paradigm', the 'Native Language Paradigm' which (Walton 1989: 16) 'provide so many definitions of the substance of language study that it becomes difficult to find a common core of agreement of just exactly what Chinese language study is all about'.

The second, which he dubbed 'instructional relativism', refers to the attitude that

> the perceived reality is that there are different reasons for learning Chinese, thus different goals, many different types of learner with different learning styles and preferences, and many different learning settings … this relativism, far from being problematic, is seen as a sign of vitality, flexibility and adaptability.
>
> (*Walton 1989: 21*)

Walton's pessimistic conclusion from this situation was that:

> Instructional Relativism, with each teacher idiosyncratically defining his or her course, combines with the Instructional Diffusion generated from the influence of the various paradigms to produce such fragmentation that we are perhaps conveying a false impression when we venture to use the term 'program' at all.
>
> (*Walton 1989: 21*)

Competing paradigms in current university Chinese teaching

Taking a cue from Walton, I will try to make sense of the variation in teaching aims and methodologies across the field by identifying three main paradigms in university-level Chinese language teaching. The use of the term 'paradigm' rather than the more narrowly pedagogical 'teaching methodology' is intended to bring out the essential point that understandings of language teaching and learning take their place within broader cultural and intellectual traditions, each with its own values and aims.

I have called the three paradigms identified here the 'communicative', already briefly examined above, the 'grammar-translation', and the 'classical'. Before we go on to look at each in detail below, let's first briefly explore the implications of the terms themselves.

- *Communicative* is often taken by its supporters as self-evidently superior to the other paradigms: if the purpose of language learning is 'communication', it is surely an obvious truism that language teaching should be 'communicative'. In practice, however, it is more narrowly defined, usually entailing an emphasis on the spoken language, particularly in the form of dialogues, often organised around the teaching of 'functions' and 'notions' (see definition quoted above).
- *Grammar-translation* refers to a methodology whereby the material is organised around a systematic grammatical progression and whose main learning strategy is translation into and from the target language. Highly influential

since the beginning of the nineteenth century in the European context, its emphasis on the passive learning of rules has seen it easily absorbed into the traditional authority-centred Chinese teaching system.

- *Classical* is an intentionally multivalent term. It refers to this paradigm's emphasis on classical Chinese, but equally stresses the ways in which this tradition draws on the classical traditions of both China and Europe in its concentration on canonical written texts and its privileging of the language and values of the literate elite.

In the following sections I will consider each tradition in more depth, identify its aims and sources, and sum up the main features of its realisation in current teaching practice in terms of the kinds of learning that it both does and does not facilitate.

The communicative paradigm

What we would now call 'communicative' approaches have the longest tradition in foreign language teaching in Europe, the earliest major example being the teaching of Greek to Roman children under the Roman Empire. Educated Romans were fully bilingual in Latin and Greek, and this educational process started at an early age, as described by Titone:

> The education of the young Roman was bilingual from infancy. In his earlier years the child was entrusted to a Greek nurse or slave; when he reached school age, he would begin learning the three R's in the two languages at the same time; later on he would follow the parallel course of the Greek *grammaticos* and the Latin *ludi magister*, and then those given by the Greek *rhetor* and by the Latin *orator*.
>
> (*Titone 1968: 6*)

Thus the Roman child would learn to speak and read and write Greek in much the same way as, and largely in tandem with his acquisition of those skills in his native tongue. Similar methods based on oral fluency were followed for most of the history of the teaching of Latin in Europe up to the modern era.

Starting from the late nineteenth century, the scope of education in Europe, and therefore that of language teaching, began to broaden dramatically. No longer was the acquisition of a foreign language confined mainly to the upper classes; no longer was emphasis put solely on mastering the classical languages and literature of antiquity, their study being replaced by that of the vernacular national languages of Europe. The same period saw the development of a more systematic approach to the analysis of language: first taking over the title of 'philology' originally confined to the study of the language and literature of the classics; later termed 'linguistics'. Modern so-called 'structural' linguistics concerned itself with all the features – sound, vocabulary, grammar, meaning – that were relevant to the description of all languages and therefore to language teaching.

The combination of the wider scope of language learning and a more comprehensive understanding of how languages worked produced a proliferation of 'methods' for teaching language: the direct method, the structural approach, the audio-lingual method, the situation method, and so on (see Finocchiaro and Brumfit 1983: Ch. 1). Language teachers were eager – perhaps too eager – to adapt the latest linguistic theories to their classroom practice, not always with the most positive results. By around 1970, according to the account given by Stern (1983: 108–112), the inevitable backlash against 'methods', particularly against the idea that any one method was sufficient for teaching languages, began to set in. At the same time, theorists started to go beyond simply designing new methods of classroom teaching to deal also with 'language teaching objectives, language content, and curriculum (or syllabus) design' (Stern 1983: 109). A whole body of research grew up around the process of second language learning itself, on the premise that we need to understand exactly how people learn other languages before we can hope to teach them successfully. Finally there was a new focus on the individual language learner, along with an attempt to 'create an awareness of the hidden curriculum of the social and affective climate created by the interaction among students and between students and the teachers' (Stern 1983: 110).

From the mid-seventies these new approaches came together under the banner of 'communicative language teaching'. The term 'communicative competence' was coined by American linguist Dell Hymes to characterise what was involved in the use of language (Hymes 1971), formulated in deliberate contrast to Chomsky's more abstract notion of 'linguistic competence' as a system of neurologically deep-wired rules (Chomsky 1965). Hymes's definition of communicative competence stressed the social context of language acquisition whereby (Hymes 1971: 277): 'a normal child acquires knowledge of sentences, not only as grammatical, but also as appropriate. He or she acquires competence as to when to speak, when not, and as to what you talk about with whom, when, where, in what manner.' A 'communicative' approach to language teaching would thus include not only knowledge of the language-internal aspects of a language – its pronunciation, vocabulary and grammar – but also an understanding of the appropriate use of a language in different social contexts.

Communicative approaches emphasise the connection between language form and language use – between text and context in our terms – in a generalised way that can be applied to a wide range of language learning needs. It is this systematic attempt to provide a context for language learning that is one of the most attractive features of communicative approaches. However, with its tendency to characterise the notion of 'situation' in fairly concrete terms, and its use of dialogues as the basic type of text, in Chinese teaching the communicative approach has found itself better adapted to the teaching of the spoken language, and particularly those instances of spoken language which take place in a clearly defined situation and with clear goals. This sort of methodology has proven less well-suited to those uses of language that are not so closely tied to a concrete situation, as with much written language.

The grammar-translation paradigm

The grammar-translation method is often regarded as representing the 'traditional' method of language teaching in Europe, with its background in the study of the classics. In fact not only does this tradition have no essential connection with the teaching of the classics in Europe, which for most of their history as taught languages were taught through repetition and practice rather than analysis, but is itself a relative newcomer on the language teaching scene, being first found in the textbooks of Germans such as Seidenstücker (1785–1817) whose *Elementarbuch zur Erlernung der französischen Sprache* [Elementary French Textbook] (1811) is described by Titone as follows:

> he reduced the material to disconnected sentences to illustrate specific rules. He divided his text carefully into two parts, one giving the necessary rules and paradigms, the other giving French sentences for translation into German and German sentences for translation into French.
>
> (*Titone 1968: 27*)

The generalisations provided by grammatical rules were seen as giving students the means to produce a wide range of linguistic patterns, but this tended to go together with the custom of 'constructing artificial sentences in order to illustrate the rule' (Titone 1968: 28), a practice whose inadequacies were well summed up by the late nineteenth-century English phonetician and grammarian Henry Sweet:

> The result is to exclude the really natural and idiomatic combinations, which cannot be formed *a priori*, and to produce insipid, colourless combinations, which do not stamp themselves on the memory, many of which, indeed, could hardly occur in real life, such as *the cat of my aunt is more treacherous than the dog of your uncle* ...
>
> (*Sweet 1899/1972: 72*)

As far as Chinese language teaching is concerned, the grammar-translation approach is a European import. From the late Qing period, Western-style grammar was enthusiastically adopted for the analysis of Chinese. Diplomat and scholar Ma Jianzhong (1845–1900), the first Chinese scholar to produce a Western-style grammar of classical Chinese based on his study of Latin grammar, considered that one of the reasons for the political and economic strength of the Western powers was the economy given to their education systems by the systematic study of grammar (Mair 1997). The study of grammar in China was seen as one of the types of Western learning that could be utilised to 'save the country' (*jiù guó*), and from the start had a close connection with language teaching. It is no surprise, therefore, to find most language textbooks in mainland China up till very recently adopting some version of the grammar-translation approach.

Furthermore, as pointed out by Ting (1987: 54), this type of 'grammar-centred' approach also fits well with the 'teacher-centredness' and 'textbook-centredness' of traditional Chinese teaching methods.

As for the specifically translation-based part of the method, this was certainly a part of the classical tradition in Europe, though more as a sideline to the main oral-based techniques. English philosopher John Locke in his *Some Thoughts Concerning Education* (1693) recommended as the 'true and genuine way' for parents to have their sons learn Latin, to find 'a Man ... who himself speaking good Latin, would always be about your son, talk constantly to him, and suffer him to speak or read nothing else' (quoted in Titone 1968: 15), in other words the traditional oral-based approach that was the norm for the learning of Latin. However, he recommends as a practical alternative 'taking some easy and pleasant books, such as *Aesop's Fables*, and writing the *English* translation (made as literal as can be) in one line, and the Latin words which answer each of them, just over it in another ...' (quoted in Titone 1968: 15). (This method of interlinear translation or glossing, which we saw in the previous chapter, is now used mainly in linguistic analyses.)

The common point of these two uses of translation, in sharp distinction to the use of translation in later practice, is the fact that they are both text-based. However, many of the advantages of such an approach are lost when dealing not with whole texts, which to a large degree create their own context, but with decontextualised isolated sentences. The exercise of translation then becomes more like an intellectual game – a kind of riddle-solving – than a practical preparation for the use of a foreign language, for which it may indeed prove a definite hindrance, in that it encourages in students the habit of attempting to *translate* everything they hear or read rather than *process* it in relation to the context. Similar concerns have been noted about the methodology of 'intensive reading' (*jīngdú*) widespread in the teaching of English in mainland China (cf. Ting 1987: 49) whereby texts are subjected to exhaustive analysis of their words and structures. Such methodologies tend to convince students that they must understand every single element of the language being used in a particular context, a requirement which is not categorical even for native speakers.

The classical paradigm

What I am calling the 'classical' paradigm has its roots in the European and Chinese traditions of the study of their respective classics. Both of these traditions were reading traditions, in which students were initiated into the study of a canon of works written in a literary language quite distinct from the vernacular, the mastery of which thus required special training. While in more recent times the teaching of classical languages in Europe at least has tended to go together with a grammar-translation teaching methodology, in fact, as Titone points out (Titone 1968: 1–2), grammar translation is a relative newcomer on the language teaching scene, and for most of its history as a taught language, Latin, the most significant classical language in Europe and the one with the longest continuous teaching tradition, was taught in a way that could, without too much violence to the term, be called 'communicative'. It was taught orally in the initial stages, often by use of simulated real-life dialogues (Titone 1968: 7), in an overall method that stressed use over analysis. The focus of teaching was summed up in a dictum of the influential seventeenth-century Czech educationalist, Jan Comenius: *Omnis lingua usu potius discatur quam praeceptis* 'Every language should be learned by practice rather than by rules' (quoted in Titone 1968: 14).

It is important to remember that Latin was used as a spoken, as well as written, language among the scholarly classes in Europe up until at least Comenius's time, and it remained the spoken language of the Roman Catholic Church up until the 1960s, not only in most of its liturgies but also in the training of its priests: I myself was taught Latin in high school by an old Jesuit priest who had originally lectured on philosophy to seminarians – in perfect Ciceronian Latin! It was only when Latin ceased to be used as a spoken language, even in such restricted settings, that a more formalistic approach to the teaching of it took hold.

The situation of classical Chinese was a little different, in that it had never been designed for exclusive use as a spoken language, nor was there a strong tradition of public speaking, as reflected in Europe, for example, in the central place given to the study of rhetoric in classical and medieval times, to encourage its use as such. However the classical language was learned through the study of a selected number of written texts which were intended to be memorised, and which once learnt became available for a restricted kind of oral use among the educated. The pathetic nature of the use by Kong Yiji, in Lu Xun's short story of the same name, of the classical *qiè* rather than the vernacular *tōu* to mean 'steal' in replying to taunts that he had 'stolen books' is due to the sad contrast of his high style with the sordid reality; but similar use in more appropriate contexts of words and phrases from the classical language was widespread among the literate elite. Furthermore, the texts were read aloud during learning – even today one of the common terms for studying is *niàn shū*, literally 'read books aloud' – and were pronounced in a modified version of the local dialect. The classical language would thus have seemed to its users like an elevated version or special register of the spoken language, rather than a dead or foreign language.

In both European and Chinese traditions, practice and memorisation were stressed throughout the learning process. In the Chinese system dating from the Han dynasty (206 BCE–220 CE), as described in Bai 2005, the first stage was the memorisation of lists of characters, which were put together into wordbooks for easy use. This stage, being the initial one of the education process, was known as *xiǎoxué*, 'minor learning', and since a lot of scholarship went into explaining and investigating the original forms of the characters, this term eventually came to be applied to linguistic studies more generally. By the Song dynasty (960–1279 CE), these wordbooks had been supplemented with elementary textbooks, containing a limited number of characters, the most commonly used being the *Sānzì Jīng*, or Trimetrical Classic, which was in rhymed lines of three syllables each, the *Qiānzì Wén* or Thousand Character Text and the *Bǎijiā Xìng* or Hundred Surnames, whose titles are self-explanatory: these three texts, according to Bai's calculation, contain a total of around 2,000 characters (Bai 2005: 47). Students were then guided through relatively simple authentic texts, such as the *Xiàojīng* (the Classic of Piety) and the *Lúnyǔ* (the Analects of Confucius) until they were ready for the higher level of learning, known as *dàxué* or 'major learning', which was the study of the Classics.

In the European system, the initial stage of learning Latin concentrated on the memorisation of long lists of word paradigms, i.e. a word in all its different inflected forms, where the different endings indicated different kinds of grammatical meanings. Students were then led through a course of wide reading in a graded sequence, traditionally starting with the terse military prose of Caesar's *De Bello Gallico* or 'On the War in Gaul', moving through prose writers such as the rhetorician Cicero and the historian Livy, and poets such as Ovid and Horace, to the peak, the epic poetry of Virgil. Both systems incorporated imitative composition in set forms – for Chinese schoolboys turning out a *shī* or *cí* poem, in Europe producing Virgilian hexameters – leading to a final literate mastery of the language across a wide range of genres.

A common feature of both these traditions was that education in them required a great deal of time and money, and was therefore restricted to the very small elite for whom the possession of a classical education was necessary for a career in the Church or in government service, or as a marker of social standing. For a certain period after the breakdown of the social systems that supported these educational traditions, that is, well into the last century, their strengths – a strong basis in the classical written language, both active and passive, and a wide reading fluency and acquaintance with a broad range of written styles – were able to be maintained at universities, and in some cases still can be as long as the student has had prior education in the language at school.

However for the majority of present day university students of Chinese, their first exposure to the language, classical or modern, is in the early years of a university course. The traditional first two stages of learning – memorising characters and reading constructed texts – are usually omitted, throwing the student straight into the complexities (not just linguistic, but also philosophical and historical) of canonical texts like the *Mèngzǐ* /Mencius or the *Zhuàngzǐ*/Chuang-tsu. Students in a three or four year university course simply do not have the time to gain the reading fluency that was the hallmark of the traditional classical scholar. Added to this problem is the fact that, by the beginning of the nineteenth century in Europe, the use of a grammar-translation method had become widespread in the teaching of both classical and modern languages, often detaching the learning of the language, in its initial stages at least, from the study of authentic texts.

Another major problem, stemming from the view of the classical language as an elevated register of the spoken vernaculars rather than a completely different language, is the lack of separation between classical and modern Chinese, well symbolised by the contents of a dictionary still widely used in my undergraduate days, *Mathews' Chinese–English Dictionary* (Mathews 1931) which lists together words and examples from all stages of the classical and modern language up to the early twentieth century. Because Chinese, at any era of its recorded history, has never been an inflected language, and as its writing system only indirectly represents pronunciation, classical Chinese looks superficially a lot more like modern Chinese ('they are both written with the same characters') than does, say, Latin like Italian. However, this surface similarity obscures significant differences in vocabulary and grammar between classical and modern Chinese, at least as much as between Latin and Italian, not to mention changes in the classical language itself over the two and a half millennia of its use. This very broad definition of what constitutes 'Chinese' is not only a problem in designing courses, but also causes confusion for students, who commonly start learning classical Chinese before they have a firm basis in the modern language.

Those parts of Chinese programs influenced by the classical paradigm provide relatively little structured teaching of the language, yet still advocate wide reading over a range of periods and styles. Unfortunately time constraints mean that it is virtually impossible for students to gain the requisite reading experience, and their relatively inexplicit grounding in the classical language, as well as confusion as to its boundaries with the modern language, mean that the final active stage of fluency in the language – even in reading, let alone writing – is seldom reached, with a consequent over-reliance on props like vocabulary lists and translations.

Competing paradigms and competing aims

It may seem from the discussion of the different paradigms given above, that what we are seeing is an historical evolution or even progression from classical through grammar-translation to communicative. I believe this would be a misunderstanding, not only because of the limitations of each paradigm as identified above, but because such an analysis ignores the different, and sometimes contradictory pressures on Chinese language courses at university level. A 'communicative' approach, at least as commonly understood, is not well-adapted for the teaching of classical Chinese; while a 'grammar-translation' approach would be largely irrelevant – if not positively counterproductive – to a course aimed at teaching spoken fluency. In practice, many university courses seem to reflect an uneasy compromise between the three paradigms I have described, a compromise forced on many course designers by what I would see as the following three requirements for a degree in Chinese studies:

- a basic speaking and listening proficiency;
- some sort of explicit understanding of the formal workings of the language;
- a reading fluency in, or at worst general acquaintance with classical Chinese.

These three requirements, while obviously related to the three paradigms identified here, should in no way be completely identified with them. The paradigms taken as a whole inevitably bring a whole lot of unwanted baggage with them based on a lack of comprehension of their original aims and teaching context: for example, the wide reading without sufficient foundation of many 'classical' style courses; the notion that explicit teaching about grammar can only be done using a 'grammar-translation' methodology and is incompatible with a communicative approach; or the common equation of 'communicative' with 'oral/aural', meaning that reading and writing tend to be taught less systematically, if at all.

Furthermore, as we will see below, while perhaps the majority of current textbooks claim to be organised in line with the communicative paradigm, in practice they tend to mix elements from all three paradigms within a overall framework whose aims and methods are often not clearly articulated and which reflect usually implicit and unanalysed assumptions about the nature of teaching and learning.

Chinese language teaching and philosophies of learning

Has the field of Chinese teaching made any progress in the two decades since Walton's gloomy judgment quoted earlier? While a recent 'state of the art' summary confidently claims to have put the teaching of Chinese on a firm footing, a closer reading reveals some doubt on this point. *Teaching and Learning Chinese as a Foreign Language* (Xing 2006) claims to be 'the first book written in English that systematically addresses all major aspects involved in teaching and learning Chinese as a foreign language' (back cover). In the author's summary, the overall aim of the book is as follows:

> The basic idea is that the communicative approach is the guiding principle and that we need to develop a system that will integrate all major factors relevant to teaching and learning Chinese into everyday practice so that teachers and students will benefit from such work.
>
> (*Xing 2006: 27*)

Xing identifies two main aims for her work: in relation to existing research in this area, and to the practicalities of teaching Chinese as a foreign language (FL). From a research point of view, her book is:

> designed to help teachers and students of the Chinese language learn the most recent developments in teaching and learning Mandarin Chinese as a foreign language ... it discusses the theoretical models developed for Chinese language pedagogy and acquisition, provides theoretical grounds for selecting teaching materials, and proposes applicable methodology for teaching and learning Chinese.
>
> (*Xing 2006: 1*)

Second, from a practical point of view, the aim of the book is to (p.3): 'serve as a manual for teaching and learning Chinese as FL at all levels, training potential Chinese language teachers, or designing a Chinese language curriculum.'

The book's intended beneficiaries are what Xing refers to as 'Chinese language practitioners', defined as 'teachers and students of Chinese as FL' (p.15) who are seen to share many common goals, as she explains using a domestic metaphor:

> Although the members of these two categories of language practice vary in terms of status/position, attitudes and personality, they engage in activities that are very dependent on goals: to teach or learn communicative skills in the target language. These two members function as if they are a married couple practicing the Chinese language. Both of them have to work hard, learn from each other and cooperate with each other to create a harmonious environment so that teachers become skilful in teaching and students become knowledgeable and competent in communicating in Chinese.
>
> *(Xing 2006: 15)*

The characterisation of teachers and students as forming a family immediately calls to mind the Confucian world view, which takes the hierarchically ordered family as the model for all other forms of social organisation; and at the same time fairly accurately reflects sinophone cultural norms, including those of the language classroom. But whether such a model is necessarily going to be appropriate in the non-Chinese contexts to which the term 'foreign language' specifically refers – as opposed to 'second language' i.e. learning a language in the host country – is a question that is rarely raised in Xing's book, and has only just begun to be raised in the Chinese teaching profession more widely (e.g. Lu 2010).

Moreover, despite its claimed communicative orientation, whereby language learning is assumed to take place in relation to social context, Xing's book shows the same inconsistency reflected in the textbook examined earlier, and summed up by educational linguist Kit Ken Loke in her analysis of recent debates about 'proficiency' in Chinese language teaching circles, that 'despite the proposed attention to "proficiency", the basic underlying view about language is still predominantly structural, not functional or communicative' (Loke 2002: 66). As Loke further explains:

> This decontexualised structural focus implies a pedagogical belief that the mastery of vocabulary and grammatical structures and rules … will automatically enable learners to use them in actual realistic communication, which has been repeatedly proven, in the applied linguistics literature, to be unrealistic.
>
> *(Loke 2002: 68)*

From the point of view of different philosophies of teaching and learning, Ting notes that communicative methodologies in the Chinese setting (Ting 1987: 55), as applied in the teaching of English to Chinese students and the teaching of Chinese to foreign students, have come into conflict with a 'fundamental approach to education' very different from that of these methodologies' European-derived roots. He identifies three 'common denominators' of such methodologies as follows:

1   learner-centred: independent, inquisitive work by the learner;
2   practice-centred: target language communication in the course of learning;
3   skill-development-centred: the development of skills in understanding, speaking, reading and writing as the goal of learning.

In contrast, as Ting points out, traditional Chinese classroom practices show a very different set of emphases, and a quite different relationship between teacher and students, which on the same model could be characterised as follows:

1   teacher-centred: dependent, reproductive work by the learner;
2   textbook-centred: reliance on the textbook as the main guide and authority for learning;
3   content-acquisition-centred: the acquisition of a specified set of words and structures as the goal of learning.

Communicative approaches in Chinese language teaching, while often regarded as self-evidently 'progressive' or 'advanced' in relation to other approaches, thus tend to operate in a general education setting which is profoundly unsympathetic to their basic philosophical standpoint. What we are seeing here in a deep-seated disjunction between the supposed adoption of up-to-date teaching methodologies and the actual retention of a highly conservative philosophy underlying teaching and learning, a disjunction which tends to produce a 'not East not West' style of language teaching we might call 'Confucian Communicative'.

'Confucian Communicative' language teaching in action

Let's come back to the textbook we looked at before (*You Can Speak Mandarin*, Lee 1993) and see how this mix of paradigms operates. The first unit starts, as is common, with greetings. A summary of the situation is first presented, followed by a dialogue:

> Peter meets Jane. They exchange names and discover that they both study Chinese. Jane identifies the teacher.

1 PETER: *Nín hǎo!*
          you:pol good = hello
2 JANE: *Nín hǎo!*
          you:pol good
3 PETER: *Wǒ jiào Peter,   nǐ .ne?*
          I be-called Peter you MOOD:open
4 JANE: *Wǒ jiào Jane.*
          I be-called Jane
5 PETER: *Nǐ xué Zhōngwén .ma?*
          you study Chinese QU:bias

6 JANE: *Wǒ xué Zhōngwén.*
            I study Chinese
7 PETER: *Tā .shì shéi?*
            s/he be who
8 JANE: *Tā .shì lǎoshī*
            s/he be teacher

(Lee 1993: 4, numbering and glossing added)

From the *situational* viewpoint around which this textbook claims to be organised, this conversation is so unlikely as to be almost impossible. Who are 'Peter' and 'Jane'? If, as seems likely from the evidence of their names, they are both English speakers, why are they conversing in Chinese? From the viewpoint of their relationship as expressed through Chinese, why do they start off using the polite pronoun *nín* 'you', and then immediately switch to the ordinary *nǐ*? What are they actually trying to do through language here, and why do they do so in such a stilted manner?

The answer, of course, is that what 'Peter' and 'Jane' are doing here is not governed by the demands of anything like a simulated context of situation: their dialogue has a purely language-internal *structural* motivation. This becomes very clear if we identify the grammatical 'themes' introduced here, those to do with the systems of person and grammatical mood (here we omit the first two moves whose grammar is largely formulaic):

move		*person*	*mood type*
3 PETER:	*Wǒ jiào Peter,*	1st person	statement
	nǐ .ne?	2nd person	abbreviated question
4 JANE:	*Wǒ jiào Jane.*	1st person	statement/answer
5 PETER:	*Nǐ xué Zhōngwén .ma?*	2nd person	yes–no question
6 JANE:	*Wǒ xué Zhōngwén.*	1st person	statement/full answer
7 PETER:	*Tā .shì shéi?*	3rd person	specific question
8 JANE:	*Tā .shì lǎoshī*	3rd person	statement/full answer

It is very clear from the above analysis that, despite its ostensibly communicative dress, the purpose of this dialogue is simply to introduce certain basic grammatical structures. As such, it falls very comfortably into the type of teaching methodology exemplified by the *Practical Chinese Reader* series of textbooks that came out in the early 1980s, whose main 'characters' Palanka and Gubo were familiar to generations of Chinese learners. However, the *Practical Chinese Readers* (Liu *et al.* 1981) were openly organised around a systematic grammatical progression, something *You Can Speak Mandarin* loses because of its ostensibly communicative framework in which grammatical information is reduced to unsystematic 'notes' to the dialogues; while at the same time, the promise implied in its title is belied in practice because you *can't* really speak Mandarin in this way, and wouldn't get very far in sinophone society if you did. Not only is the relationship of dialogue to situation – of text to context in our terms – very unclear, even within the bounds of the dialogue itself the language forms are often not the expected ones: for example, the 'full answer' forms of moves 6 and 8 would be very unlikely in any sort of colloquial register.

Let's try creating a context where this kind of exchange would be more plausible, and coming up with the kind of text which would be appropriate to it. We can turn 'Peter' into 'Piotr', i.e. a Russian, and make him and 'Jane', who can be Australian, both foreign students in China, for whom their only common language is Chinese. Having already studied Chinese in their respective home countries, they have just arrived in China for further study at a Chinese educational institution and meet up outside the classroom on the first day of classes. What they could say, trying not to go too far away from the language of the original dialogue, might go something like this:

PIOTR: *Èi, nǐ hǎo!*
         eh you good
JANE: *Nǐ hǎo!*
         you good
PIOTR: *Nǐ yě .shì xué zhōngwén .de .ma?*
         you also be study Chinese SUB MOOD:bias
JANE: *Shì .ya.*
         be MOOD:excl
PIOTR: *Wǒ .shì Piotr.*
         I be Peter
JANE: *Èi, nǐ hǎo,*   *wǒ jiào Jane*
         eh you good   I be-called Jane
PIOTR: *Nèiwèi .shì wǒ.men .de lǎoshī .ma?*
         that MEAS be we SUB teacher MOOD:bias
JANE: *Shì .ya,*   *nà .shì Lǐ lǎoshī*
         be MOOD:excl   s/he be Li teacher

From a communicative point of view this is all very well, one might object, but from a language learning point of view, this contextually appropriate text contains all sorts of grammatical features which would be too complex for a beginning student. For instance, there is the use of the nominalised structure [*nǐ*] *.shì* [*xué zhōngwén*] *.de* where the basic action clause *nǐ xué zhōngwén* 'you study Chinese' is turned into an identifying clause which has the implication of something like 'you are a Chinese studier' – appropriate for a question where Piotr is in fact claiming the same identity for himself and Jane – not to mention the structural complications of Piotr slipping a *yě* 'also' just after the beginning of that structure and the mood particle *ma*, used for 'biased' questions expecting a positive answer, at the very end of it. But on the other hand, if the aim of learning language in a communicative way, as opposed to the old-fashioned grammar-translation method, is precisely to enable people to communicate, what is the purpose of using the dialogue form in such a strained and awkward fashion? Why not just go back to a *Practical Chinese Reader* style grammar-translation method and be done with it?

Of course, it is not the case that the content of this one dialogue exhausts the information about Chinese language and culture provided by the lesson. After the presentation of the dialogue itself, in both pinyin and mixed character-and-pinyin form (p.4), and a vocabulary list of about half a page (pp.4–5), then follow about four pages (pp.5–9) of 'notes', both linguistic and cultural. However, a close reading of these 'notes' shows up further problems. In line with the 'functions and notions' style of communicative methodology being used here, the first few of these notes are organised around various 'functions', things you can do with language, such as (pp.5–7): *saying hello; saying 'good morning'; saying 'good evening'; telling people your name; asking someone's given name; asking someone's surname; telling people your surname; asking someone's surname (informal).*

A quick look at this list suggests that what is on offer here is in fact a series of *translation equivalents* from anglophone societies: the use of times of the day in greetings, for example, is not a feature of sinophone societies to any great extent; while from a sinophone point of view, the use of the surname is far more prominent, and strategies for eliciting it thus far more important, than the use of a given name – the reverse of the order given here. Although notions of 'formal' and 'informal' are mentioned, something that is crucial in the area of greetings, they are not explained in a way that gives the student access to the dynamics of sinophone societies, and a couple of references to 'honorifics', a peripheral though still significant feature of contemporary sinophone societies, are dropped in without any explanation beyond the remark that they function 'to show respect for the other person' (p.7). To do it justice, *You Can Speak Mandarin* does make a consistent attempt to provide its Australian target learners with the sort of Chinese expressions that they can use in their home context: however, the result is often a kind of 'Englese' that would never actually be used in a sinophone context.

Then follows another series of 'notes' (pp.7–9): *asking if something is so; saying that something is so; asking who someone is; identifying a person.* Here it would be clear to the experienced language teacher that we have crossed over from 'functions' into 'notions', in other words from a situational to a grammatical/lexical focus. However the student is given no clues that a different kind of information is on offer here, except for the sudden appearance of – mostly unexplained – terms, obviously technical ones like 'interrogative' and 'affirmative', and commonsense terms being used in technical senses like 'statement' or 'question'. All these 'notes' are dressed up as commentary on the situation, pointers towards the communicative use of the language being presented, but in fact they are framed in such a way as to give the student systematic access neither to authentic sinophone social contexts nor to authentic sinophone ways of speaking.

You Can Speak Mandarin is only one textbook, and I am in no way claiming it as 'representative' of the field as a whole. But the fact that it does embody some of the contradictions in the understandings of Chinese language teaching current in the field can be verified from a perhaps unexpected source. In 2004, a limited edition book was produced whose Chinese title *Àoyùn Hànyǔ 100 Jù*, literally

'Olympic Chinese 100 Sentences', indicates very clearly that its ostensible aim was the practical one of providing 'survival Chinese' for foreign participants in the upcoming 2008 Beijing Olympics; as well as reflecting the influence of the 'accumulative' model of language learning noted earlier, whereby successful language earning is understood as 'acquiring' a sufficient stock of words and structures.

The book is published by the prestigious People's Education Press and compiled by the National Office for Teaching Chinese as a Foreign Language, widely known by its Chinese abbreviation as the Hanban, the same organisation responsible in the past few years for setting up a series of Confucius Institutes around the globe. One would therefore expect a highly professional production, informed by the latest in language teaching methodology, and within a very clear conception of how the texts presented – inevitably in the form of dialogues – related to their respective contexts. What one actually gets is the same awkward mixture of grammar-translation and communicative styles within an overall 'Confucian' style teacher-centred, content-based model that we saw in *You Can Speak Mandarin*.

Lesson 9, *Checking in a Hotel* (sic), starts with the following list of *jīběn jù* 'basic sentences' (glossing and numbering added):

1 *Wǒ yùdìng .le fángjiān.*

   I book ASP:compl room

2 *Qǐng chūshì nín.de hùzhào.*

   please present you:pol. SUB passport

3 *Nín zhù 234 hào fángjiān*

   you:pol. stay 234 number room

4 *Zhè .shì fángkǎ*

   this be room card

It is presumably these sentences that are the real focus of learning, with four of them in each of the 25 lessons making up the '100 sentences' of the title. From a language teaching point of view, however, it is unclear whether these sentences are intended as *jùxíng* 'sentence types', i.e. sentence patterns which through substitution and expansion exercises would form the basis for a much larger repertoire of expressions, as would be expected in a formal textbook; or whether they are simply *chángyòng cíyǔ* 'frequently used expressions' such as would be found in a traveller's phrase book.

In any case the question seems moot, since the actual situation as created in the following *huìhuà* 'dialogue', divided into parts 1 and 2, shares the same air of unreality – or at least alternative textbook-style reality – as the example from *You Can Speak Mandarin* quoted earlier (glossing added):

Part1

MIKE: *Nǐ hǎo, xiǎo.jiě.*   *Wǒ yùdìng .le fángjiān.*

            you good miss   I book ASP:compl room

CLERK:	*Nǐ hǎo!*	*Qǐngwèn*	*nín jiào shén.me míng.zì?*
	you good	please-ask	you:pol be-called what name
MIKE:	*Wǒ jiào Mike,*	*cóng Měiguó lái.*	
	I be-called Mike	from America come	
CLERK:	*Qǐng shāo děng*		
	please little wait		

Part 2

CLERK:	*Xiān.shēng,*	*qǐng chūshì nín.de hùzhào.*	
	sir	please present you:pol. SUB passport	
MIKE:	*Gěi nǐ*		
	give you		
CLERK:	*Xiān.shēng,*	*nín zhù 234 hào fángjiān.*	*Zhè .shì fángkǎ.*
	sir	you:pol stay 234 number room	this be room-card
MIKE:	*Xiè.xiè*		
	thank-you		

In relation to the situation, a number of questions immediately come to mind. Why are the participants speaking Chinese in the first place, since a foreign hotel is just where one would expect English to be spoken? Why does the hotel clerk ask the guest only for his given name rather than surname ('Mike' is in fact throughout the book only ever identified as such), strange even in an anglophone setting and positively bizarre in a sinophone one; and why does she seem to accept that, along with a bald 'I'm from America', as sufficient identifying information, only afterwards asking for his passport? As for the language of the dialogue itself, why does it show the same formal over-completeness: e.g. *Qǐng chūshì nín.de hùzhào* 'Please present your passport', where a simple *Nín.de hùzhào?* 'Your passport?', using the polite second person pronoun *nín*, would be quite sufficient?

Taking stock: opening gateways to the development of sinophone identities

In analysing textbooks such as these, it is hard to avoid a strong sense of puzzlement. From the point of a student of Chinese, it would seem that, far from facilitating their entry into sinophone culture, textbooks seem to be designed to make that process as difficult as possible!, and to prevent the 'outsider' from ever becoming 'insider'. While working for an English-language television station in Beijing in 2003–2005, I was often jokingly moved to remark to one or other of my Chinese colleagues when editing a script they had written: *Zhǐyǒu yí.ge Zhōngguó, bú.shi zhǐyǒu yí.ge Wàiguó!* 'There is only one China, there isn't only one "Foreign!"'. The Chinese habit of dividing the world into two parts – commonly expressed as *guónèi* 'inside the country' and *guówài* 'outside the country' – is a pervasive one, and is supported by a whole discourse: *wǒguó* 'my/our country' versus *yìguó* 'foreign countries'; *chū guó* 'leave the country/go abroad' versus *huí guó* 'return to the country'. It is also reflected in the name of the country itself – *Zhōngguó* – which historically corresponds not to 'The Middle Kingdom', as it is normally translated, but 'The Central States', the cluster of polities around the Yellow River in what is now northern China in the first millennium BCE, which shared many linguistic and cultural similarities, in contrast to the 'barbarians' to the East, West, South, and North.

This historically salient sense of 'us' and 'them' was of course only intensified by the shock created by the military, economic and cultural challenges at the hands of foreign powers starting from the 1840s, and since the success of the Chinese Communist Party in expelling foreign powers from Chinese soil was and is still claimed as one of their greatest achievements, it is not surprising, perhaps, to find an unconscious desire to 'keep the foreigners at a distance' permeating the field of language teaching in mainland China and beyond, even in the face of a professed desire to achieve the opposite. Language textbooks may no longer carry the blatant propaganda of the Mao era, when foreigner learners were taught language like 'Chairman Mao is the Red Sun that lives in our hearts', but a more subtle, though equally excluding, type of discourse often still operates.

In fairness, it must also be acknowledged that the Chinese language teaching 'industry' has had only a fraction of the time and resources and expertise devoted to it that English language teaching has, and that particularly at university level, many of those teaching Chinese are doing so only because it is a requirement of their job, not because they have any particular training or even interest in it. Nevertheless, if we are to take seriously the goal of helping contemporary students of Chinese to become sinophone, we need to be sensitive to the contradictions within the discourses of language teaching as reflected in Chinese language textbooks, and question their aims and methods in relation to students' needs, as well as becoming more explicit about the kinds of texts and contexts that will actually help students to become sinophone.

「我一直想stay In touch with Chinese,
我报给了我一个学习华文的空间。」
郭英华 Leslie Kwok - 前国家游泳选手/商人

Language ambassador

3

LEARNING CHINESE THE LEE KUAN YEW WAY

The social and political context of language learning

Introduction: the challenges of being multilingual

The photo opposite and its caption – 'I always intend to *stay in touch with Chinese*, My Paper has given me a space for studying Chinese' – tell us something about the multilingual context of current-day Singapore, where it is so natural to use more than one language that, even when specifically talking about the desire to maintain his Chinese language skills, Chinese Singaporean Leslie Kwok cannot resist the temptation to mix in some English. This kind of 'hybrid' discourse, though not at all uncommon among bilinguals the world over, including those in sinophone contexts, tends to be frowned upon by policy makers and educational authorities. It would certainly *not* attract the approval of the man who more than any other has shaped official policy towards language and hence the language environment itself in Singapore. In this chapter we will look at this particular language learner in relation to his language environment, and see how the process of language learning has played out in his case. Let's first see how he regards multilingualism:

> I used to carry a multi-purpose plug for my tape-recorder when I travel. When I get to a new destination, I had to adjust the plug pins. This will give me a clue on whether or not to change the voltage on the tape-recorder from 240 to 110. But when I have to switch between English, Mandarin, Hokkien and Malay – never mind Tamil – the mental transformers have even more work to do than the multi-purpose plug.
>
> *(Chua (ed.) 2005: 125 [10 Feb 78])*

This striking image comes from a list of 'quotable quotes' included in a book by Lee Kuan Yew, former Prime Minister and now Minister Mentor of Singapore, called *Keeping my Mandarin Alive*. The collection of interviews and comments is described by its editor, Chua Chee Lay, one of MM Lee's Chinese teachers, as follows (Chua (ed.) 2005: iv): 'This is not a book of MM Lee's language theory or his language policy. Instead it is a detailed description of his Chinese language learning journey, one that is fraught with difficulties and obstacles.'

Lee's book provides a useful window into the experiences of a highly successful individual language learner, as well as providing insights into some of the commonsense understandings of the language learning process. (In quoting from Lee's book, extracts from the interviews will be identified by (page number) in parentheses; extracts from earlier speeches in addition by [date of original use] in square brackets.) In relation to the aims of this book, Lee's detailed descriptions of his own learning experience, as well as his forthright opinions about that experience, raise in very accessible form many of the questions facing the university student as potential sinophone. Obviously, the Chinese-learning aims of the potential sinophone addressed in this book will not always coincide with those Lee puts forward, and the sorts of answers suggested here may well differ from Lee's in many cases. Nevertheless his articulate and wide-ranging account poses these questions in a way that allows them to be properly discussed.

In this chapter we will also use Lee's reflections on his language learning experience to examine some of the social and political contexts relevant to learning Chinese, considering the questions:

- What varieties of Chinese are spoken in the sinophone sphere, including multilingual contexts where more than one language is an option, and what different statuses do they enjoy?
- What variety or varieties of Chinese should students learn or be exposed to?
- What sorts of linguistic, social and cultural contexts do these different varieties of Chinese operate within, and how are potential sinophones to position themselves in relation to their own use of Chinese?

These are the sorts of questions Lee Kuan Yew's account of how he has 'kept his Mandarin alive' is particularly suited to helping us explore.

Lee Kuan Yew: a sociolinguistic autobiography

The title of this section deliberately echoes that of an article by one of the most influential Chinese linguists of the twentieth century, Yuen Ren Chao, who in 'My Linguistic Autobiography' (Chao 1976) describes the mixed dialect background in which he grew up in the final years of the Qing dynasty in northern China. This multilingual type of context is still a very common one in Chinese-speaking communities around the world, much more common than is generally acknowledged in the Chinese teaching profession. Lee Kuan Yew, though a Chinese of Hakka (Kèjiā) background, grew up speaking *no* Chinese at all, which makes his story of how he came to learn the language even more relevant for the potential sinophone. I will start by letting Lee tell the story in his own words, with some interpolated comments, and then provide some biographical and historical background to his complex sociolinguistic background.

Lee's own language learning experiences

> I started to learn Chinese in 1942, probably in March or April. The Japanese captured Singapore in February and suddenly the notices were in Japanese, in kanji. I didn't want to learn Japanese because I disliked them; they were very brutal. So I decided to learn Chinese to understand what they were writing. I bought several 'Chinese taught through English' books. ... After each lesson, there was a glossary explaining the Chinese characters in English. ... I mastered about 2000 characters, but in a superficial way. I only knew the meaning of the characters and that a combination of the characters meant something else. I didn't learn how to pronounce the words, because I had no teacher.
>
> *(pp.17–19)*

Characteristically, Lee starts learning Chinese for an entirely practical but fiercely personally motivated reason: to be able to read the Chinese characters – 汉字 or *kanji* in Japanese – on official notices in Japanese-occupied Singapore. For this reason, he uncritically equates 'Chinese' with 'Chinese characters' – a common conflation in popular discourse – but is well aware that 'mastering about 2,000 characters' – the precise awareness of the exact number of characters known also being a common theme among foreign learners of Chinese – only gives him a 'superficial' access to the language. Lee's understanding at this point is that of someone who knows some of the basic building blocks of the language, and some of the ways they may be combined into larger units, but has no ability to string them together to make meaningful discourse, like someone who has memorised the basic ciphers of a code but has not yet learned the rules for putting them together into messages.

> Looking back now, I think I made a mistake. If I had looked for a teacher, I would have found one. I had a neighbour living opposite me who was the nephew of a civil servant. ... He came over to teach me. He was a *Chaozhou ren* [... Teochew] (chuckles). His Mandarin had *Chaozhou de qiangdiao* [... a Teochew accent]. I was very particular that if I had to learn, I wanted to learn the correct pronunciation and not a dialect pronunciation, so I erased this teaching. Then I became a clerk at a Japanese textile firm. I had to copy Japanese words – *katakana*, *hiragana* and *kanji*. So my writing in *kanji* was consolidated. ... I did not keep up with my Chinese; I just read *kanji* which was necessary to understand Japanese.
>
> *(p.19)*

Lee explains how he passed up an initial opportunity to get access to the spoken language because of his insistence on acquiring a standard accent – what he refers to as 'correct pronunciation'. This again is very characteristic of attitudes among

Chinese learners and in the Chinese teaching profession generally; but far from characteristic of the sinophone sphere more broadly, which tolerates an enormous amount of variety in pronunciation, comparable to that of English across the whole English-speaking world. In Lee's emphasis on 'consolidating' his knowledge of Chinese characters, we see him much more concerned to attain mastery of the written medium.

> By 1951/52, I started to learn Mandarin. I learnt it with my friend Hon Sui Sen. We got a man who was supposed to have a Beijing accent. … We tape-recorded him on a very small Grundig tape recorder with a spool tape. It was a dictaphone. The reproduction was very poor. The teacher got suspicious because once (the lessons were) recorded, he thought we would not need him (chuckles). He wasn't keen on recording. He wasn't very successful, so we dropped him. That lasted for probably about eight or nine months. That gave me a slight basis and revived my memory of the *kanji*.
>
> *(p.20)*

Lee's first foray into learning 'correct' spoken Chinese fails because of the inadequacies of the teacher, despite the latter's possession of a standard Beijing accent. It is interesting to note, however, that the main result Lee remarks on from this attempt is that the teaching 'revived [his] memory of the *kanji*': once again the picture seems to be emerging of Chinese characters being regarded as the basis for all language learning – an attitude that is very prevalent in the Chinese teaching world.

> Then in 1955 I contested elections in Tanjong Pagar. There were two opponents, one was a Raffles College boy … the other was … from Chinese High School, a Hakka like me. He challenged me to a debate in Mandarin in Tanjong Pagar which included at that time Niu Che Shui [… Chinatown]. Of course it could have been a calamity for me and so I evaded him. It was my first shock and I had to make a speech at a rally in Banda Street. … I got hold of a journalist…to assist me. … And he did one page. I practised very hard for a few days (laughs). He used one phrase: that we were honest people, that were were an honest party, and the others were not trustworthy – that they were *gua yang tou mai gou rou* [挂羊头卖狗肉, to palm off something inferior to what it is purported to be] – so I practised that speech. … The crowd knew that I was learning, so they cheered me – it went well.
>
> *(pp.20–25)*

What finally propels Lee into aiming for fluency in the spoken language is another eminently pragmatic reason – political necessity. As someone from a political party which drew much of its support from Chinese-educated voters, the English-educated Lee needs to be able to communicate with his electorate in

Mandarin. Although at this stage not feeling up to taking part in a 'debate in Mandarin', Lee works hard on acquiring enough fluency to deliver a speech in the language. Culturally speaking, it is significant that the main thing Lee remembers from his first speech is a proverb, what is known in Chinese as a *chéngyǔ* or 'fixed expression'. Mastery of *chéngyǔ* is seen as one of the marks of the educated person, and the ability to use the appropriate *chéngyǔ* for a situation gives the speaker considerable rhetorical authority. It may reflect the down-to-earth nature of the political rough and tumble that this particular *chéngyǔ* is not in the classical *wényán*, as are many such phrases, but in the vernacular *báihuà*.

> Then I picked up Mandarin. ... As the secretary-general of the party I had to meet many Chinese-educated, young workers. Many of them were left-wingers who spoke either dialect or Mandarin. So I decided to concentrate on Mandarin because there are so many dialects. ... By 1955/59 I could make speeches in Mandarin without difficulty, but of course I was always looking for new words and phrases, because my English vocabulary was much bigger than my Chinese.

In the consolidation of his learning of Mandarin, Lee again stresses the pragmatic focus of his language needs – hence his concentration on 'useful words and phrases'. The period of time he singles out here, 1955–1959, is when Singapore was moving towards independence from Britain and what would turn out to be short-lived political union with Malaysia, a time when Lee was obviously thinking of fluency in Chinese largely from the point of view of its political utility rather than the overriding cultural value he later ascribes to it.

Lee's sociolinguistic background

What was the kind of linguistic background in which Lee grew up, and what was the broader social and political context in which he made his language learning choices? In the following discussion I draw on an early biography of Lee by fellow Singaporean T.J. George, published in 1973, to give an idea of the sociolinguistic world that gave Lee his initial linguistic repertoire and largely shaped his attitudes to language learning, both in conformity to and in reaction against that background.

George sums up the sociolinguistic situation of Singapore at the time, at least in regard to the majority ethnic Chinese population, as follows:

> The society in which he lives is predominantly Chinese, but very complex: the Singapore Chinese consist of many different dialect groups with totally different manners. Although all of the Chinese community in Singapore derives sustenance from the same basic culture, it is diverse, atomistic and mutually uncomprehending. Its most important division is into two main streams, the Chinese-educated and the English-educated.

> Lee Kwan Yew rode to power on the backs of the first and has increasingly sought to buttress his position with the backing of the second, but he has never won the complete trust of either. The Chinese-educated are so much a world apart that he has never fully understood them. Throughout Southeast Asia Chinese schools teach Chinese *mores*, Chinese nationalism, Chinese patriotism.
>
> *(George 1973: 28–29)*

The background of the 'Chinese-educated' to which George refers could not be more different from Lee himself, who falls very clearly into the 'English-educated' category. In the previous generations of Lee's family there are two major influences: linguistically, English, and culturally, Malay; nowhere does Chinese language or culture figure to any great extent. Lee's family thus falls into that linguistic and cultural hybrid ethnicity known in Malay as *peranakan* or 'born locally', otherwise known as 'Straits Chinese', referring to those ethnic Chinese settled around the Straits of Malacca since the seventeenth century, and who though retaining many Chinese customs, have largely dropped the use of Chinese in favour of either Malay, the mixed Chinese–Malay creole known as Baba Malay, or in more recent times, English (see further discussion in Chapter 9).

Lee's grandfather had had an English education, and did business out of the British colony, trading mostly with Indonesia, as a *chin chew* or 'sub-agent' with a big shipping line. Lee's father worked in a foreign commercial firm selling petroleum, a job which 'enjoyed tremendous prestige' and 'equated with high social status'. Though from a Chinese family, Lee's mother's great-grandfather had 'married a Malay', and 'the family thereafter was culturally Malay'. Lee himself was the first child in his generation and his birth was 'a major event in the Lee family', causing his grandfather to proclaim that he 'should be educated to be the equal of any Englishman', an 'instruction' that the proud parents 'never forgot' (George 1973: 17–18). The baby was given the Chinese name of Kuan Yew (in Mandarin *Guāngyào*) 光耀 'Light that Shines' but he 'grew up as Harry. In all probability the parents followed the common overseas Chinese practice of giving children two names – one English, one Chinese. Lee dropped his English name only after he became a politician.'

As a prosperous *peranakan* family, it was natural for the Lees to want their grandson to be educated in the language and culture of the colonial power, Britain. As George remarks:

> Their elders' yearning to make model Englishmen of their children was typical of the times. The British were the ruling class, the fount of all power and therefore the repositories of all wisdom. … The closer the Asian got to the standards and style of the Englishman, the better would be his position socially and economically. To be English-educated meant to go up in life; to be educated in England itself meant becoming part of the truly privileged set, having the world at your feet.
>
> *(George 1973: 20–21)*

The fact that English was the language of the colonial power meant that with the surrender of the British garrison to the Japanese in 1942 – the event that as we have seen spurred Lee's first foray into learning Chinese – and then with the gradual withdrawal of British control during the 1950s, culminating in independence in 1959, the status of English in Singapore was also affected. However, the divide between 'English-educated' and 'Chinese-educated' continued to be one of the most significant within the education system for at least another twenty years, and in Singaporean society more widely even to this day.

Although Lee's initial education was at 'a small Chinese kindergarten near the Lee home', his 'regular schooling':

> began when he was eight, at the Telok Kurau English School. There were plenty of Malay boys in this school and Kwan Yew's friends were mostly Malay. ... Already, his strong point was English ... . Four years later, at twelve, Kwan Yew moved to the Raffles Institution. This school ... had always been the most important educational institution in the city. It was synonymous with aristocracy, prestige and power. Everybody who was anybody in Singapore went to Raffles. It had to be the school for Kuan Yew, marked out from birth for the best England itself could offer ... . People who knew him at this stage say that although he looked very Chinese he seemed more Malayan in his ways. ... Kuan Yew finished the course in 1939 with medals and honours. This was the time the parents had chosen to send him off to England ... . War intervened. With Europe in turmoil there was no question of sending the boy on the perilous journey to England. So he entered Raffles College, later to become the University of Singapore.
>
> *(George 1973: 20–21)*

Again what is striking from this account of Lee's education is the prominence of English and secondarily Malay in his linguistic repertoire, and the almost complete absence of Chinese. While Lee later came to see this cultural hybridity as highly problematic, there is no hint at this stage that he was doing anything but following the socially and culturally accepted path for someone of his background and class in the multilingual and multicultural atmosphere of colonial Singapore.

In the colonial society of the time, Lee's background and education made him well equipped to get ahead in that world, but at the same time, by the contradictory standards of that time, left him part neither of the English-speaking world nor of the Chinese-speaking one:

> Born into a Chinese family ... he was brought up not to be an ordinary Chinese. Equipped with English as his first language, with easy access to English culture and style of behaviour, he is not English. He once described English-educated Chinese as a devitalised people, speaking and thinking in a language which was not part of their being – and his problem

is that he himself is one of them, yet cannot quite identify even with them because of the special circumstances of his careers.

(George 1973: 28)

Although it very much reflects Lee's current thinking, one might note with wonder, from a cultural point of view at least, why someone '[e]quipped with English as his first language, with easy access to English culture and style of behaviour' is nonetheless regarded as 'not English'. Both George and Lee seem to ascribe to a view of language and culture as inextricably linked to ethnicity, so that someone of Chinese background who 'looks Chinese' cannot possibly be anything other than Chinese.

The answer, of course, has to do with cultural politics, perhaps even racism, obvious hangovers from an ethnocentric colonial mentality. From this point of view, Lee's Chinese roots and yellow skin make him, in his own eyes and those of many Singaporeans, 'essentially Chinese', and simultaneously prevent him from being 'really English'. Such an automatic equation of language and ethnicity is not particularly helpful for the potential sinophone, and as we will see in the discussion below, the kinds of 'objective evidence' often adduced in its support, in relation to language learning at least, rest on rather shaky grounds.

Becoming sinophone: the cultural imperative

There are several reasons why we want to keep Mandarin. The overriding reason is cultural and the question of self-esteem. You need a sense of your own identity. Next the economic value. In our business with China and Taiwan, you must know the language for your own self-esteem.

(p.128)

Despite his own immediate reasons for learning Mandarin being mainly pragmatic, Lee is adamant that the chief motivation today for one of Chinese background like himself to learn Chinese is 'cultural … self-esteem' and 'sense of identity'. Lee takes a firmly 'essentialist' view of ethnic identity, combined with an almost Kiplingesque sense of an unbridgeable gap between East and West:

I may speak the English language better than I speak the Chinese language because I learnt English early in life. But I'll never be an Englishman in a thousand generations and I have not got the Western value system inside me; it's an Eastern value system with the Western value system superimposed.

(p.126 [13 Aug 78])

From this viewpoint, Lee might well find the notion of cultural and/or linguistic hybridity as put forward in this book profoundly unsympathetic, something to be avoided rather than embraced by those like himself, and other ethnic Chinese whose stories we will read in Chapter 9, who live with this kind of disjunction between their ethnicity identity and sociolinguistic repertoire. On the contrary, for Lee and many ethnic Chinese, the fact that Chinese is not in their existing culture repertoire is seen as a lack to be remedied:

> I say a person who gets deculturalised – and I nearly was, so I know this danger – he loses his self-confidence. You feel a sense of deprivation. For optimum performance, a man must know himself, know the world. He must know where he stands.
>
> *(p.126 [13 Aug 78])*

Here and below Lee makes a clear equation between Chinese ethnicity and fluency in Chinese, so that a person who does not speak the language is somehow not fully Chinese (p.5 [21 Sep 84]): 'Only a Chinese Singaporean who cannot speak or read it, and who has been exposed to discomforture or ridicule when abroad, will know how inadequate and how deprived he can feel.'

Another prominent theme in Lee's discussion, something which has also played a large role in the Singaporean government's policy of 'mother tongue' education, is that knowledge of the ethnic or ancestral Asian language somehow provides a bulwark of tradition against the corrupting influence of Western-introduced modernity:

> It is not just learning the language. With the language goes the fables and proverbs. It is learning a whole value system, a whole philosophy of life, that can maintain the fabric of our society, in spite of exposure to all the current madness around the world.
>
> *(p.3. [5 Nov 72])*

By implication for Lee, then, the cultural necessity for knowing Chinese is confined to those of Chinese ethnicity. And although from the point of view of maintaining cultural traditions, one of the dialects of Chinese more commonly spoken in Singapore such as Hokkien (*Fújiànhuà* 福建话 or *Mǐnnánhuà* 闽南话), Teochew (*Cháozhōuhuà* 潮州话), Cantonese (*Guǎngdōnghuà* 广东话) or Hakka (*Kèjiāhuà* 客家话) might be seen as providing a more direct line to the traditions and practices of local Chinese, as opposed to Mandarin which has traditionally been mainly a language of education in South-East Asia, we will see below that Lee is firm that the only version of Chinese worth learning is Standard Mandarin.

Becoming sinophone: the economic imperative

> Singapore's language climate will never be static. There will always be a backward and forward drift between the English language and the Chinese language. As China becomes a more important economic factor in our lives, the position will drift towards a greater use of the Chinese language.
>
> *(p.133)*

Coming from a commercial background, and as founding Prime Minister of a country which since secession from the Malay Federation in 1965 has had little or no natural resources within its own borders, it is natural for Lee to stress the economic aspects of language fluency. Lee's characterisation of Singapore's economic situation as a dynamic and ever-changing one has clear implications for language policy. It is interesting here to note that, despite his own background as a fluent Malay speaker, and the significant minority of Singaporeans who are ethnically and linguistically Malay, not to mention the fact that Singapore is surrounded on all sides by the Malay-speaking countries of Malaysia, Indonesia and Brunei, Lee seems to see no significant role for Malay in the Singaporean linguistic economy. The contrast here is striking with the description quoted above of Lee as a school-boy who 'looked very Chinese [but] seemed more Malayan in his ways'.

This attitude also contrasts sharply with statements made by Lee in the 1950s and 1960s, when he laid more emphasis on the place of Singapore as part of the South-East Asian region than the ethnic roots of its Chinese population. In an address to Parliament in 1956, speaking against the then current emphasis on the English language in the education system, Lee lays out a very different kind of educational path for his son from that which was arranged for himself:

> My son is not going to an English school. He will not be a model Englishman. I hope, of course, that he will know enough English to be able to converse with his father on matters other than the weather. I hope also that in time to come I will know enough Malay to converse with him on the problems of humidity and heat control in the tropics. But whatever the difficulties in family relationships, he is going to be part of Asia, part of Malaya.
>
> *(George 1973: 65)*

In the decade following that speech, political union within Malaysia was first achieved and then lost, but even after independence in 1965, Lee's thinking on this subject still stressed the local context, rather than Chinese background, of Singapore's Chinese population. In a speech to an American audience in 1967, Lee had this to say:

> I am no more a Chinese than President Kennedy was an Irishman. Slowly the world will learn that the Lees, the Tohs, the Gohs, the Ongs, the Yongs, the Lims in Singapore, although they may look Chinese and speak Chinese, they are different. They are of Chinese stock and not apologetic about it. But most important, they think in terms of Singapore and Singapore's interests, not of China and China's interests.
>
> *(George 1973: 16)*

In 1967, Lee was speaking just after a long-running Communist insurgency in Malaysia, and Communist agitation in Indonesia, both of which were largely carried out by local Chinese communities with support from the Communist government in China, so he was obviously anxious to reassure his American listeners that the Singaporeans were not 'that kind' of Chinese. He was also speaking at a time when Singapore, like the United States, had no diplomatic relations with the People's Republic of China; but within the short space of five years, that was all to change with the PRC's entry into the United Nations and President Nixon's dramatic visit to Beijing, leading to the eventual establishment of full diplomatic relations. In the following decade, China began its 'Open Door' policy and started on its long journey towards its current status as economic powerhouse of the world. In line with these changes, by 2005 Lee has come to regard the Chinese language as an economic necessity (p.138): 'China now makes it [Chinese] a language with economic advantages. So we do not have to tell parents, better do that. When we talked about culture, roots, they were thinking of jobs, security, future …'.

At the same time Lee continues to stress the importance of English as the 'working language' of Singapore as a whole, Chinese and non-Chinese:

> [W]e must make a living in Singapore, we have decided and, I think rightly, that English is our working language. Otherwise, Singapore would divide, clash, collide, collapse. Non-Chinese would not be able to survive. So, how do we keep Chinese alive? And it is very important that we keep Chinese, not just for economic reasons, but for reasons of identity, sense of self, and pride in our own culture and civilisation.
>
> *(p.42)*

Nevertheless, as is clear in the end of the above quotation, although Lee emphasises the economic need for both Chinese and English, the cultural imperative for Singaporean Chinese to learn Chinese is equally, or perhaps even more stressed:

> There are several reasons why we want to keep Mandarin. The overriding reason is cultural and the question of self-esteem. You need a sense of your own identity. Next the economic value. In our business with China and Taiwan, you must know the language for your own self-esteem.
>
> *(p.128 [2000])*

There seems to be a contradiction here in that, from a strictly economic point of view, these days it would seem reasonable to give as many Singaporeans as possible access to Chinese as well as to English, not to mention Malay. But with official policy, particularly education policy, strictly 'rationing' each Asian language to its respective ethnicity, what seem like fairly rigid cultural considerations win out over economic ones, and this despite leaving ambiguous the status of many Singaporeans of whatever ethnicity whose mother tongue, like Lee's own, is in fact English.

Learning to be sinophone: the pedagogical process

As a learner of Chinese, Lee reflects widely on the nature of his own learning experiences, as well as those of people around him. Although he naturally does so as a lay learner, rather than from the professionally informed perspective of a pedagogical expert, his comments nevertheless give us insights into a number of aspects involved in the language learning process, as well as reflecting many common ideas about language learning that are, as it were, in the air. Below I will go through a selection of Lee's thoughts on this topic, drawing out their implications for the potential sinophone. I have divided Lee's comments into four main areas: critical learning period, bilingualism, contexts of language use, and brain as computer hard disk.

Critical learning period

> The younger one learns to speak a language, the more permanently it is remembered.
>
> *(p.127)*

> Therefore the lesson is: learn it when young. So it is important to make the effort. Have the roots to sink into your mind and it will be a lifelong asset. It is something I have missed which I cannot recover now.
>
> *(p.87)*

Lee shows himself here a firm adherent to the claim, widely held as a common-sense view and also supported by much academic opinion, that there is a 'critical learning period' for language: in other words, up to a certain age, children learn languages relatively quickly and painlessly, but from teenage on into adulthood, language learning becomes a rather slower and more painful process. Lee never ceases to lament the fact that he did not learn Chinese until well after this critical learning period, and to encourage Chinese Singaporeans to 'have the roots sink into [their] mind' as early as possible. This would seem to be a rather dispiriting reality for the majority of potential sinophones, who will take up the language only at university, or in a still small number of cases at or before high school.

However, there are reasons for thinking that the notion of a critical learning period is not as significant for language learners, at least for second language learners, as commonly thought. The reasons why children tend to pick up languages relatively quickly and easily may be summed up in three words: motivation, opportunity and time. Children are highly *motivated* to learn the language or languages in their environment because language gives them the key to an enormous amount of meaningful activity going on around them from which they would otherwise be shut out. Children also receive an enormous amount of support and reinforcement for their first stumbling attempts at the adult language, and are continually encouraged and rewarded for their success.

This brings us to the next component: *opportunity*. From birth, and even to a limited extent while still in the womb, children are able to hook into an enormously rich and highly patterned language environment. They are exposed to language, not in the dry decontextualised manner of many textbooks designed for adult learners, but in an intimately context-linked fashion. They experience language first as linked to clear material and social contexts in which language use is highly functional, and where many other modalities such as gaze, body language and gesture reinforce the linguistic meanings being made. Gradually over a period of years, they also learn to understand language which is not tied to an immediate context, a prime example being the written registers they are exposed to in school. Finally, perhaps the most often overlooked consideration is the sheer amount of language children are exposed to over the period of years it takes them to become fully fluent in the adult language. Children have long periods of *time* in which to listen to others talking and try out the language themselves, including through seemingly trivial play activity such as nursery rhymes and playground language games which reinforce key aspects of their linguistic repertoire.

It must be painfully obvious that on all three of these considerations – time, opportunity and motivation – your average adult learner operates at a severe disadvantage compared to the average child. Adults are notoriously busy people, and lack the stretches of 'play' time which allow children to try out new skills in a non-threatening way. As far as the university classroom context experienced by the potential sinophone is concerned, the amount of time actually hearing, let alone speaking, Chinese is usually in the region of five hours a week, possibly supplemented by language laboratory work or private tutoring. The opportunities for adult language learning also tend to be impoverished in comparison to the rich situation-linked context of child learning. Language learning often takes place as a decontextualised exercise, in which students are required to master aspects of pronunciation, vocabulary and grammar, and writing, often without language use being linked to a genuine communicative context, and usually without anything like the reinforcement from other modalities that support language use in a natural context.

Finally, in terms of motivation, adults who already possess a fully functional language adequate for all their needs have to overcome several practical and psychological barriers to find appropriate contexts for using another language and to feel comfortable in doing so. As we will discuss at the end of this chapter and again in Chapter 9, there are also identity issues attached to speaking another language fluently, and reasons why a second language learner might *not* want to become too proficient in another language. We probably all know of immigrants who have taken to their new language context like a duck to water, gradually becoming indistinguishable in their language use from the native born, while others who may have been in the country longer, nevertheless stick obstinately to their original language and/or carry over features of that language to the second language. So, while it is true empirically that most adult learners often do not have the opportunities Lee proposes to be of such benefit to young learners, they are nevertheless able to bestow meaning on their learning and if diligent and assiduous in providing opportunities for themselves to hear and use it, there is in principle no reason why the adult learner should not eventually become as fluent in the language as one who has spoken it from infancy.

Bilingualism

> [I]f you want good Chinese, you must be prepared to let your English go down to 90, 80 odd percent. Then you can reach 50, 60 or 70% in Chinese. Or you can go to Chinese schools ... then your Chinese can go up to 80%, and your English will go down to 50 or 60%. Very few can do both at the same level; 100% for each, I'd say that's possible only for a few who are specially gifted.
>
> *(pp.39–40)*

Lee here seems to regard language learning as a zero sum game: the more you gain of one language, the less you retain of another. However, the experience of Lee himself and Singaporean Chinese of his generation, as well as ethnic Chinese just over the border in Malaysia, would tend to suggest differently. It is not at all uncommon for older generations of Singaporean Chinese, or older and current generations of Malaysian Chinese, to be fluent in several dialects of Chinese, as well as in English and Malay. However, it is true that what research suggests is that the case of the person who is *fully* bilingual or multilingual, i.e. has the same level of proficiency in each language, is rather rare.

The more common sociolinguistic situation is that in which people use the different languages in their repertoire in different contexts and for different purposes. It is thus widely attested that people have a 'home' language and a 'work' language, or a 'local' language and a 'national' language. From both a pragmatic and an identity point of view, each language performs different functions and carries different values for speakers and their interactants. One might indeed wonder what would be the use of having two languages that *were* totally interchangeable on all levels. But this is not how sociolinguistic contexts usually work: instead, people do different things, take on different identities, and even to an extent display different personalities in each language. We will come back to these issues when we explore the multilingual persona in more detail in Chapter 9.

Pragmatic uses of language

> The Mandarin that I learnt was special for what I wanted to say. The words that I know best are the ideas that I wanted to put across either in politics, the economy, society or whatever.
>
> *(p.31)*

> Given that we wanted the bulk of our Chinese Singaporeans to achieve reasonable proficiency in Chinese language, we had to create a widespread need to use Chinese language. For our students, Chinese language has to be a 'live' language, as opposed to a classroom subject.
>
> *(p.11 [17 Jul 04])*

As we have seen in Lee's own account of his Mandarin learning trajectory, his immediate motivations for learning were very pragmatic albeit highly emotionally charged ones, directed to specific goals, and his Mandarin use therefore concentrated on 'special' uses of the language, or what technically are known as 'registers', i.e. particular varieties of language for particular uses. Thus his economic and political vocabulary in Mandarin, and his ease in discussing such topics, would naturally be far greater than for, say, literature or philosophy. Related to this point is another with particular relevance for the potential sinophone, that there needs to be a 'widespread need to use Chinese language'. A language that is regarded primarily as a 'classroom subject' is likely to remain largely confined within the bounds of that context, with proficiency in that language seen as useful mostly for academic purposes such as tests and exams. When Lee remarks on the teaching of Chinese in Singaporean schools, '[f]or our students, Chinese has to be a "live" language, as opposed to a classroom subject', his implication that the learning of a language needs to be functional and meaningful in the life of the speaker, not just some sort of game, is a clear one for the university Chinese learner on the road to becoming a functioning sinophone. Whether in relation to Chinese communities in the home country, or through immersion programs in places within the sinophone sphere, the language learner needs to have a living context and practical motivation for using Chinese.

The brain as computer hard disk

> Every day I'll read the newspapers for 10 to 15 minutes … . But … just reading the newspapers, it's passive learning not active. … when you stand up to make a speech, you have to speak out the words. That means it must be in the active part of your vocabulary – on immediate recall, on the hard disk. That's the difference being on the hard disk and on the CD-ROM.
>
> *(pp.51–53)*

> If I were a computer and I had all the information in my PC, I 'control F', I will find what I want. It's different with the brain, 'control F', I will only find what I have been using frequently and it is an immediate recall.
>
> *(p.87)*

> PC is convenient, it helps, it is a tool, you press the button, it can be repeated several times and you can put it into your mind. But a language must live in people and the people must be our people.
>
> *(pp.93–94)*

In every generation, scholars and lay people have searched for analogies to understand the seemingly inexplicable complexities of the human brain. Since the 1980s, with computers becoming as common a part of the ordinary household as the fridge or the TV, and with the exponential growth in their range of functions and ease of use, the personal computer or PC has come to be seen as providing a natural model for the functioning of the human brain, and Lee draws on this model to make several points.

The first is a distinction between the active control of, versus the less direct access to language forms, comparable to the difference between the 'hard-wired' hard disk of a computer, that is immediately accessible, and the 'insertable' CD-ROM which can be accessed at need, but more slowly and less dependably. Lee also compares the more contingent nature of human memory, which works by strengthening the connection to knowledge more frequently accessed, but weakening that to knowledge only rarely accessed, with the more mechanical 'control F' or 'find' function on a computer which, provided that the kind of knowledge required is expressed in a searchable form, will automatically make its way through the whole computer in order to find it.

All analogies, of course, break down eventually, and Lee shows himself well aware of this when he points out that, for all the 'convenience' of the PC, 'a language must lie in people', that is, in the ongoing interactions of human societies. Although we are far from understanding everything about the functioning of the human brain, it seems clear that it is a far more complex entity than the most sophisticated computer, able to perform many operations simultaneously, storing information in a number of different places 'distributed' across the neurones and synapses that are its 'hardware', and with an amazing capacity for adjusting to new situations in the world which it is continually processing, or even to repair trauma or injury to itself. There is no evidence to suggest that it is somehow possible to reach the full capacity of our brain, or that – in an attitude most famously expressed by the fictional detective Sherlock Holmes – new knowledge *in* must mean existing knowledge *out*. The reasons why most people do not attain full fluency in more than one language are more easily explained by the factors of time, opportunity and motivation discussed above, rather than by any inherent limitations on brain capacity.

Mother tongue versus master language: the nature and functions of a standard language

> Language requires that we understand each other. Grammar must always be correct. As in English, you can speak with different accents, but if the grammar is correct, it can be understood. To do all that in Singapore, we have to stick to English and Mandarin. Don't go into dialects, it will ruin the bilingual policy we have.
>
> *(p.67)*

> You cannot learn English and Mandarin and speak dialects at home at the same time – it's not possible. I know it's not possible because it takes up more brain space, more 'megabytes' in the brain.
>
> *(p.31)*

If you have no master language, and you cannot absorb your mathematics, history, science, geography, either in English or Chinese. You are done for.

(pp.136–137 [25 Nov 2004])

It [Hokkien] is not congruent with the written Chinese script. Present-day written Chinese is Mandarin reduced into script ... . If Hokkien prevails, then the standard of written Chinese will go down.

(p.124 [23 Dec 77])

In Lee's pronouncements on the 'mother tongue' versus what he calls the 'master language', we see many of his previous concerns arising again: his emphasis on the pragmatic aspects of language use; his model of the brain as a computer hard disk; and his stress on 'correctness', not this time of pronunciation but of 'grammar'. We also see an emphasis on 'norms' and 'standards' as a prerequisite for efficient communication and an explicit identification of the standard language with the 'written ... script'.

There are a number of complex and inter-related issues that need disentangling here. First, despite Lee's insistence that '[y]ou cannot learn English and Mandarin and speak dialects at home at the same time', again we need look no further than just over the border in Malaysia for a living refutation of this claim. As noted above, there is no reason to think that learning a new language involves a diminution of an existing language, at least not in relation to the brain's capacity. If the new language does gradually take over many of the functions originally associated with the existing language, then this stems from the nature of language use as being inextricably linked to context, not from the supposedly inherent limitations of brain capacity.

Second, the idea that 'correct grammar' is necessary to enable efficient communication is also a rather narrow one. What we find in most languages is a range of what are technically known as *registers*, or functional varieties of language, on a range from commonsense to technical on the one hand, and from casual to formal on the other. In a very real sense, each register has its own grammar as well as its own vocabulary, in that a particular cluster of preferred choices of words and structures is normally regarded as appropriate to that register and rules governing their use may be tighter or looser in different genres. From this point of view, it is more useful to replace a rigid concept of 'correctness' with the more flexible notion of 'appropriateness'. Just as you would quite naturally and unconsciously speak differently to your teacher, to fellow students, or to family members, so different registers of a language are appropriate for different situations. When we characterised language learning in Chapter 1 as learning what kinds of language are appropriate to different contexts, we were in fact talking about mastering an increasing repertoire of registers.

This brings us to the notion of a *standard language*. While all societies distinguish different linguistic registers, societies which are literate, i.e. where one or more of the languages used in that society has a written form, tend to go beyond this to single out a single language, or a single register of a language, as the standard or norm. The existence of a written form allows this standard language to be described and codified in a way that is less easy, if even possible, with the more ephemeral spoken language. This standard written form then becomes the basis for formal education and both influences and is influenced by the more formal registers of the spoken language.

In this regard, Lee is quite accurate in pointing out that a certain amount of variation is acceptable in pronunciation, as in the different 'accents' of English; and in fact the same argument also applies to grammar and vocabulary. In both the sinophone and anglophone spheres, while a wide range of variation is acceptable in the spoken language, though more so in relatively casual and commonsense registers than in the more formal and/or technical ones, there is a much more restricted range of variation tolerated for the standard written form. As a native speaker of Australian English, in spoken registers I may well use certain pronunciations and choices of words that may not be immediately comprehensible to native speakers of other dialects of English. However, in most written registers, apart from informal ones like personal letters or emails, I will tend to produce something much closer to that which would be recognised as 'standard written English' in the United Kingdom or the United States or most other parts of the anglophone sphere.

In Chinese, as Lee correctly points out, the standard written form is based on the standard dialect of Chinese, i.e. Mandarin, and is to a large extent 'not congruent' with a non-standard dialect like Hokkien – a point usually lost on many boosters of the so-called 'supra-dialectal' nature of the Chinese writing system. But in the sinophone sphere, for political and historical reasons, different varieties of 'Chinese' that would be regarded as different 'languages' in say a European context, are regarded as 'dialects' of a single 'language' because they share a single standard written form and are spoken within the borders of a single country. The sociolinguistic situation in China is analogous to a hypothetical case in which the Western Roman Empire had never broken up, and thus speakers of Italian, Spanish, Portuguese, French, Romanian and many other regional forms of speech were all regarded as dialects of a single language 'Romance'. As we saw in Chapter 1, the standard written register of contemporary Chinese is still heavily influenced by the 'Chinese Latin' that is *wényán* or classical Chinese, and quintessentially written forms such as public notices are not infrequently written in almost pure classical Chinese.

From the point of view of the potential sinophone, the implications are clear: you will need to learn a range of registers of Chinese, both spoken and written, and the registers you learn will be intimately associated with the contexts in which you use the language, and the specific functions for which you use it. A greater adherence to specific norms is likely to be required in more formal and/or written registers, but a huge variety is likely to be encountered – and accepted! – in many other registers. You will need to be familiar with standard spoken and written registers of the language in order to operate successfully in the widest range of sinophone contexts, but only as one part of your sociolinguistic repertoire.

Conclusion: every learner is unique

MM Lee has proven to be a very forthright and stimulating guide through various aspects of the language learning process. Indeed, he has given us a rare opportunity to look at the language learning process from the learner's point of view, the principal object of language pedagogy but one not often given the chance to speak for him or herself. Nevertheless, for our purposes, Lee's reflections are limited by the very fact that makes them useful: their particularity. Every language learner comes to the experience with their own background, their own abilities – both strengths and weaknesses – their own needs, and their own goals for learning the language. Language textbooks, and to a large extent the language teaching profession, tend to pass over these complexities, much as they pass over the sociolinguistic complexities of the sinophone sphere itself, in favour of a mechanical standardised model that treats both the language input and the recipient of that input as conforming to a fixed common set of specifications.

MM Lee's account is also limited by the status signalled by the two letters before his name, i.e. by his role as an influential politician and policy maker, who has had sustained input into the development of Singaporean language policies over a period of decades. Politicians, like many educationalists, like to stress conformity if not uniformity: it makes the implementation of bureaucratic processes easier to carry out and assess. Likewise the language learning process embodied in many current textbooks assumes that all learners start from the same point and end up at the same stage. Much of this is unavoidable, but the particularity of each learner also needs to be emphasised, and each learner needs to be aware that what they bring to the learning process is just as important as what they will receive during that process: indeed that there is a constant and mutually informing interaction between the two. We will come back in Chapter 9 to take another look at the learner focusing on that particularity from the point of view of identity and personality as expressed or developed through the use of another language. In the meantime, the account of one special learner, Harry Lee Kuan Yew, reminds us that ultimately *every* learner is special.

PART B

Drawing battlelines over language

In Part A we examined the contemporary state of Chinese studies from the point of view of learning and teaching Chinese. While this account of the 'state of the art' did involve some discussion of the historical roots of the current situation, especially in Chapter 2 on different language teaching paradigms, it is in Part B that we will focus specifically on the different historical traditions that have fed into Chinese studies, this time from the point of view of the analysis of language, i.e. linguistics. Over the last century and a half of the development of modern Chinese studies (see Honey 2001 for an account of the origins and development of its 'philological' traditions), at least three overlapping divisions have emerged which are still current and relevant to an understanding of ideas about language in the field. First there is a division between the 'old-fashioned' sinology and the Area studies which 'replaced' it (and which is now becoming 'old-fashioned' in its turn); next there is a division between the philological text-based approach characteristic of sinology and the social science methodologies which 'super-seded' it (with a similar disclaimer); and finally there is a division between what could be broadly characterised as a 'humanistic' approach towards the Chinese language and the 'scientific' linguistic methodologies that exist in an uneasy truce with it. These divisions are not always recognised by those studying or working in the field of Chinese studies, and certain scholars do of course operate across these divisions, but they still determine to a significant extent where one positions oneself in the field.

We start off in Chapter 4 by looking at what is perhaps the most obvious manifestation of these divisions, the phenomenon I have dubbed 'character fetishisation', by examining arguments within Chinese studies over just how important Chinese characters are in the understanding of Chinese language and culture, arguments that go beyond linguistics to literary theory, philosophy and even history. Chapter 5 goes back in time, first to the late 1930s and then to the early 1960s, to examine a couple of debates that in effect aimed to define the nature of the field: the first debate specifically over the nature of characters and whether it was sound or meaning that was more important in their creation and interpretation; the second not focused on the characters as such but regarding them, explicitly or implicitly, as crucial in marking off the study of China from that of other parts of the world.

Chapter 6 shifts to scholarship on language in China itself from the late nineteenth century. The sheer inertia of Chinese tradition under the late Empire seemed to be dragging the country close to destruction, and this sparked radical proposals for a wholesale rejection of the Chinese cultural inheritance, including the language and its writing system, in favour of Western imports. Such extreme solutions brought in their turn conservative reactions, and the pull between full-scale adoption of Western concepts and technologies and their wholesale rejection continues to the present day. In the case of linguistics, the inextricably mixed nature of modern Chinese linguistics as a hybrid of native Chinese and imported Western traditions has caused and continues to cause significant ideological as well as practical problems for the understanding and use of Chinese. This chapter also picks up on some ideas put forward during one of China's key modernising periods in the 1910s and 1920s for Chinese characters to be discarded, and discusses some of the ideological issues involved in more recent revivals of those ideas.

Multilingual polity

4

CHARACTER FETISHISATION

The *modus operandi* of orientalism in Chinese studies

Introduction: the historical background to orientalism in Chinese studies

The kinds of discourses to be explored in this chapter are commonly characterised, using the coinage of scholar Edward Said (1978), as *orientalism*: that is, cross-cultural ideological constructs involved in the (mis)representation of the 'East' by the 'West'. Such claims have deep historical roots, and may also operate in reverse, a process more recently dubbed 'occidentalism' (Buruma and Margalit 2004). Before we plunge into the discussion of how this phenomenon shows up in contemporary Chinese studies, it would be useful to get a flavour of these discourses and the historical background to their emergence. Below I present three extracts from three different kinds of 'travellers' accounts' which identify some of the common themes in such discourses, and hint at some of the reasons for the reluctance of many Western – and Chinese – scholars to treat things Chinese as on a par with other languages and cultures.

The first extract comes from a late nineteenth-century work by a missionary scholar as part of a chapter on 'Western Opinions' on the Chinese language, in which the author includes, seemingly indiscriminately, speculations on the descent of the Chinese race from one or other of the sons of Noah alongside scholarly discussions on the relationship of the Chinese language to the languages of Tibet and Assam:

> [T]he language and literature of China can never among people remote from that country arouse any enthusiastic interest such as that with which some of the Semitic and Indo-European languages have been studied by western scholars. ... It cannot be maintained, however, that the language and literature of China have failed to arouse the interest of Western students.

Nor should we expect it to be otherwise, as least as to the language, when we think on its nature and the way in which it is written, so unlike all that we are familiar with in other languages ... . [I]t was not until about the end of the sixteenth century that important and authentic information about China and its language began to be acquired by European scholars, and the works written by these show how the language puzzled and enchanted them. One of its great charms for them at first seems to have been found in its written characters.

(Watters 1889: 2)

We may note that, among the aspects of Chinese culture that 'charmed' Europeans, the 'way in which [Chinese] is written' is singled out for special mention, something that has been a prominent theme in European discussions of China since the pioneering accounts of the Jesuit missionaries started to trickle back from China in the early seventeenth century.

Philosopher Chad Hansen identifies the other side of this exoticism, a kind of 'excuse' for the strangeness of Chinese thinking, which earlier scholars of China, commonly known as *sinologists*, had dubbed 'Chinese logic':

Talk about 'Chinese logic' emerged in a much earlier generation of sinologists. It is charitable to assume that it was initially motivated by a sincere effort to understand ... [by] giving rationales for Chinese philosophical doctrines. But the doctrines themselves often appeared so bizarre (especially to the missionary generation of interpreters) that they could be characterized as reasonable only if logic were suspended or altered beyond our normal recognition ... . So 'special logic' was originally thought of as a descriptive claim with a frankly racist content: people who are racially Chinese have different (and incommensurable) dispositions to draw conclusions from premises. The special logic claim was used to demand tolerance from Westerners who found Chinese philosophical theories – in a word which has become almost a specialized vocabulary item for things Chinese – inscrutable. Saying Chinese were illogical had a dual effect. It allowed us both to acknowledge our inability to understand the ideas and yet to regard those ideas as a 'profound' alternative to our own world view.

(Hansen 1983: 10–13)

Hansen notes that the metaphor of 'inscrutable', literally 'unable to be interpreted' and often applied in the first instance to facial expressions, has been so often applied to the case of China as to become a stereotypical description of Chinese culture generally.

Evidence that such attitudes are not confined to China can be seen from the following rather jaded comment from a long-time Japan resident who sees a very similar thing going on in Japan, albeit with a strange twist:

Ever since the 'discovery' of Japan by the West, Western visitors have gone out of their way to emphasize as many of the unfamiliar aspects of Japanese life as they could, partly because by doing so they made their own stay there sound all the more intrepid ... .The most difficult myths to dispel are those concocted by the Japanese themselves: for example, the curious and universally credited myth that Japan is a small country. Of Japan's four main islands, the largest, Honshu, is slightly larger than all of Great Britain. ... Or there is the equally pervasive belief in Japan's 'uniqueness', a quality taken for granted whenever Japanese people attempt to define their country and the ways in which it differs from everyone else's. For example ... 'The Japanese language is subtle and poetic. Japan is unique. Therefore all other languages are crude and merely "logical".' These and similar articles of faith can be encountered at all levels of the social spectrum – in unthinking youths for whom they are reinforced nightly by television quiz shows, as well as in educated 'opinion makers' who write books 'proving' the Japanese to be totally unlike all other human beings. This class of literature is called *nihonjinron* (literally 'Japan People Discussions'), examples of which regularly rank among the nation's best sellers.

(Booth 1991: 10–11)

Booth comments upon the motivation of Western travellers for emphasising the strange aspects of Japan, something that has also been characteristic of Western travellers' tales of China since at least Marco Polo, and the fact that this has to do with raising their status in their own culture. This should remind us that such judgments are never made in isolation – there are always cultural, economic or social reasons behind them. What we also see in this extract is that the Japanese, following the lead of the West in this as in so many other areas, have in effect 'orientalised' themselves, by claiming a kind of 'uniqueness' – again a key term in these kinds of discourses – which they could only have in the eyes of others. This kind of 'nativised orientalism' is something we will see in relation to the kinds of discourse about language in the Chinese context in Chapter 6.

The foundation stone of orientalism: 'characters real'

So from where did these distortions about China in the eyes of Europeans initially derive? And why did the writing system play so prominent a role in them? Some initial answers can be found in one of the earliest formulations of the foundational myth about the Chinese written language, found in the works of English philosopher Francis Bacon. This is the idea which so appealed to seventeenth- and eighteenth-century scholars like Bacon and Leibniz, watching with alarm the decline of Latin as the common language of scholarship in Europe, that Chinese represented a sort of *universal language*:

[I]t is the use of China, and the kingdoms of the High Levant, to write in characters real, which express neither letters nor words in gross, but things or notions; insomuch as countries and provinces, which understand not one another's language, can nevertheless read one another's writings, because the characters are accepted more generally than the languages do extend; and therefore they have a vast multitude of characters, as many, I suppose, as radical words.

(Bacon 1605: 82–83)

This claim contains at least two half-truths, each of which is taken up in different ways by two modern scholars. Philosopher Chad Hansen characterises the written language as follows:

Written Chinese has no alphabet. Each character has a one-syllable pronunciation. The character was viewed as the basic unit of language and was the natural focus of interest for anyone who was literate in ancient China. The characters provided a shared mode of communication among the different Chinese languages since it did not represent any particular pronunciation. Thus, as in China today, people speak different languages but write and read 'the same.'[27]

27. Chinese language in archaic times, as at present, differed not only in pronunciation but in grammar and idiom. These differences tended to show up as discernible differences in written style.

(Hansen 1983: 47, 179)

The first half-truth, as expressed by Hansen, is that in traditional China, 'as in China today, people speak different languages but write and read "the same"'. Even Hansen's scare quotes around 'the same', referring us to an endnote, don't really soften his claim in any significant way, recognising merely 'discernible differences in written style'. This seeming concession disguises the raw fact that in modern Chinese, the written language is a register of one particular 'Chinese language', that is, Mandarin. A Cantonese speaker, for example, when learning the standard written form is obliged to learn a new language, admittedly one related to his or her own (see Bauer 1988), but with significant differences in vocabulary and grammar, alongside the perhaps more obvious differences in pronunciation concealed by the non-phonemic writing system (on which more below). In imperial China the gap between spoken and written styles was even wider, where the written standard, now known as *wényánwén* 文言文 or 'written language', was based on *none* of the contemporary spoken languages, but was rather a register based on a group of written texts of the period around 300 BCE (the Chinese 'Classics'), whose mastery required a long period of education for the elite class who could afford it. The modern written standard, *báihuàwén* 白話文 or 'vernacular language', has also been heavily influenced by this earlier standard in phraseology and to a certain extent in grammar. Thus the advantages of this supposed 'universal language', even if its range has shrunk from Bacon's 'countries and provinces' to Hansen's 'China today', would appear to be severely limited ones.

The second half-truth persists in a form perhaps even closer to Bacon's original formulation of the Chinese written symbols as 'characters real, which express neither letters nor words in gross, but things or notions', as shown in the following quotation by literary theorist James Liu:

> [A]lthough traditional Chinese etymology postulates 'six scripts' (*liushu*) ... two of these concern variant forms and phonetic loans, so that actually there are only four kinds of characters: simple pictograms, simple ideograms, composite ideograms, and composite phonograms. These characters are not arbitrary signs representing what Saussure calls the 'sound-images of words,' as are the letters of a phonetic script. In the terminology of C.S. Pierce, the simple pictograms are icons, because they resemble their referents. For example, the simple pictogram 日 (ancient form ⊟) is an icon for the sun; it is *not* a sign representing the sound of the word *ri*... whose archaic pronunciation has been reconstructed as *niet*.
>
> (*Liu 1988: 16–17*)

Liu's claim that 'the simple pictograms are icons, because they resemble their referents' seems very close to Bacon's notion of 'characters real', i.e. symbols or descriptions of reality, a concept Liu simply dresses up in modern semiotic terminology. This, together with Liu's related claim that 'characters are not arbitrary signs ... as are the letters of a phonetic script', takes some disentangling, and shows how complex are the issues involved.

The notion of a sign, in the terminology of American philosopher C.S. Pierce most commonly in use, divides into three main types: *icons*, which resemble what they refer to; indexes or *indices*, which are related in time or space to what they refer to; and *symbols*, which are related only by convention to what they refer to (Pierce 1931–1958: 2.275). If we are talking about ordinary signs such as road signs or warning signs, we can easily find examples of all three kinds: the icon of a car on a high-angled line which means 'steep ascent/descent'; the index of a jagged lightning bolt which refers to electricity; or the symbol of a circle with a line across it (often superimposed on an icon or index) which means 'no ...'. All these three types of sign are *conventional*: that is, they are established within and only interpretable by a particular community of sign users. However, among these three types, icons and indices are *motivated*, since they have an independent connection to what are known in philosophical terminology as their *referents*, i.e. what they refer to; while symbols are *unmotivated*, also known as 'arbitrary', since their only connection to their referents is the social convention that links them. Such signs may thus be used across different language communities, but precisely because they are not linked to a particular language, they are limited to easily recognisable features of the experiential world or those which have a close link to material action.

However, as soon as language becomes involved in sign interpretation, something which allows a much wider range of meanings to be expressed, the relationship between sign and referent becomes transformed into a relationship between the sign and a unit of the language. To take one of Liu's examples, the circle with a dot which he says is 'an icon for the sun': it is doubtless true that those who initially devised this character did so on the basis of the iconic relationship between its shape and that of the sun. But as soon as this picture came to be used as a *graph*, i.e. as a visual form which is part of a writing system, in order to function as part of that writing system it must represent some unit of a language: in other words, it must refer in the first instance, not to the outside world, but rather to a particular sound-shape and/or word-shape.

This is a complex point that needs to be probed further. How do we know that this character means 'sun'?: precisely because in modern Mandarin it 'has the reading', as the traditional phraseology would have it, *rì*, one of whose meanings is 'sun'. This is not the secondary fact Liu implies it to be, but rather is crucial to the sign's interpretation. If for the moment we accept Liu's logic, we would have the following equivalence between sign and referent:

日 is in an *iconic* relationship with that bright circular object in the daylight sky.

Alongside this, there is in fact another meaning which attaches to the graph 日, a meaning which appears in the earliest texts, that of 'day'. This would give us the further equivalence between sign and referent:

日 is in an *indexical* relationship with the period of time it takes for that bright circular object to cross the daylight sky.

You will note that in each case the referent has deliberately been expressed using a clumsy paraphrase in order to bring out the paradox of Liu's argument: that in providing the interpretation of this sign he unhesitatingly uses *an actual word of a language*. In this case, of course, because he is writing for an English-speaking readership, he does not use any form of Chinese or other languages which have traditionally used Chinese characters, but rather the linguistically and culturally very distant English, a language for which the iconic referent 'sun' is appropriate, but in which the indexical referent 'day' corresponds to a completely different word. So where does this leave Liu's argument?

We can avoid such apparent paradoxes by recognising that 日, unlike our road sign examples, was from its earliest uses linked to an actual word of a language, the Old Chinese word Liu gives as *niet*, borrowed into Japanese as *nichi* (its *on* or 'sound' reading), with the graph also linked to the native Japanese word *hi* (its *kun* or 'interpretation' reading), and so on with similar cases in other languages that have borrowed Chinese characters such as Korean and Vietnamese. Giving a 'reading' to a Chinese character, to use the traditional phraseology of sinology, simultaneously does two things: it identifies how that graph is to be read out in connected text; and it identifies the word or word-element to which that graph corresponds. In technical linguistic terminology, Chinese characters as graphs correspond both to the smallest unit of sound that can be comfortably pronounced in isolation, the *syllable*; and also in most cases to the smallest meaningful combination of speech sounds, the *morpheme*.

In Old Chinese (also called 'Archaic Chinese' as by Liu above), the stage of the language when the writing system was devised, the majority of morphemes corresponded to single syllables and at the same time to independently functioning *words* – this 'one word = one syllable' feature gave rise to the 'monosyllabic' tag often applied to Chinese. It was this double characteristic that allowed the system to work as well as it did, because each written character could be interpreted as both a spoken syllable and a grammatical word. There were also at this stage of the language some instances where a morpheme corresponded to more than one syllable, something that is far more common in modern Chinese, but the way the writing system dealt with this situation in fact provides further confirmation for the characterisation of the writing system given here, as we will see below.

However, when this system was borrowed for other languages, it could *not* work, except with major modifications, for languages like Korean and Japanese that did not share this syllable = morpheme = word feature, and even for languages like Vietnamese that did. The speakers of such languages adopted two basic strategies in order to adapt Chinese characters to their own use: they *borrowed the word along with its graph*, modifying its pronunciation to the phonology of their own language, as in the *niet > nichi* example above. Alternatively, they *used the graph to represent a native word*: either one of similar *meaning* to the Chinese original, as in the Japanese example of the *kun* or 'interpretation' reading of 日 as *hi*; or one of similar *sound,* as in the example of the characters used in their *on* or 'sound' readings, whose simplified forms eventually gave rise to the Japanese syllabary, the *kana*: e.g. 世 Ch. shì, せ Jp. se. In either case, the transfer was made from a word or word-element in the one language to a word or word-element in the other: at no stage did the process take place directly through *ideas*.

This is a claim which may seem absurd to most of us for whom 'meaning' and 'idea' are synonyms. The traditional view of linguistic meaning in the European tradition stemming from Aristotle is that the elements of a language are only meaningful insofar as they are symbols for ideas, and that while these symbols may differ from language to language, the underlying ideas are the same for all humankind (Cook 1938: 115). Swiss linguist Ferdinand de Saussure replaced this simple, commonsense picture with something far more radical and counterintuitive. For the absolute, unchanging notion of an 'idea', Saussure substituted the relative notion of meaning or 'signification' as a relationship between concept and sound (Saussure 1916: 104): that is, it is precisely in the conventional relationship between each concept and the sounds which represent it that each language provides its speakers with the means to distinguish objects and events in the world (see further discussion on this point in Chapter 5). The implication of this for the current case is that each language defines its own 'ideas' through a mutual delimitation of concept and sound: there are in fact *no* pre-existing ideas to which words, or graphs, may attach themselves; there are only sounds and concepts mutually delimited into meanings. Thus the concepts which any language expresses are precisely those for which it has distinct sound expressions.

To come back to the example of 日 'sun', the most economical explanation is not, despite Liu's claim, that it is an icon, nor in the meaning 'day' an index, but rather that it is a graph for the word whose reading in modern Chinese is *rì*, whose Old Chinese form had those two meanings; and likewise for its Korean, Japanese and Vietnamese analogues. If we look at how it is actually used in connected discourse, this is perfectly clear. It appears in such combinations as *rìluò* 'sun fall – sunset', *rìshí* 'sun eat – solar eclipse', *dì sān rì*, 'number three day – the third day', is reduplicated to give *rìrì* 'every day, daily', and so on. All these functions are features of the morpheme *rì* not of the character: in simpler terms, of the word functioning in a particular language. To try and argue from the nature of the character to the meaning of the word is putting the cart before the horse: despite recent Western theoretical arguments about the priority of writing over speech which have been eagerly seized upon by certain sinologists (see discussion of Derrida in the following section), the Chinese writing system, like all writing systems, is based on a spoken language, not vice versa.

The fact that this spoken language has changed hugely since the time most of the characters were first devised only reinforces this point: if we want to understand classical Chinese texts, or for that matter modern Chinese texts, we need to relate them to the particular form of the language at the time they were written. Chinese characters no more represent unchanging ideas than the letters of the Roman alphabet represent unchanging sounds – you only have to look at how the Roman alphabet is used to write Latin as opposed to one of its modern descendants like Italian or Spanish, let alone the distantly related English which took over the 'same' alphabet, to be convinced on this point.

The linguist George Kennedy, in his introduction to working with classical Chinese texts, describes these complex relationships with characteristic care and precision:

> The units of Chinese writing are called *graphs*. The sounds attached to a graph are called its *readings*. The reading or readings may vary greatly with the dialect of the reader, and the phonetic representation of that reading will vary greatly again according to the system of romanization used. In this Guide each graph introduced is provided with the conventional reading given in the work itself, spelled in capital letters. This gives a maximum of general information about the sound for that graph. In the space following, the student will insert the proper reading in the dialect of his choice, and in the system of romanization preferred by him. Graphs through their readings represent syllables of speech that are words or parts of words. These should be written with lower-case letters. When the student has filled in a reading for his dialect, he has represented a *morpheme* in his dialect. This morpheme can then be defined by one or more English equivalents enclosed in single

quotation marks. … The morphemes in the Chinese name of the work, in accordance with the above, are entered as

1 辭 ZI [cí] N 'a phrase, a word'

2 海 HOJ [hǎi] N 'sea'

(Kennedy 1953a: 1–2, emphasis original,
modern Mandarin 'readings' inserted)

Note that Kennedy does not once refer to the graphic shape of the characters, though he is careful to stress the range of pronunciations that can be attached to them. Kennedy thus emphasises the sound connections of the characters while effectively dismissing as irrelevant the graphic features which have caused the most excitement among Chinese and Western scholars.

Chinese characters as disciplinary identifier in Chinese studies

Let's try and summarise what we've seen so far, and understand how such arguments might relate to the question of how Chinese studies defines itself as a field. Whatever answer you give to this question, and it is in the nature of any field that those within it are likely to have different, even contradictory answers, there is no doubt that any definition will have the Chinese language at the core (as we will see in Chapter 5). Therefore it is the attitude towards the Chinese language, particularly in its canonical 'classical' written form, that positions individual academics and theoretical schools on either side of academic boundary lines. So how does the classical Chinese written language work? Is it, as claimed for example by a well-known and influential pair of philosophers, 'unique' (that word again!) 'being sharply distinct not only from all other non-Sinitic languages but from spoken Chinese as well (ancient and modern)' (Ames and Rosemont 1999: 289–290)? Or does it, as asserted in the most closely argued treatment of the origins of Chinese writing in recent years (Boltz 1994), operate in exactly the same way as all other historically attested writing systems such as Sumerian cuneiform, Egyptian hieroglyphs or the recently deciphered Mayan writing system?

Such arguments tend to centre around the notion of 'ideograph' (also called 'ideogram'), i.e. a written symbol that represents an idea, i.e. Bacon's 'characters real', and whether or not that term may legitimately be applied to Chinese characters. Debates on the 'ideograph' have a long history, going back at least to Peter du Ponceau (1838), who was reacting to notions widely held in seventeenth- and eighteenth-century European scholarship by scholars of the stature of Bacon and Leibniz. The notion of ideograph has proved of limited use in understanding how Sumerian cuneiform worked, even less so for Egyptian hieroglyphs, and actively misleading in delaying for some decades the successful decipherment of Mayan writing (see Coe 1992). However, in Chinese studies and related fields, this term and the conceptions of Chinese writing lying behind it still have many adherents.

The idea of the ideograph as the defining characteristic of the Chinese writing system is also invoked in the case of other languages which have traditionally used or still use Chinese characters in their writing systems, such as Vietnamese, Korean or Japanese. What is often ignored, or downplayed, is the fact that these societies not only borrowed Chinese *characters*, they also borrowed the classical Chinese *written language*, *wényán* or 'classical Chinese', which formed the basis of education in these societies, as in China, up until the early decades of the twentieth century, and contributed many words through borrowing to all three languages.

Nevertheless, we need to acknowledge that all such claims derive from actual usage at particular historical periods: in other words, they are based on historically situated understandings of the nature of Chinese characters as a writing system, understandings which cannot merely be dismissed as 'mistaken'. The intellectual justification of such classifications is essentially the following: *whether Chinese characters exist as a meaningful system separately from their relationship to any particular form of a language*. This is not just an intellectual claim about the nature of Chinese characters, and by implication writing systems in general, but an ideological stance which can be used to set off the Chinese writing system, and by implication Chinese language and culture, from all other languages and cultures in the world.

The positive answer to this claim, I would suggest, assigns a false independence to Chinese characters as, in effect, a language in themselves, a claim based on arguments about the nature of their construction as written forms. In this chapter I argue for the opposing claim that, in actual usage, Chinese characters are and always have been interpreted in relation to a particular language, and that in this function, *the principles of a character's composition are irrelevant to its interpretation*. In other words, once Chinese characters become used as elements of a writing system in order to represent a particular language, their interpretation is determined by their connection to specific units of that language, not by any 'inherent' meaning they may seem to possess in themselves.

A useful framework for understanding ideologies about language in the Chinese context is put forward in Hodge and Louie's application of the insights of Cultural studies to Chinese studies, *The Politics of Chinese Language and Culture* (Hodge and Louie 1998), a book written in large part in order to take on the deep-seated ideologies relating to the study of China such as those involved in the ideograph debates. Hodge and Louie set out from a thought-provoking distinction between *sinology* and what they call *sinologism*. The earlier self-descriptive term for the field, 'sinology' is now, as they point out, more commonly replaced in English-speaking circles by 'Chinese studies'; while their coinage 'sinologism', by contrast, refers to a 'branch of "orientalism"', 'a set of knowledges and assumptions about the study of China' (Hodge and Louie 1998: 13). Their definition of this 'ism' is worth quoting, since it identifies many of the tendencies that have dogged the long-running debates about the nature of the Chinese language:

> [T]he China constructed by Sinologism is not simply a Western invention. The key assumptions of Sinologism are partial truths, which makes it

especially important to address them and disentangle them from the forms in which they are packaged in classic Sinology. Sinologism takes major tendencies within Chinese culture and turns them into absolute values, essential truths about Chineseness or 'sinicity': an ideology above dispute, not a set of provisional, contested hypotheses and generalisations in need themselves of further examination and enquiry.

(Hodge and Louie 1998: 13)

Hodge and Louie go on to critique the complex of values commonly associated with the Chinese language in popular discourse, identifying an 'ideology of language' whose 'most important assumption is that there is only one form of the Chinese language, with different methods of encoding it' (Hodge and Louie 1998: 75). They suggest a classification which would replace the notion of a 'single Chinese language' by an 'ordered set' of different forms of 'Chinese', whereby the upper term of each division is taken to possess more 'social value' than its lower counterpart, and likewise more leftward sets take precedence over those to the right (Figure 4.1):

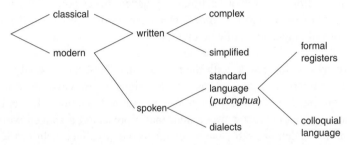

FIGURE 4.1 Typology of kinds of Chinese (Hodge and Louie 1998: 76)

We have already seen in Chapter 3 how Lee Kuan Yew, coming to the learning of Chinese in mid-twentieth-century Singapore, gave clear priority to the written form over the spoken, and to the standard language over the dialects; and in the sinophone sphere more broadly, classical Chinese tends to carry greater rhetorical weight than modern Chinese – so it is the former that tends to be used in the *chéngyǔ* 'set phrases' or 'proverbs' that are such a distinctive feature of sinophone discourse. According to this ideology of encoding identified by Hodge and Louie, all these different forms of Chinese are 'controlled' by the characters, in that it is the characters that are regarded as providing the ultimate source of meaning; and in their book they give cogent analyses of examples of these kinds of discourses.

In the same spirit, in the following sections we will examine various discourses within Chinese studies exhibiting the particular form of sinologism I have dubbed *character fetishisation* (漢字崇拜主義 *hànzì chōngbàizhǔyì*): that is, an exaggerated status given to Chinese characters in the interpretation of Chinese language, thought and culture. This status is used to shore up ideological claims about the Chinese language which basically come down to the positing of the uniqueness of the Chinese world view and its incommensurable differences from a supposed Western world view. The notion of character fetishisation characterises a discourse process, the linguistic creation of a kind of 'uniqueness' for the Chinese situation that both operates through and reinforces a series of half-truths.

Discourses of character fetishisation will be explored in this chapter in relation to the three broad fields of traditional humanistic studies in China which many sinologists have traditionally moved across – literature *wén* 文, history *shǐ* 史, and philosophy *zhé* 哲, using three main examples: the literary theorising of James Liu, the ideological historicising of William Jenner, and the linguistic philosophising of Roger Ames and Henry Rosemont Jr. My characterisation of the work of these scholars in such '-ising' terms is intended not to demean their work but rather to stress the process-like, discursive nature of their separate theoretical and descriptive enterprises: in other words, to analyse how they use this understanding of Chinese characters as part of their overall argument about Chinese culture.

Character fetishisation in action: language and literature

Following on from his previous claim, Liu broadens his critique of Western 'misconceptions' of the nature of Chinese characters into an attack on the Western conceptions of language that lie behind them:

> Western philosophers, with their logocentric bias, have usually regarded Chinese written characters as arbitrary signs. Even Saussure, who recognized that the Chinese written system is not phonetic, still thought that each written character was a sign that represented a spoken word. This opinion is demonstrably incorrect and also contradicts traditional Chinese views. In general, whereas Western thinkers concerned with the nature of language conceived of writing as a representation of spoken language, which was in turn conceived of as an intermediary between the world and human beings, the Chinese saw a direct relationship between writing and the world, without the necessary intermediacy of spoken language. It is therefore misleading to call Chinese characters logograms or logographs, as some scholars do, apart from the fact that it sometimes requires *two* characters to write one word.
>
> (*Liu 1988: 17–19*)

Liu bolsters his attack by using Derrida's critique of the whole tradition of Western philosophy as 'logocentric' (Derrida 1974), a critique in which Derrida singled out Saussure as a major target. Derrida criticised Saussure and others for the sin of 'logocentrism', the fetishisation of language, in the particular form of 'phonocentrism', the fetishisation of speech over writing. Whether or not this accurately represents Saussure's views, it could be argued that Derrida's solution simply reverses the direction of fetishisation by prioritising writing over speech; and in any case, in the Chinese context it plays right into the existing misconceptions about the nature of Chinese characters already identified above.

We need to be careful here to draw a distinction between what is shown by a careful linguistic analysis of the Chinese language and its writing system – most of which analyses derive ultimately from traditional Chinese scholarship – and more fanciful ideas about the language also current in the Chinese tradition. It is no real contradiction, nor, in such a culturally loaded area as language should it seem surprising to note, that from the earliest major work on the Chinese writing system, Xu Shen's *Shuōwén Jiězì* 說文解字 (100 CE), hardnosed analyses and fanciful mythmaking have existed side by side. In the *Shuōwén*, as it is usually abbreviated, Xu Shen put forward a classification of six principles of character formation, the so-called *liùshū* 六書, of which various versions had been in existence since at least a century before Xu Shen's time.

In fact Xu's listing of then current characters shows clearly that it was only a minority of characters that fell into the categories which have so excited the imaginations of latter-day sinologists. These character types, translated by Liu as 'simple pictograms, and simple and composite ideograms' (in Xu's terms, *xiàngxíng* 象形 'imitate shape', *zhǐshì* 指事 'indicate thing' and *huìyì* 會意 'combine meanings') have from the *Shuōwén* onwards occupied the least space in the character dictionaries, the majority falling into the category Liu translates as 'composite phonograms' (*xíngshēng* 形聲 'form (and) sound'), where one part of the character is another character *used exclusively for its sound value*.

It is worthwhile exploring the principle on which the 'composite phonograms' were formed, a principle which finds almost exact equivalents in the historically comparable writing forms like Egyptian hieroglyphs or Sumerian cuneiform (Boltz 1994: Ch.3). The key here is one of the categories of character that Liu, very significantly, dismisses as irrelevant: the 'phonetic loan' or *jiǎjiè* 假借 'borrowing'. This category's principle of use is a simple one, and again closely related to one of the characteristics of Old Chinese. Although, as Karlgren points out (Karlgren 1926: 31), Chinese 'already at a very early stage lost its faculty of forming new words by means of derivative affixes', it still showed remnants of this morphological process in the form of alternations of initial consonant and/or tone in related pairs like *chuán* 'to pass on' and *zhuàn* 'that which is passed on – commentary, biography', *cháng* 'long' and *zhǎng* 'to become long – to grow' (compare English *bath – bathe*, or *long – length*). Since in most cases the context would make clear which word was intended, the most economical principle was to write both with the same character, a strategy which continues to this day with the *chuán/zhuàn* 傳 and *cháng/zhǎng* 長 doublets (cf. English *house* 'residence' and *house* 'to provide housing for').

This principle was also extended to words that were morphologically unrelated but had similar pronunciations. Many of the more abstract or grammatical words in Old Chinese were represented by these sorts of phonetic loans: the character for *jī* 'basket' 其 was borrowed for the pronoun *qí* 'his/her/its/their'; *zhī* 'go' 之 for the subordinative particle *zhī* '...'s, of ...', *lái* 'wheat' 來 for *lái* 'come', and so on. Numbers of such characters were later confirmed in their borrowed senses, with the original words represented by a variant of the original character 'expanded' by the addition of a semantic 'determinative': thus 箕 *jī* 'basket', with the 'bamboo' determinative 竹; and 萊 *lái* 'wheat' with the 'grass' determinative 艹.

What is significant here is the extent to which *the sound features of the language were utilised from the very beginning in devising written forms*. The use of sound in devising characters goes beyond even such well-known cases, affecting even the *huìyì* type of character (Liu's 'compound ideograms') whose construction is traditionally thought to have no direct relationship to their pronunciation at all (Boodberg 1937; Boltz 1994: Chs 2–3). Boltz claims that there were two main types of character variation in the early script. The first is the familiar *jiǎjiè* or 'borrowing' discussed above, characterised by Boltz as a *paronomastic* ('side-naming') method, i.e. using an 'established graph' to stand for a 'semantically unrelated but phonetically similar or identical word' (Boltz 1994: 61). Alongside this type of variation, where the sound was similar or constant but the meaning changed, was another kind – not recognised as one of the *liùshū* and largely disguised by subsequent developments in the writing system – which Boltz dubs *parasemantic* ('side-meaning'), where a particular graph 'may be used to write a second word the *meaning* of which is readily suggested by the *depictive quality* of the graph itself' (Boltz 1994: 62, original emphasis).

Take the character 口: according to Boltz, this was originally used not only paronomastically to represent the word *kǒu* 'mouth' and words of similar sound; but also parasemantically to represent the word *míng* 'to call, to name' and related words. In the first case, the process of *jiǎjiè* 'borrowing' is still clearly recognisable in the contemporary script, with 口 *kǒu* 'mouth' also used paronomastically as a phonetic in characters like 扣 *kòu* 'button up, buckle', with the semantic determinative 手 / 扌 *shǒu* 'hand', and 叩 *kòu* 'to knock', with the semantic determinative, now obsolete as an independent character, of a kneeling man. In the second case, the original character 口 has itself been supplemented with the phonetic determinative 夕 to give 名 *míng* 'call, name' (where the phonetic is an abbreviated form of 明 *míng* 'bright') the same character also used parasemantically to represent related words like 鳴 *míng* 'bird call', with 鳥 *niǎo* 'bird' as semantic determinative, and 命 *mìng* 'order' with semantic determinative 令 *lìng* 'order'.

The significance of this for the ideograph debate is that such analyses largely dispose of the *huìyì* 'composite ideogram' category as an independent type; although I remain less convinced than Boltz that *all* such cases can be explained this way. Such a reinterpretation would grievously undercut many discourses of character fetishisation, since this is the very category on which such accounts are most inclined to become creative, even willy-nilly dragging many *xíngshēng* 'composite phonograms' into that class. Boltz puts the matter quite bluntly:

> There is no way a character can be 'invented' by putting together constituent elements none of which is intended to have any phonetic

function ... . When characters occur with two or more constituent parts, and none appears to be phonophoric [i.e. 'sound-bearing', 'phonetic' EMcD], we must assume that there is a phonetic element in the character somewhere that we have not yet uncovered ... . As a rule, we cannot but insist that 'phonetic-less' characters simply do not exist.[19]

19. Many of the 'classic' cases of this kind of thing, i.e. characters constituted of two or more elements allegedly based only on the meaning of the elements, not the sound, are after careful analysis explicable as phonetic compounds ... .

(Boltz 1994: 72)

If Boltz's argument is accepted, it has the effect of demonstrating that Chinese characters do not, after all, constitute a special case, since they clearly followed the same principles as all the other writing systems in the world.

Further evidence that sound has always played a crucial role in the interpretation of Chinese characters comes from Kennedy, who notes a surprising fact about the graphs for the names of insects in Chinese as far back as we can trace: none of them are pictograms. This would seem, on the face of it, an inexplicable fact: surely insects are among those features of the natural world which would most easily lend themselves to being represented by pictograms? Well, the other surprising fact noted by Kennedy is that, in all of these cases, the names of insects *have two syllables*: thus, in their modern Mandarin forms, *zhīzhū* 'spider', *xīshuài* 'cricket', *húdié* 'butterfly', and so on. Now this type of fact, dismissed by Liu as a side issue – 'apart from the fact that it sometimes requires *two* characters to write one word' – is immensely significant, because it provides a negative confirmation of the principle that works for the majority of words in Chinese: that is, the equation of one syllable = one word. To return to Liu's original example, why could the word *rì* 'sun, day' be represented by what looks like an icon of the sun?: precisely because this morpheme had only *one* syllable, and therefore could be easily read out from a text as such. And so why could the word *zhīzhū* 'spider' not be represented by an icon of the insect?: because it had *two* syllables, and thus could only be represented by two other existing characters with similar sounds, in this case 知 *zhī* 'know' and 朱 *zhū* 'cinnibar', used simply for their sound value, with the addition of an 'insect' determinative 虫 to each, thus 蜘蛛.

Nonetheless, it could be claimed that what scholars such as Liu and Hansen are arguing for is simply an acknowledgment of traditional Chinese views about the nature of the characters. It is true, as Kennedy points out, that certain features of the script do lend themselves to mythmaking of this sort: as in the case of the Chinese scholar who indulged in 'false etymologising' with regard to the word *xīshuài* 'cricket', inventing two separate insects on the basis of the two separate characters, and remarking gravely that 'the crics eat ... the stems while the kets eat the leaves' (Kennedy 1951/1964: 116 – see the end of Chapter 5 for another example). I think, however, we should be sceptical as to whether the 'traditional Chinese views' were in fact as Liu represents them, at least across the board; and in any case Liu and Hansen fail to draw a distinction between describing and mythmaking, either in their sources or in their own work.

Liu, for example, puts forward an elaborate argument about attitudes towards language based on his mistaken characterisation of the writing system. To repeat part of the quotation from his work given above:

> In general, whereas Western thinkers concerned with the nature of language conceived of writing as a representation of spoken language, which was in turn conceived of as an intermediary between the world and human beings, the Chinese saw a direct relationship between writing and the world, without the necessary intermediacy of spoken language.
>
> *(Liu 1988: 17–19)*

I am not disputing the accuracy of Liu's understanding of traditional Chinese thinking, but just as in an earlier work Liu himself took issue with certain mistaken ideas about Chinese characters put forward by American poet Ezra Pound and widely taken up in Western Modernist literature (Liu 1962), it is important to distinguish in principle between (ideological) claims about the language and (more or less objective) descriptions of how the language works. Similar confusions are found in the work of Chinese linguist Shen Xiaolong, whose ideas will be discussed in more detail in Chapter 6. Using some of the same classical texts as Liu, he builds up a very strong claim for the primacy of meaning over form:

> On this unique relation between form and spirit in the Chinese language, there is ample discussion among ancient thinkers. The unity of heaven and men in philosophy took as its standpoint people's subjective experience and awareness. Therefore among the dichotomies such as form and spirit, word and meaning, pattern and principle, the spirit, meaning and principle aspects of language were primary, and the contrasting formal aspects of language had no independent existence. An important theme of ancient Chinese philosophy was 'Language does not exhaust meaning'.
>
> *(Shen 2001: 3)*

Liu and Shen's claims suggest that there may be a kind of institutionalised blindness about the Chinese language in various areas within and beyond Chinese studies. The supposed complexity of the writing system may be one factor in this, but there may also exist a more serious misunderstanding of language in the Chinese tradition that works against attempts to understand it. Just as an over-concentration on the graphic features of Chinese characters has led many scholars astray in their understanding of the Chinese language, it is an over-emphasis on 'meaning' as opposed to linguistic 'form' which supplies one of the key underlying supports for the over-simplifying of linguistic issues which we find in Chinese studies generally.

Shen, whose work is largely concerned with the paradoxical task of 'proving' that Chinese is clearly distinct from 'Western languages' (see Chapter 6), uses arguments of these kinds to argue, yet again, for Chinese 'uniqueness' (that word again!), as shown in the quotation above. Now again it is a moot point whether, as in the case of Liu and Hansen's interpretations, 'ancient thinkers' really thought of these pairs of concepts as the 'dichotomies' (*yí duìduì máodùn fànchóu* 一對對矛盾範疇) which Shen considers them to be. It is certainly true that the 'famous analogy' from the classic Taoist philosophical text the *Zhuangzi* quoted by Shen can be interpreted this way:

> The *Zhuangzi* has a famous analogy in regard to the relationship between language and meaning: 'The purpose of the trap lies in the fish; when you get the fish, you forget the trap. The purpose of the snare lies in the hare; when you get the hare, you forget the snare. The purpose of words lies in the meaning, when you get the meaning, you forget the words' ... . Here 'words' are only a trigger for expressing meaning. It has meaning, but it cannot exhaust meaning.
>
> *(Shen 2001: 3; translation from Liu 1988: 11)*

However, while it is obvious that the *Zhuangzi* regards the fish as more important than the trap, it is also clear that without the trap, you have no way of getting the fish in the first place. For Shen to claim that the words 'are only a trigger for expressing meaning' is throwing the baby out with the bathwater. The further conclusion he goes on to draw, that '[the trigger] has meaning, but ... cannot exhaust meaning' restates the priority in a different manner, using what have become proverbial expressions in Chinese thinking about language, *yán bú jìn yì* 言不盡意 'words do not exhaust meaning' and *dé yì wàng yán* 得意忘言 'when you get the meaning, forget the words'. These proverbs sum up a whole attitude towards the creative use of language, i.e. poetics, and by implication towards the analysis of language, i.e. linguistics. We can accept the validity of experience upon which such statements on language are based without needing to take such claims at face value in our understanding of Chinese language and literature.

Character fetishisation in action: history

Such misunderstandings about the nature of the Chinese writing system are not simply confined to describing the workings of the language itself, or of literature written in that language; they are used as a basis for all sorts of larger claims across the field of Chinese studies, as the following 'harangues' show:

> [W]hat is wrong with China is to be found in the core of the heart and mind of the average Chinese, ... China has failed and may always fail, as a racial entity, to meet modern conditions, not because of a lack of opportunity to prove her capacity, nor because of repression from without, but because her development was arrested more than two thousand years ago ... what is really wrong with China and will continue to be wrong with her, is that the Chinese are children, that their world is a child's world of make-believe;

and that they have no more right, in their own interest or in humanity's larger interest, to govern themselves or shape their own course of education, than the pupils in a school have to boss the faculty and dictate what they will learn and what they will not.

(*Gilbert 1926: 45*)

[T]he present high culture is in its essentials the continuation of the high culture – the civilization – of imperial China; ... while there are many elements of it that present and future cultures will draw on with profit, this cultural formation has outstayed its usefulness and does not really work any longer; ... while it is not dead yet, it is dying, and in the process, blocking the emergence of cultures with life in them; ... its end will have profound and all-pervasive effects in every aspect of Chinese life; ... only fundamental and, in historical terms, rapid reordering of the inherited tradition can liberate the peoples of China from its crushing weight.

(*Jenner 1992: 210–211*)

Since the Opium Wars of the 1840s began the long and painful process of destroying China's traditional political and cultural ascendancy in its own region, a process whose effects are arguably still being worked through in both the political and intellectual spheres, the question 'What's Wrong with China', to use the title of the source of the first extract above, has been a commonplace among both Chinese and foreign intellectuals. A common answer to this question would be the one given by the title of the second, 'The Tyranny of History': in other words, that the long weight of Chinese tradition, from many points of view of course a source of great admiration and pride, has now become a 'deadweight' on the further development of the culture.

The two works extracted above exemplify this discourse of 'China in decline' in response to different historical circumstances, and driven by different ideological imperatives. The author of the first, Rodney Gilbert, an American journalist working in China, claims to be carrying out a necessary scolding of the 'winsome but temperamental jade' (Gilbert 1926: 7) that is China in his eyes. Writing in the mid-1920s when the inadequacies of the early Republic were fully in evidence, and the Kuomintang had yet to restore an at least partial unity and stability to the country, his tirade nevertheless sounds both shrill and arrogant to a modern reader. This combined with his open racism – 'China has failed and may always fail, as a racial entity, to meet modern conditions'; and more than patronising assumption of superiority – 'the Chinese are children ... their world is a child's world of make-believe', makes it easy to dismiss his work as the rantings of an imperialist with a Chinese bee in his bonnet.

Given this, it may seem more than a little offensive of me to use what Geremie Barmé, quoting Mao, refers to as 'reactionary editing' (Barmé and Jaivin 1992: xviii), to place alongside Gilbert's harangue the far more thoughtful and measured remarks of William Jenner, a well-respected literary translator and cultural commentator on China, writing in the wake of the Protest Movement of 1989 which came to an end so tragically in Tian'anmen Square in June of that year, and gave many commentators, including Jenner, cause to despair. However, just as with the parallels drawn above between Francis Bacon and James Liu or Chad Hansen, it seems to me that there are certain discursive strategies, as well as underlying assumptions, which are common to both Gilbert and Jenner. Two further quotations specifically dealing with the language may show this up more clearly:

> An inexact and illogical language has led to inexact and illogical thinking among the masses of the people. It is against reason to suppose that a people using a primitive medium of expression can think anything but primitive thoughts. The average Chinese is as incapable of sustaining a logical argument in his own tongue as he is of whistling a tune ... . The Chinese speaker, who has acquired the vocabulary and phraseology to express himself eloquently, has already achieved so much that he is much more taken up with the form of what he is saying than with the sense of it; and his hearers also are too busy being impressed by his style to worry much about the truth of his statements or the soundness of his arguments.
>
> (*Gilbert 1926: 93*)

> Written Chinese can be as precise and specific as its user wishes it to be, provided one is prepared to be inelegant, but it will admit, and even encourage, a degree of imprecision and unspecificity that is structurally impossible in a European language. ... Although modern written Chinese is not quite as vague as the classical forms from which is has evolved, it still inhibits analytical, logical thinking and sharp definitions, encouraging instead the juxtaposition of powerful but fuzzy images. It impedes, but does not prevent, the linear development of an argument or a narrative in strong, simple, uncluttered language. ... Let me state clearly that I am not saying that Chinese people have any greater difficulties in thinking logically than other nationalities: far from it. ... Nor is there any reason to believe that spoken Chinese is inherently resistant to clear thought and argument. ... The problem lies in the writing system.
>
> (*Jenner 1992: 212–214*)

While the unrelenting negativity of Gilbert's harangue becomes almost comical – probably the best way to regard such discourse – the reader's amusement may be suddenly brought up short by noticing that some of Gilbert's claims are uncomfortably close to those made by Jenner. While no longer characterised as an 'inexact and illogical language' whose speakers cannot 'think anything but primitive thoughts', Chinese is nevertheless, in Jenner's formulation, a language whose written form 'inhibits analytical, logical thinking and sharp definitions'.

When Jenner goes on to raise the 'awkward question' of whether 'the structures of the Chinese written language inhibit clarity of expression and thought' and the related query of whether they 'encourage acceptance of what is written in assertive rather than analytical ways' (Jenner 1992: 215), a reader unacquainted with the long tradition of such sinologistic discourse – see Haun Saussy's aptly titled *Great Walls of Discourse* (Saussy 2001) for an extended discussion of the discursive creation of a 'lacking' Chinese language in relation to European languages – may wonder just exactly why the language itself is being blamed for problems that on the face of it would seem to have more obvious political or cultural explanations.

Character fetishisation in action: philosophy

To move on now to philosophy, Ames and Rosemont's 'philosophical translation' of that key literary and philosophical text the *Analects* (of Confucius), spends some time, as do many such translations, giving a glossary of what they call in this context 'The Chinese Lexicon': in other words, the key philosophical terms used in the *Analects*, and how they should be understood and thus rendered into English. Their exegesis of the term 道 *dao*, which they characterise as 'very probably the single most important term in the philosophical lexicon', is very representative of their methodology as a whole:

> The character has two elements: *chuo* 辶 'to pass over', 'to go over', 'to lead through' (on foot), and *shou* 首, itself a compound literally meaning 'head' – hair and eye together – and therefore 'foremost'. *Dao* is often used as a loan character for its cognate, *dao* 導, 'to lead.' Thus the character is significantly verbal, processual, and dynamic. The earliest appearance of *dao* in the *Book of Documents* is in the context of cutting a channel and 'leading' a river to prevent the overflowing of its banks. Even the *shou* 'head' component has the suggestion of 'to lead,' or 'give a heading'.
>
> (*Ames and Rosemont 1999: 45*)

This kind of argumentation is what Creel, in a series of textbooks of classical Chinese (see Creel *et al.* 1938–1952), called the 'inductive method': that is, examining the structure of the character in order to derive insights about the meaning of the word it represents. If we accept, as I have argued we should, that the principles of a character's composition are irrelevant to its interpretation, of course such a methodology falls down immediately. But even on its own terms, this 'inductive' method seems on rather shaky ground. Let's first compare how the *Shuowen* explains this character (quoted in Huang 1997: 14, formatting modified and characters added): 'The road one walks on, composed of 之 *zhi* "to walk" and 首 *shou* "head", signifying "that by which one walks all the way to one's destination".'

Ames and Rosemont's definition differs from the *Shuowen* in small but significant ways. First of all it identifies the first component not as 之 *zhi* 'to walk'
but 辶 *chuo* 'to lead through'. Why Ames and Rosemont make this substitution is
not clear. The word *zhi* quoted by the *Shuowen* in the meaning 'go' is also used as
a loan character for two homophonous grammatical words, the third person pronoun 'he, she, it' and the possessive particle 'of ..., ...'s'; perhaps Ames and
Rosemont felt that this polysemy (multiple meaning of a single character) somewhat 'muddied the waters' of their argument, and thus chose a variant form of the
same character. Next they analyse the second component 首 *shou* 'head' as itself a
'compound' which is 'literally' 'hair and eye together' and 'therefore "foremost"'.
This sort of combinatory logic could be set out as follows:

> hair + eye = foremost
>
> foremost + pass over = to lead
>
> to lead (dynamic) → that which leads one (static) = way

The inductive method, which Creel, then Professor of Chinese at Chicago, made
the main selling point of his series of textbooks of classical Chinese, was critiqued
by Kennedy in a review of Creel's third volume of the series as being structured
around the 'basic assumption that a Chinese graph is a more or less eternal symbol
for an idea, from which it follows that the most useful information about it is given
through an analysis of its technique of ideal representation' (Kennedy 1953b: 490);
and similar types of argument have of course been dealt with in earlier sections of
this chapter. In the case of the analysis of the character for *dao* 'way', what Ames
and Rosemont provide is a kind of 'Just So Story', which may well be pedagogi-
cally useful, but has no grounding in the actual usage of the term in texts.

If we now compare a number of other definitions appended to different translations of the *Analects*, we find that they concentrate on the *meaning* of the word,
rather than the *construction* of the character, in explaining the term. A slightly
earlier translation, Huang 1997, first cites the *Shuowen* definition quoted above,
and then goes on to explain it as:

> a road or way. From this root meaning is derived the connotation 'a theory,
> doctrine, or body of principles upheld and followed by a group of believers'.
> The English word 'way' fits both the literal and the metaphorical meaning
> of the Chinese character nicely.
>
> (*Huang 1997: 14*)

If we compare now an earlier treatment, attached to Waley's 1938 translation,
cited using Wade–Giles romanisation as *tao*, we find no mention of the form of
the character at all:

> [T]*ao* has not in the Analects a technical or peculiar meaning, but is used
> there in just the same sense as in early Chinese works in general. *Tao*

means literally a road, a path, a way. Hence, the way in which anything is done, the way in which, for example, a kingdom is ruled; a method, a principle, a doctrine.

(*Waley 1938: 30*)

Likewise another more recent translation than Ames and Rosemont's, Slingerland's, does not seem to feel the need to call on the form of the character in order to justify its explanation:

Referring literally to a physical path or road, *dao* also refers to a 'way' of doing things, and in the Analects refers to *the* Way: that is, the unique moral path that should be walked by any true human being … , endorsed by Heaven and revealed to the early Sage-Kings. More concretely, this 'Way' is manifested in the ritual practices, music, and literature passed down from the Golden Age of the Western Zhou.

(*Slingerland 2003: 243*)

If we come back to Ames and Rosemont's definition, apart from its Creel-like 'inductive method', we can also note another rhetorical strategy: a 'dynamic interpretation' of Chinese characters which claims that 'the great number of these [Chinese] ideographic roots carry in them a verbal idea of action' (Fenellosa and Pound 1920: 59, quoted in Kennedy 1958/1964: 448). This notion was first put forward by American japanologist Ernest Fenellosa, and after his death it was taken up by American poet and literary polemicist Ezra Pound as part of his manifesto for his own poetic school of Imagism. This 'dynamic interpretation' of Chinese characters has also been critiqued by Kennedy (Kennedy 1958/1964: 443–462) in a devastating analysis of Pound's interpretation of a poem which shows that the Chinese language's supposed preference for expressing dynamic actions is, at least on Pound's own evidence, a complete myth, foisted upon it by the demands of Pound's own aesthetic theories. Analysing one Chinese poem of twenty syllables, which Pound–Fenellosa hold up as an example of the notion of 'dynamic action', Kennedy finds 'eleven of the twenty are defined as nouns, three as adjectives, two as copulative variants, one as an intransitive verb, two as of doubtful classification, and only one, "admire", as a transitive verb with fairly low dynamics' (Kennedy 1958/1964: 449). As Kennedy remarks wryly: 'the notion that Chinese poetry is overloaded with strong transitive verbs, is, to put it mildly, shot to hell' (Kennedy 1958/1964: 450).

In an appendix to their translation, entitled 'Further remarks on language, translation, and interpretation', Ames and Rosemont lay out the understandings of the Chinese writing system and written language underlying their 'inductive' and 'dynamic' characterisation of it. Their basic starting point is that (Ames and Rosemont 1999: 289): 'the classical Chinese written language … is unique [sic!], being sharply distinct not only from all other non-Sinitic languages but from spoken Chinese as well (ancient and modern) …'. The basis of this difference supposedly stems from the peculiar nature of the Shang oracle bone inscriptions,

our earliest extant examples of the script. First they call on the Shang script's supposedly non-phonetic nature in claiming that:

> many of the thousand-plus characters that have been identified thus far ...
> are importantly pictographic and ideographic in construction. ... These
> characters are thus to be interpreted basically as representations of objects
> and ideas respectively, and though they would likely have some relation-
> ship to the pronunciation of these same objects and ideas, they are not
> merely representations of sounds.
>
> (*Ames and Rosemont 1999: 290*)

Such a claim takes us all the way back to Bacon and his 'Characters Real', and
even goes beyond the old confusion between 'characters' and 'words', whose
separation has been one of the main aims of modern Chinese linguistics, into
confusing words and their referents: how, for example, can 'objects and ideas'
have a 'pronunciation'? Second, Ames and Rosemont identify the ostensibly very
limited circumstances of use for the early script. As they argue, given that:

> the excavated inscriptions are written on divinatory or other materials that
> are religious, not secular, in nature ... [c]onsequently the development of
> the written forms must have been under the direct and powerful influence
> of extralinguistic factors, especially the religious and other beliefs of the
> early Chinese people. ... The written characters, for instance, may have
> been thought to possess magical qualities which it would have been defil-
> ing or even dangerous to apply regularly in nonreligious contexts.
>
> (*Ames and Rosemont 1999: 291*)

There are a number of good reasons for being sceptical of such claims. First, as
Ames and Rosemont themselves acknowledge, there may be very simple practical
reasons for the lack of non-secular inscriptions: that they 'could have been written
on less durable artefacts' (Ames and Rosemont 1999: 291). In the case of comparable early writing systems like Sumerian cuneiform or Egyptian hieroglyphics,
modern researchers have been aided by the relatively dry climates of those two
areas which have preserved a large amount of texts of different genres, texts which
the wetter climate of eastern China may well have destroyed (compare the later
texts preserved in quantity in the desert conditions of Dunhuang in the drier west
of the country). Furthermore, if we take the examples of those other two
ancient scripts, the fact that they demonstrably *were* used for secular purposes
does not seem to have ruled out the sorts of 'magical' uses Ames and Rosemont allude
to; similar usages are attested to this day for the Hebrew script in the long tradition
of the Qabbala, and for the Greek and Latin scripts. It is obviously not necessary
for a script to 'look' meaningful in order for it to be assigned magical properties.

The work of fellow philosopher A.C. Graham lays several of Ames and
Rosemont's bugbears to rest:

> Classical Chinese is a language of mainly monosyllabic words, each syllable with its own written character, organised by word-order and the placing and function of grammatical particles. The script is not, as used to be supposed, ideographic; different monosyllabic words, however near they approach synonymity, are written with different graphs, and particles like other words have their own graphs. The combination of graphic wealth with phonetic poverty has the result that the etymology of a word and its relation to similar sounding monosyllables is displayed in the structure of the graph rather than of the vocable.
>
> (*Graham 1989: 389*)

Graham accounts for the downgrading of sound in favour of meaning on the part of scholars like Ames and Rosemont, insofar as it derives from traditional Chinese thinking on language, by noting that the 'combination of graphic wealth [in the character] with phonetic poverty [in the syllable]' explains why Chinese scholars are apt to draw conclusions about the nature of the language from the structure of the graph, forgetting that it is the underlying meaning of the syllable/morpheme which is responsible for any insights character shape may give us.

Conclusion: a site for reconciliation – trusting the evidence of the text

The grand claims of these scholars' 'sinologism' – though of course I am not presuming to characterise all or even most of their work as such – contrasted with the careful and nuanced explanations of Kennedy and Graham's 'sinology', show up very well the difficulties for Chinese studies in understanding the Chinese language. On the one hand, the facts themselves are complex and not easy to get right; on the other, there is what often seems like a compulsion to be interested not in establishing facts, but rather in perpetuating myths. All the scholars critiqued above are quite legitimately concerned to combat what they see as distorted Western views of Chinese language and thought, but in their anxiety to redress the balance they fall into the trap of 'reactive relativism' (see Chapter 6), by trying to show that Chinese is everything Western languages are not.

But whatever the specific motivation of scholars like Hansen, Liu, Shen, Jenner, and Ames and Rosemont within and beyond Chinese studies for putting forward their points of view, their arguments are able to draw on a whole reservoir of character fetishisation discourse which has to some extent become the commonsense of the field. Furthermore, since scholars critiquing these tendencies, such as Boodberg and Kennedy, and more recently DeFrancis (1984, 1989) and Unger (2004), have tended to take a dismissive if not polemical tone towards such arguments, the effect of the ensuing debates seems to have been largely one of drawing battle lines between the linguists and the non-linguists within the field (see discussion in Lurie 2006).

However in a different context, Ames and Rosemont themselves show that they do not need to call on discourses of character fetishisation to justify their understanding of the text. This can be clearly seen in their discussion of the key semantic field of 'change' in classical Chinese, based on their interpretation of the passage from the *Analects* translated by Legge as 'If for three years he does not alter from the way of his father, he may be called filial', but by themselves as 'A person who for three years refrains from reforming the ways of his late father can be called a filial son' (Ames and Rosemont 1999: 280). Their justification for this interpretation is given in an explanation worth quoting at length:

> The emphasis in this passage as we understand it is on reforming the ways of the father only after having fully embodied and understood them, and then only with due deliberation. Our translation implies that the son must first honor the ritual traditions seriously, but must then reappropriate them for himself, and in the course of time, attune them to make them appropriate to his own particular circumstances. Philology will not entirely settle the matter for *gai* 改 has been conventionally rendered 'to change,' 'to alter,' 'to correct,' 'to amend' or 'to reform,' and the negative *wu* 無 can thus equally be linked to *gai* as 'does not alter,' 'makes no change,' or 'refrains from reforming.' We hedge and say philology will not [sic] 'not entirely' decide the case because translating *gai* as 'change' in this instance is within the semantic tolerance, although it might not be sufficiently specific to convey the intended meaning. ... A translation of this passage needs to distinguish among several different senses of 'change': 1) *bian* 變 is to change gradually across time, 2) *yi* 易 is to change one thing for another, 3) *hua* 化 is to transform utterly where A becomes B, 4) *qian* 遷 is to change from one place to another, and 5) *gai* 改 is to correct or reform or improve on *x* on the basis of some other standard or model *y*.
>
> *(Ames and Rosemont 1999: 280–281)*

Ames and Rosemont's interpretation here is an exemplary instance of traditional philological exegesis, whether of the European or Chinese stripe, as well as, might I suggest, of a social semiotic analysis of the Hodge and Louie kind (see Chapter 8 for more discussion). It is semiotic, in the sense strongly insisted on by Saussure, that words only have meanings *in contrast to each other* (Saussure 1916/1957: 107–120): it is therefore impossible to understand the particular force of *gai* in Chinese without knowing the other terms with which it is in contrast. It is social because it extends the semiotic explanation towards an understanding of the society Confucius was describing or envisaging: in terms of Ames and Rosemont's own explanation, in the way that philosophy gives us access to 'different "worlds" with which we can come to terms' (Ames and Rosemont 1999: 315). And furthermore we can note that here, in contrast to the earlier example quoted, the translators make absolutely no reference to the form of the relevant characters: a character-based 'inductive' explanation is simply not necessary.

This suggests more generally that Ames and Rosemont are in fact gilding the lily by calling on character-based analyses in other contexts. If their explanations are grounded in a detailed understanding of the text, and of the system of terms defined and contrasted within, then there is simply no necessity for them to go any further. It would seem that their dependence on what has here been dubbed a discourse of 'character fetishisation' has more to do with their predetermination to see 'the classical Chinese written language' as 'unique' (Ames and Rosemont 1999: 289), using a term which like the earlier use of 'inscrutable' for China itself (cf. Hansen 1983: 13) would seem to have become almost stereotypical for the Chinese language.

The notion of an 'inscrutable China' and its contribution to Western thinking has been subjected to trenchant critique in an article by Rey Chow in which she points out how Derrida, through the misunderstood notion of Chinese writing in his early work, casts 'Chinese writing as *the* metaphor for difference from Western phonocentrism' (Chow 2001: 70, original emphasis). She broadens her critique of what may seem merely an intellectual gambit on the part of an iconoclastic Western philosopher into a conclusion with implications for the sorts of discourses examined here, as well as for the broader fields of Chinese studies and Asian studies:

> Translated into the context of high theory and philosophy, 'inscrutable Chinese' is no longer simply the enigmatic exterior of the oriental but also *an entire language and culture reduced to (sur)face, image and ideogram.* ... The face of the Chinese person and the face of Chinese writing thus converge in what must now be seen as a composite verbal stereotype – *the other face* – that stigmatizes another culture as at once corporeally and linguistically intractable.
>
> (*Chow 2001: 72, original emphasis*)

Applying Chow's critique to the discourses of character fetishisation examined in this chapter, the paradox emerges that such discourses stem not from philosophers like Derrida or poets like Pound (Fenellosa and Pound 1920/1936) whose relative ignorance of Chinese language allows them to reshape it in their own desired or required 'image'; but rather from scholars such as Hansen, Liu, Ames and Rosemont, who have dedicated their professional lives to learning about and trying to come to grips with the genuine differences between 'home' and 'the other'. Even would-be iconoclasts like Hodge and Louie end up reproducing in their own analyses the very ideology they are attempting to deconstruct, reaffirming the centrality of Chinese characters as 'semantic primes ... that determine – and control – all other meanings expressible in the language' (McDonald 2000: 216).

Chinese scholars Zhan Xuzuo and Zhu Liangzhi (Zhan and Zhu 1995) trace the historical process by which Chinese characters, to quote the English subtitle of their article, have been used to 'verify beliefs and ideologies' throughout the history of the traditional Chinese state. It is this very role of 'verification' that some scholars in Chinese studies see as a continuing one for Chinese characters, a role that allows their promoters to preserve the notions of 'inscrutability' and 'uniqueness' that have been an inherent part of Western sinology since its beginnings. If we can understand the substantive issues involved in how Chinese characters work, a crucial question still remains. Will there be the willingness within the field, among the linguists, the philosophers, the historians, the literary theorists and everyone else, to discard the exaggerated status ascribed to the characters both positively *and* negatively and see cultural China as 'distinctive' rather than 'unique', as 'interpretable' rather than 'inscrutable'? This chapter has tried to suggest some of the ways out of the current intellectual standoff, but ultimately the question is one only the field as a whole can decide.

Iconolatry

5

IDEOLATRY VERSUS PHONOLATRY?

Chinese characters as disciplinary identifier

Introduction: the continuing relevance of historical debates

Just over seventy years ago a debate was initiated in the pages of one of the founding European sinological journals, *T'oung Pao*, between proponents of two sharply contrasting views on the nature of Chinese characters. Professor Herrlee Glessner Creel of the University of Chicago, fresh from his first-hand researches among the newly discovered archeological remains of the Shang dynasty in northern China, called for a reevaluation of the role of ideography versus phonetics in the interpretation of the evolution of the characters (Creel 1936). Professor Peter Boodberg from the University of California at Berkeley countered with a call for a recognition that phonetics played a much greater part in the creation of characters than traditionally thought (Boodberg 1937). As the debate unfolded in mounting miscomprehension and scholarly polemic on both sides (Creel 1938; Boodberg 1940), it became clear that what was at stake was not simply a radical divergence over the nature of Chinese characters, but an argument about the particularity of the Chinese situation, a related clash between a 'humanistic' and a 'scientific' world view, and in some sense a battle for control over the field of sinology or Chinese studies itself.

Just under thirty years later, another debate took place in the American *Journal of Asian Studies*, the flagship journal of the then relatively new area of Asian studies which was seen as incorporating the traditional narrowly defined sinology, japanology, indology, etc., within a broadly based modern, social scientific field. This debate derived from a symposium organised for the 1964 annual meeting of the Association of Asian Studies on the question of the relationship between, to use the symposium title, 'Chinese Studies and the Disciplines'. The discussion was subsequently published by the *Journal*, including not only the papers written by the members of the panel, but also some reflections and follow-up comments by other participants, and revolved around whether the question of whether the old-fashioned 'sinology' and its text-based philological approach should be preserved, or rather replaced by different disciplines working within and beyond the field of Chinese studies, and bringing to that field all the up-to-date rigour of their social scientific methodologies. Although language was not the main topic of discussion in this debate, it was definitely present as a major sub-theme, in a way that echoed some of the concerns of the earlier debate in a different context.

Coming down another forty years, despite the fact that the label 'sinology' has all but completely given way to 'Chinese studies' on the contemporary academic scene in anglophone circles at least, the relics of 'sinologism', in Hodge and Louie's sense, are still clearly to be seen. From the evidence put forward in the previous chapter, one of the major manifestations of sinologism in contemporary Chinese studies is found in discourses of 'character fetishisation', that is, an inordinate if not hegemonic – to use an appropriate political metaphor – status given by many sinologists to Chinese characters in the interpretation of Chinese language, thought and culture. As we saw in the previous chapter, supporters of the kind of views put forward by Creel can be found across the field in areas as diverse as literary theory (Liu 1988) and philosophy (Hansen 1983; Ames and Rosemont 1999); while negative recastings of Creel's claims, which however leave their basic tenets ultimately unchallenged, show up in history (Jenner 1992) and even Cultural studies (Hodge and Louie 1998). A recent collection critiquing ideographic views of the characters (Erbaugh 2002) identifies what Boodberg referred to caustically as 'the ghost of Ideography' not just haunting 'the platform of sinological Elsinore' where Boodberg had noted its presence (Boodberg 1940: 266), but beyond sinology proper in disciplines like psychology and education and theoretical enterprises like deconstruction.

The key ideological underpinning of such discourses is the desire to prove the uniqueness of the Chinese situation, neatly summed up by Ames and Rosemont in their characterisation of what they call the 'classical Chinese written language', which in their definition corresponds to the language of the earliest records of written Chinese scratched on oracle bones during the Shang dynasty. As they claim, in a very strong statement given at length in the previous chapter, 'the classical Chinese written language … is unique, being sharply distinct not only from all other non-Sinitic languages but from spoken Chinese as well (ancient and modern)' (Ames and Rosemont 1999: 289–290).

It is of course perfectly understandable that sinologists, or any other area specialists, would wish to stress the particularity of their own area of study, but when this causes them to go beyond what the evidence will support to erect ideological chimaeras which are of little or no use to their main purpose, it would seem to call for some explanation. In fact a modern scholar working on

Chinese is confronted with a whole 'commonsense' discourse, not only about the 'uniqueness' of the Chinese language but the concomitant 'uniqueness' of Chinese history and culture. This ideological complex had its beginnings in the mis- or over-interpretations of the pioneering reports of the Jesuit missionaries which represented modern Europe's first detailed accounts of China (see Mungello 1986); and its development up to the present is well covered in Saussy's detailed study with the felicitous title of *Great Walls of Discourse* (Saussy 2001). This complex, given wider circulation in the early twentieth century by literary theory under the polemical aegis of Ezra Pound (Fenellosa and Pound 1920/1936, Pound 1934/1951), and then used as a convenient stick to beat the Western 'logocentric' dog at the hands of deconstructionists like Derrida (1974), provides anyone describing Chinese with a ready-made set of arguments, either to draw on or to react against, whose basic premises have not shifted one inch since the time of Creel and Boodberg. An examination of this debate is therefore not merely of historical interest but may be able to cast some light on why discourses of 'character fetishisation' have such staying power.

In this chapter I would like to use a re-examination of the Creel–Boodberg debate to cast some light on these still unresolved issues in contemporary Chinese studies, not just by dealing with the substantive issues, something that has already been done in great detail elsewhere (DeFrancis 1984; Erbaugh 2002), but by analysing and critiquing presuppositions and biases on both sides and identifying their respective rhetorical strategies. It may seem paradoxical that with over a hundred years of historical scholarship on Chinese characters since the seminal discovery of the oracle bones at the turn of the twentieth century, no agreement has yet been reached on their nature as a writing system; but this is only paradoxical if we ignore the huge ideological and cultural value attached to the characters and their defining role both for Chinese culture generally and the field of Chinese studies that feeds off it. It is not necessary to go any further than the extensive literature on the alphabet, and the intellectual and cultural benefits claimed from its use in the history of Western culture (e.g. Logan 1986, 2004), to find an example of a similarly elaborate ideological complex erected on as flimsy a basis.

Creel's opening salvo: 'characterising' the Chinese writing system

At issue in the first instance is what may seem like a rather trivial debate over whether 'ideographic' or 'logographic' is the best term to describe the essential nature of Chinese characters as a writing system. The substantive disagreements, as well as the passions aroused, by this choice of nomenclature are well-rehearsed in the following rather tendentiously expressed comment on the issue by one of Ames and Rosemont's fellow philosophers:

> The characterisation of Chinese as pictographic or ideographic is under nearly constant attack from Chinese linguists who seem to prefer the term *logographic*. It is hard to understand the passion and intensity of their arguments on the choice of a word to denote a range of languages that includes exactly one! In any case, we need not find any way to resolve the issue. What is important for the present argument is that Chinese themselves view their own written language as conventional representations of the semantic content, that is, pictures or diagrams. The written forms of the pre-Han period were even more 'picture-like' than is the regularized modern (post-Han) script. In fact, the vast majority of Chinese characters have phonetic components. But Chinese etymologies tend to interpret these ideographically too, and with some justification. There is usually a range of choices of phonetics available for a particular use, and the choice of the phonetic component probably does reflect semantic concerns as well as phonetic ones.
>
> (*Hansen 1983: 179, footnote 25*)

What is interesting here is that the uniqueness of the Chinese case is treated as absolutely unarguable; and furthermore apparently supported by complete unanimity on the part of some uncharacterised 'Chinese themselves'. Any possibility that the Chinese writing system may be – at least partially or indirectly – phonetically based, like all other historically and currently existing writing systems, is resolutely pushed to one side. This suggests that what is at stake in the choice of term is not simply a definitional issue in the narrow sense but rather a demonstration of allegiance in the study of China, whereby one nails one's standards either to a 'particularist' or 'universalist' mast.

As in many such scholarly debates, because the participants fail to agree on definitions of key terms, they very often end up speaking at cross purposes. The Creel–Boodberg debate is stymied from the start by a failure on the part of the two scholars to ensure that they are actually talking about the same things. In the case of Creel, it is only because he settles on vague definitions of such key terms as 'language', 'writing', and 'meaning', as well as resisting the *reductio ad absurdum* implied by his position, that he is able to go on insisting, in the face of much phonetic evidence to the contrary, that the ideographic principle deserves the dominant position he gives it in the interpretation of Chinese characters. Although Boodberg, by contrast, is very careful to define his terms, he does not make the effort to debate Creel directly on *his* definitions, and his generally dismissive attitude towards what he describes as Creel's 'impossible thesis' (Boodberg 1937: 330, footnote 2), means that he fails to present the step by step rebuttal that would be needed to carry conviction. The two combatants thus never really come to grips with what exactly they disagree on.

Creel opens the debate with a foreshadowing of the 'logocentric' and 'phonocentric' nature of Western thought that will be developed three decades later by Derrida:

Language has been defined as 'any means of expressing feeling or thought'. Of the five senses, three – hearing, sight and (for the blind) touch – are the media of elaborate systems for the communication of human ideas. It is a curious fact that in all of our Western culture the use of two of these senses, sight and touch, has been reduced to purely secondary position, mere conventional representation of the sounds which make up the primary aural system. This has been true for so long that we tend to consider it the normal state of affairs.

(Creel 1936: 85)

A warning bell is rung here by the unworkably broad definition of 'language', which if taken literally would include all sorts of signalling systems, including such classic non-human examples such as the vervet monkey calls and the bees' honey dance (see Dunbar 1996; Deacon 1997), and later proves to give Creel more than enough conceptual rope with which to hang himself. Creel then immediately goes on to make an implicit identification of 'language' with 'writing', and to characterise the latter as consisting of two types – those which 'notate sounds' and those which 'represent thought':

It is a further and even more curious fact that we Occidentals have come, by long habitude, to think that any method of writing which consists *merely* of a graphic representation of thought, but which is not *primarily* a system for the graphic notation of sounds, in some way falls short of what writing was foreordained to be, *is indeed not writing in the full sense of the word*.

(Creel 1936: 85, my emphasis)

The sting in the tail here is in the two 'hedging expressions' *merely* and *primarily* which signal the same method of arguing by half-truths so prevalent in discourses of character fetishisation. The notion introduced by the *merely*, that of 'graphic representation of thought', harks back to Creel's original (unsourced) definition of language as 'any means of expressing feeling or thought', and like it makes the fatal mistake of ignoring the crucial contribution of the 'means' of expression, and indeed the whole constitutive rather than 'merely' reflective nature of language in relation to thought. As shown by Saussure's pioneering work on language (Saussure 1916/1957) – work, however, whose conclusions are still widely resisted within linguistics and philosophy – language plays a key delimitative role in making links between an amorphous region of thought and a variable field of sound. The role of gesture in sign languages, something which was not well understood in Saussure's time, may seem to provide an 'iconic', 'natural' mode of expression similar to what has been claimed for Chinese characters. In fact, *gesture* in *signed* languages has been shown to play exactly the same role as *sound* in *spoken* languages: although many 'signs' are clearly iconic or indexical in origin, like some of the characters examined in the previous chapter, again as elements of a sign language they have exactly the same symbolic function as sounds in spoken languages (Johnston and Schembri 2007: 22–26). Thus, paradoxically, there are no pre-existing 'ideas' for language, or writing, to express, and the concepts which any language expresses are precisely those for which it possesses delimited expressions through sounds or gestures (see the discussion of Saussure's concept of 'signification' below).

The notion introduced by *primarily*, that of writing as a 'system for the graphic notation of sounds', makes the same mistake from the other end. For users of alphabetic scripts, it may seem commonsense that an alphabet 'notates', to use Creel's telling verb, the sounds which they produce as speakers of a language. In fact, however, even the notion of 'notation' is a very slippery one, as shown both by the need for the distinction among linguists and phoneticians between 'narrow' and 'broad' transcriptions, i.e. a more versus less detailed representation of fine phonetic differences, as well as by the frequent impossibility of drawing that distinction (International Phonetic Association 1999: Ch.5); and demonstrated even more clearly by instrumental analyses of speech which reveal that, acoustically speaking, it is impossible to divide up the stream of sound into clearly distinct units like those which alphabetic scripts present to us, the closest we can get to this being the notion of 'transitions' between different articulatory postures (Ladefoged 2001: Ch.15). But just as it is a mistake to ignore the role of sound in expressing thought, or as I would prefer to say (see below), in creating meanings, it is also a mistake to ignore the role of meaning in delimiting different sounds. The reason why a language we don't understand seems to us like a flow of gibberish is that we are unable to break up the stream of sound into meaningful segments; thus just as sound is crucial in expressing meaning, so too is meaning crucial in delimiting sound.

It is, nevertheless, easy to see why Creel is taking this stance in defence of Chinese writing as the fully developed system it is, rather than allowing it to be dismissed as 'not writing in the full sense of the word'. In some further quotations he gives from various standard works on writing from the late nineteenth and early twentieth centuries, he quite rightly takes issue with the bias explicit in such claims as '[the Chinese] never carried the art of writing to its legitimate development in the creation of a perfect phonetic alphabet', or in characterisations of Chinese characters as 'phonetic characters in-the-making ... long since arrested in [their] development ... at an early stage' (Creel 1936: 85–86). Again rightly he rejects the progressivist ideology implicit in such remarks, where the 'successive stages in the evolution of writing' go from 'pictographic or iconographic' to 'ideographic or hieroglyphic' to the 'highest' stage, 'phonetic' writing; and remarks pointedly: '[i]n philosophy, in the study of society, in biology, we have at last abandoned the theory of unilinear evolution' (Creel 1936: 86). (Interestingly enough, some sixty years later, on the basis of archeological finds made since the 1970s, Boltz's treatment of the origin and development of the characters (Boltz 1994), in a section headed 'Why the Chinese script did not evolve into an alphabet', argues that Chinese writing *was* developing in the direction of a syllabary, i.e. with characters representing syllables rather than morphemes, but this development was blocked by conservative Confucian scholars motivated by the kinds of ideologies about writing as directly representing the world which were described by Liu in the previous chapter (Boltz 1994: 168–177).)

It is, however, possible to understand what Creel is doing as simply replacing the 'phonetic progression' model of writing with an 'ideographic progression' model, by putting 'ideographic'– in itself a very slippery concept – in place of 'phonetic' at the top of the heap. In doing so, as a close student of the earliest records of written Chinese, the oracle bones, he is careful not to make the mistake of claiming that Chinese writing is merely or primarily 'pictographic', another slippery term which tends to predominate in popular discussions of Chinese characters, discussions which, like Creel, tend to fudge the crucial distinction between 'language' and 'writing system':

> Chinese is not, and was not three thousand years ago, a pictographic language in the sense that it consisted of writing by means of pictures all or most of which would be readily understood by the uninstructed. If the Chinese, in developing their writing, took a direction quite different from that of most other languages, preferring to continue along the pictographic, symbolic and ideographic path rather than to specialize on phonetics, the reason does not seem to lie in any particular principles on which the Chinese formed their earliest and simplest pictographs. ... It was in part because the Chinese gave up pictorial writing that they were able to develop a practicable pictographic and ideographic script, with comparatively little help from phonetic principle.
>
> *(Creel 1936: 91–93)*

As argued in the previous chapter, there is, in fact, no such thing as a 'pictographic language', only 'pictographic graphs', whose principles of graphic composition just like those of the 'ideographic' or 'phonetic' graphs shown in Chapter 4, are equally irrelevant to their interpretation as elements of a writing system.

Once Creel has established Chinese characters as a valid writing system – a point on which he is of course completely justified – he then goes on to raise doubts in relation to the Chinese case concerning another tenet of Western thinking on language, dating back at least to Aristotle, and later to be identified by Derrrida as the key underpinning of 'logocentrism': that written language is the representation of spoken language:

> It seems altogether probable that the earliest materials which we could properly call Chinese writing would be ... purely pictorial writing, not yet an attempt to represent the sounds of speech nor even to represent every word in a spoken sentence by a graphic symbol. ... It is altogether probable ... that there was a very considerable degree of correspondence between the Shang bone inscriptions and the spoken language of the time.

But was there complete consonance? More important, were the characters engraved on the oracle bones regarded primarily as records of ideas, or as records of sounds? This is an extremely difficult question.

(*Creel 1936: 113–114*)

The distinction put forward here, again introduced by the 'hedging' word *primarily*, again casts as a dichotomy what should really be seen as a complementarity: the relationship between the 'ideographic' and the 'phonetic' principles, or as I would say, between meaning and sound, in the creation of writing systems. Creel goes on to put forward in summary form the main theses of his study:

1   It is probable that the earliest Chinese writing was pictographic and ideographic, the phonetic element having entered only gradually.
2   There is some evidence which would indicate that at the time of the Shang bones and even later the ideographic aspect of the script was considered paramount, while the phonetic element was in some instances treated with carelessness.
3   Throughout the history of the language there has been a steady (though no doubt unconscious) insistence upon retaining the ideographic value of the characters; when the script has threatened to become merely phonetic, the ideographic element has in some cases been reduplicated to prevent such a result. And down to the present day Chinese scholars in general consider the ideographic rather than the phonetic content the essential element of the script.

(*Creel 1936: 114–115*)

In attempting to dissolve this dichotomy, we need to understand not just the traditional explanation of linguistic meaning in the Western tradition stemming from Aristotle but also the radical reconceptualisation of this notion by Saussure. To start with Aristotle (died 322 BCE), 'The Philosopher' explains linguistic meaning in terms of words functioning in a process of *symbolisation* of images of our experience:

Spoken words are the symbols of mental experience and written words are the symbols of spoken words. Just as all men have not the same writing, so all men have not the same speech sounds, but the mental experiences, which these directly symbolize, are the same for all, as also are those things of which our experiences are the images.

(On Interpretation, *trans. Cook 1938: 115*)

Aristotle starts off from the two facts – seemingly unarguable to him and many others since – that, on the one hand, different 'men' – in the sense of 'peoples' or 'nations' – speak and write differently, but on the other hand, these different peoples nevertheless live in the same world and are able to communicate with each other. Aristotle explains this in terms of identical *images* of experience that reside in the brains of every human being, with spoken words being 'symbols' – in the original Greek sense 'tokens' or 'substitutes' – of these mental images, and written words in turn 'symbols' of spoken ones.

Saussure (died 1913) replaces Aristotle's commonsense view of symbolisation with a far less intuitive characterisation of language as not *reflecting* but rather *making* meaning through the mutual delimitation of concept and sound that he calls *signification*:

> [I]n language there are only differences *without positive terms*. Whether we take the signified or the signifier, the language contains neither ideas nor sounds that pre-exist the linguistic system, but only conceptual differences and phonic differences that have issued from the system.
>
> *(Saussure 1916/1957: 120, original emphasis)*

Saussure sees the fundamental relationship in language as holding, not between the mental image of experience and the word that represents it, but between a *concept*, a signified, and a *sound pattern*, a signifier. To put this view in slogan form, *meaning is constituted by language as an interface between thought and sound*. The radical implication of Saussure's position is that there are in fact no pre-existing ideas to which words, or graphs, may attach themselves: there are only sounds and concepts mutually delimited into meanings. These meanings form a network or framework of classifications which each different language lays on the world of experience, and which speakers of that language use to make sense of their experience and act on and in it (Ellis 1993: Ch.3).

Thus, far from Chinese writing, or any other writing system, directly representing ideas, there are in fact no language-independent ideas for it to represent. An 'ideographic' script in this sense, as argued by Sampson in his linguistic description of writing systems (Sampson 1985: 34), is in fact a theoretical and practical impossibility. Formulations such as the following by Creel, as well as its many predecessors and descendants, betray a crucial ignorance of this key point:

> We may safely infer that the Chinese had a quite fully developed spoken language before writing was thought of and that Chinese writing began with the drawing of pictures. But were the Chinese who drew those first pictures (from which writing later developed) trying to represent objects, or were they trying to represent spoken words with pictures. Was the man who first drew a picture of a horse trying merely to draw a horse, or was he trying to make a graphic representation of the sound *ma*, 'horse' (i.e. its ancient equivalent)? The latter alternative seems doubtful. It is much easier to imagine a preliterate man as desiring to draw a picture of a horse, than to imagine him as suddenly and without preamble giving mental birth to the concept of writing, the graphic representation of the spoken word, and proceeding to carry it out by drawing a picture.
>
> *(Creel 1936: 112)*

Although Creel's little 'just-so story' has a certain superficial plausibility – cf. Kipling's whimsical *Just So Story* of 'How the Alphabet Was Made' (Kipling 1902: 93–111) which expresses similar 'commonsense' ideas in a manner intended for a child audience – nevertheless, if we reject the notion that it is possible for 'ideas' to exist without 'words' to express them, then the notion of the early Chinese attaching a picture to the idea of horse becomes far *more* implausible than their linking of a graphic image to a pre-existing word. Creel puts forward, merely in order to dismiss, the extreme position that the graph could be a direct 'graphic representation' of a sound, which in the Chinese case it indubitably is not; but the more nuanced position that a graph might represent a 'word', that is, a linking of a sound and a concept, is something which he does not seem to consider.

Boodberg's return volley: 'ideas' versus 'words'

Boodberg, by contrast, makes the definition of the *word*, and its characterisation in relation to the *graphs* (written forms) of the writing system, the very centrepiece of his argument, and takes a firm stand against those scholars who would neglect this crucial relationship in their discussion of the then still recent discoveries of Shang dynasty Chinese writing:

> The investigation of the corner-stone problem of Chinese epigraphy, the relation of graph to vocable, has indeed been rather retarded than advanced by the new finds. Most students in the field have chosen to concentrate their efforts on the exotically fascinating questions of 'graphic semantics' and the study of the living tissue of the *Word* has almost completely been neglected in favor of that of the graphic integument encasing it. As to the later (Chou) forms of the Chinese written language, they continue to be interpreted according to the principles laid down by native didactic and classificatory works, while less orthodox sources and evidence bearing chiefly on the 'phonetic' aspects of the script are consistently disregarded.
> *(Boodberg 1937: 329)*

Boodberg perceptively identifies part of the problem as stemming from an academic territoriality dispute, with the 'epigraphists' coming from or identifying themselves with the Chinese tradition of *wenzixue* or 'graphology', while the 'phoneticians' represent the vanguard of Western science:

> It is, perhaps, inevitable that in the investigation of ancient 'ideographic' scripts the 'phonetician' and the 'epigraphist' should often work at cross purposes. ... While such 'phoneticians' as Karlgren have successfully invaded the domain of the 'epigraphists', the latter have shown some reluctance in availing themselves of the findings of the rival branch and exhibit a strange impotence whenever called to apply these findings to the

study of graphic forms. The fundamental problem of the relation of graph to word, or 'symbol' to 'sound', has not even been definitely formulated.
(Boodberg 1937: 330; see also discussion of a similar situation in Lurie 2006)

Boodberg sets himself the task of rigorously formulating this relation, doing so with a level of precision and technicality that immediately marks him out as belonging to the 'scientific' camp:

1   Any single symbol (or *Graph*) in so-called 'ideographic' writing should ideally have only one significance (represent only one *Semanteme*) expressed in the living speech by only one vocable (or *Phoneme*).[3]...

    3   When referring to Chinese, the term *phoneme* is used by the writer to refer to a *syllabic phoneme*.

2   Pictograms [graphic representations of natural objects] and symbolic signs do not constitute in themselves Graphs, i.e. elements of a written language. In order to become such, they must be conventionally and habitally associated with certain semantic-phonetic values. Thus the pictogram 馬, originally the picture of *a horse-like animal* was not necessarily the graphic equivalent of the Chinese word for *horse* until it became definitely associated with this semanteme and was supplied with the appropriate phoneme (Chin. *ma*, not [Gk.] *hippos*, [Lt.] *equus*, [Gm.] *Pferd*, etc.). ...

3   The habitual association of a graph (G) with the corresponding semanteme and phoneme (SP) which culminates in the apprehension of the graph by the reader of the language of which it forms an element as a single complex GSP can be achieved only through a long usage of the language and the particular graph and only after conventions have been firmly established.
(Boodberg 1937: 331–332)

Boodberg introduces these definitions under the common scientific banner of universality, describing what he is doing as 're-affirming some of the general principles which determined the evolution of practically all known forms of writing' (Boodberg 1937: 330). Yet it could be argued that, if Creel takes the written *character* as the fundamental unit of his analysis, Boodberg in effect simply replaces this with the *word* – in his terms, the combination of a single meaning, the *semanteme* (S), and a single sound, the *phoneme* (P) – but which to all intents and purposes is the same unit as Creel's: i.e. that represented by a single character, Boodberg's *graph* (G). It is telling that, in contrast to the usual definition of phoneme as 'minimal speech sound' (e.g. Catford 1988: 198–200), i.e. normally a single consonant or vowel, Boodberg immediately tailors his definition to the Chinese context by making the minimal unit equivalent to a syllable, what he calls a 'syllabic phoneme'. There are in fact strong phonological reasons for arguing that this should be the case, at least for modern Mandarin, (see Halliday 1990/2006), but although Boodberg later goes on to deconstruct the SP unit into its component S and P, and show how the two combine variably in the use of a single graph G to represent more than one word, he never shows how the individual examples of S and P are delimited from each other in the first place. This leaves him vulnerable to Creel's 'commonsense' arguments that a character must of course represent an 'idea' rather than a 'word', since if there were no pre-existing idea how could there be a word to convey it?:

> To Professor Boodberg's categorical statement [in a footnote discussed below EMcD (Boodberg 1937: 332 n.5)] that 'this does not mean that the graph *represents* the "idea" or "concept" behind those words', it is instructive to contrast the dictum of no less great a linguist than William Dwight Whitney: 'That *a word is the conventional sign for a thought*, not its depiction or inseparable reflection, is a fact that underlies also of necessity the constant change of every language; and the latter is unintelligible without its full and formal recognition'[1].
>
> 1 William Dwight Whitney, Max Müller and the Science of Language: A Criticism (New York, 1892), 41.
>
> *(Creel 1938: 272–273, the italics are mine)*

Creel's interpretation of Whitney's dictum here is rather strategic: what Whitney really seems to be stressing is the *conventional* as opposed to natural character of linguistic signs, something Saussure also took up in his own work. Whitney (1827–1894), Professor of Sanskrit at Yale and President of the (American) Oriental Society, was one of the great figures of late nineteenth-century linguistics. Saussure was well acquainted with and influenced by his critique of then current linguistic theory (Whitney 1875); and the two actually met once in Leipzig, the centre of mainstream linguistics at the time. Saussure developed this notion of his older contemporary by giving a principled basis for the role of convention in language, arguing cogently that, despite the commonsense view of language deriving from Aristotle discussed above, words were symbols of mental experience, in other words, ideas which pre-existed their verbal expression and were moreover common to all humankind, the reality was in fact the exact opposite: words in effect created ideas, and each language did so in its own distinctive and ultimately incommensurable way.

Although Boodberg never mentions Saussure's work, he is unlikely, in the intellectual milieu of the day, to have been completely unaware of it. However, in contrast to Saussure's practice, but in line with then common usage among linguists, he tends to use 'speech' as more or less equivalent for 'language' (cf. the subtitle of American linguist Edward Sapir's 1921 work *Language: An Introduction to the Study of Speech*), and thus leaves the rhetorical space open for Creel to argue that Chinese characters do not in fact represent 'speech', in the sense of spoken language, but some more abstract form of 'language', one mediated through images rather than sound:

Writing, as practised in ancient China, was probably not considered an adjunct of speech. It was apparently regarded as a separate discipline, just as we do not consider the plans of an architect to be the writing down of spoken words. To be sure, a house-plan may be discussed before it is drawn, and after it has been set down on paper we may look at it and say words like 'window' and 'door' and 'wall'. But we have not 'read' a blue-print when we have vocalized some words. A blue-print is a thing which must be seen to be appreciated; hearing or talking are quite inadequate to convey it. So it was with ancient Chinese, and so it is to a large extent with modern Chinese writing. If the Chinese have not written phoneti-cally, then, it is not so much because they have been unable to as because they have preferred to write ideographically instead. That Chinese writing was unconnected with speech, in its beginnings, is a logical certainty.

(*Creel 1936: 124–125*)

Creel's 'logical certainty' is in fact a logical impossibility. His analogy of the house-plan is misplaced, since it assumes the (at least potential) existence of a concrete house to which the plan might correspond, but in the case of language, there is no separate world of ideas to which words might refer. The cases usually cited in this connection, for example that of the 'picture writing' shared by some North American Indian tribes who had no common language, are not applicable here either, since the graphic forms there formed 'picture narratives' which *were* closely dependent on certain easily identifiable features of the natural world, like the modern road signs discussed in Chapter 4: there is nothing comparable in even the earliest Chinese texts available to us, which clearly are a comprehensive representation of a particular language, grammatical particles and all. However, the closest Boodberg comes to refuting Creel on this point is tucked away in a footnote, where he insists on the superiority of the term 'logograph' as opposed to 'ideograph' for describing Chinese characters, an insistence that we have seen in the quotation from Hansen in the previous section, was still being dismissed as unimportant decades later:

The term 'ideograph' which is so widely used by both layman and scholar, is, we believe, responsible for most of the misunderstanding of the evolution of writing. The sooner it is abandoned, the better. We should suggest the revival of the old term 'logograph'. Signs used in writing, however ambiguous, stylized, or symbolic, represent *words*. If we associate with a graph several related words, unable to determine which of them it is supposed to represent exactly, this does not mean that the graph *represents* the 'idea' or 'concept' behind those words. Whatever be the significance of these vague terms in psychology, in linguistics they mean absolutely nothing. Linguistic science deals first and last with the word, its only reality. The 'disembodied word' which is generally what is meant by 'idea' or 'concept' does not exist for the linguist. For him, 'les idées ne viennent qu'en parlant' [ideas come only in speaking].

(*Boodberg 1937: 332, n.5, original emphasis*)

Here we seem to have reached a classic rhetorical dead end: Creel insists that he is talking about 'characters', while Boodberg insists that *he* is talking about 'words'; and neither is prepared to debate the other on this basic unit of their analysis. Boodberg does go on to discuss in great, perhaps excessive, detail, the problems relating to the interpretation of characters in cases of what he calls polysemy – more than one meaning to a graph, polyphony – more than one sound to a graph, and even polygraphy – more than one graph to the same word; problems familiar to learners of English orthography who have to negotiate exactly comparable pitfalls such as *bank* 'side of river' versus *bank* 'financial institution', *lead* 'to take along' versus *lead* 'soft metal', and *metal* versus *mettle* (etymologically, at least, the same word). But it is clear that he too has his own scale of priorities, since he introduces at the very opening of his argument a clear value judgment in his contrast between the authentic 'living tissue of the *Word*' as opposed to the derived 'graphic integument encasing it' (Boodberg 1937: 329).

If we are to move beyond such proclamations of basic tenets of faith, which would seem from their rhetoric to be equally important and unarguable for both Creel and Boodberg, we need to go back to Saussure and understand exactly how it is that meanings – Boodberg's 'semantemes' – and sounds – Boodberg's 'phonemes' – are on the one hand delimited from other meanings or sounds, and on the other hand linked to a particular written character – Boodberg's 'graphs'.

It should help to make these complex but crucial points easier to understand if we apply one of the complementarities Saussure put forward as basic in defining the meaning of linguistic elements, that between *paradigmatic* and *syntagmatic*. Saussure saw that, in order to work out what a word in a particular language means, we had at the same time to distinguish it: a) from other words of similar sound or meaning *associated* with it – hence the 'associative', now more commonly known as 'paradigmatic' (from the Greek for 'displayed beside'); and b) from the other words which appeared in *combination* with it – hence the 'syntagmatic' (from the Greek for 'arranged with'). In the quotation from Saussure given above there appeared what may have seemed at the time like the rather mystical statement that '[i]n a language there are only differences *without positive terms*'. The complementarity between paradigmatic and syntagmatic explains how negative differences can create a positive.

We can see how this works in relation to the example of 日 *rì* 'sun, day' discussed in the previous chapter. We first need to be clear that *rì* is a *wording*, that is, to adapt Saussure's formulation, a stretch of sound mutually delimitated with a stretch of meaning. So how do we know what *rì* means? Well, *paradigmatically*, by what it is *not*. From the viewpoint of *sound*, *rì* is not *sì* 'four'/ is not *chì* 'red'/ is not *zì* 'word'/etc., etc.; while from the viewpoint of *meaning*, *rì* 'sun/day' is not *yuè* 'moon'/ is not *tiān* 'sky'/ is not *yè* 'night'/ etc., etc. If we were able to list all the wordings with which *rì* contrasted both in sound and in meaning, then we would have defined it paradigmatically, in the sense of mapping out its place in the system of possible contrasts. But of course a wording like *rì* does not exist in isolation, but in the combination with other words: so to answer our question *syntagmatically*, we know what *rì* means by what it is *with*. We know *rì* means 'sun' because it appears in combinations like *rìluò* 'sun fall – sunset' and *rìshí* 'sun eat – solar eclipse' etc., etc.; and we know that *rì* also means 'day' because it appears in combinations like *dì sān rì*, 'number three day – the third day' *rìrì* 'every day, daily', etc., etc. Once we have listed all the wordings with which *rì* could be combined, then we have defined it syntagmatically in the sense of mapping out its place in the structure of possible combinations. If we put these two perspectives together, we will find that we have defined *rì* entirely *negatively*, without the need for positing an 'idea' that it represents or expresses.

This kind of argument also renders irrelevant arguments like Creel's which would see Chinese characters as constituting a language-free or language-neutral system, like the North American Indians' picture writing, which can be 'shared' between languages or dialects: as Creel hails it (1936: 105): 'something unique among the literary languages of the world, a system by which ideas are presented directly to the mind by visual images, with little assistance from the phonetic principle.'

Here we see the force of Boodberg's insistence on the *word*, i.e. the meaning–sound or semanteme–phoneme (SP) combination, in interpreting the graphs (G) (repeated from above, Boodberg 1937: 332):

> 3 The habitual association of a graph (G) with the corresponding semanteme and phoneme (SP) which culminates in the apprehension of the graph by the reader of the language of which it forms an element as a single complex GSP can be achieved only through a long usage of the language and the particular graph and only after conventions have been firmly established.

Boodberg stresses the role of *convention* in establishing links, not just between the semanteme and the phoneme, as Saussure did with his notion of the concept/ signified and sound-image/signifier (Saussure 1916/1957: 66–67), but also between the semanteme-phoneme SP combination and the graph G to which is it 'attached'. The force of the notion of convention is that any GSP complex must relate to a particular speech community, that is, a group of speakers who share a similar system of contrasts, and although each system of contrasts may be more or less accessible to other speech communities, words and their meanings can not plausibly be seen to be directly 'attached' to objects or categories in what is naively called the 'real world' without reference to a particular language system.

It is in relation to the nature of this 'attachment' that the inadequacy of Creel's account becomes glaring. Despite his insistence that the earliest form of written Chinese 'was unconnected with speech, in its beginnings', when Creel comes to give an example of how this might have happened, to repeat part of the quotation above (emphasis added) – 'Was the man who first drew a picture of a *horse* trying merely to draw a *horse*, or was he trying to make a graphic representation of the sound *ma*, 'horse' (i.e. its ancient equivalent)?' – he is despite himself, like Liu in the similar situation discussed in the previous chapter, forced to quote examples of *words*, i.e. actual SP combinations. Creel also takes descriptive fiction for linguistic reality in his use of another type of convention, that of linguistic gloss-ing, whereby the sound of the word is represented in italics, i.e. *ma*, and its mean-ing in inverted commas, i.e. 'horse'. Despite the equivalence implied by this convention, *ma* and *horse* are not in fact 'the same word', much less 'the same idea', but isolated SP(G) combinations torn from the fabric of the separate lin-guistic systems which give them meaning. What is important for the present argument is to see how in all cases what is being related to graphs are actual *words* of a language, and cannot be understood in any meaningful sense as *ideas* detached from a particular language.

Sinology gives way to Area studies: Chinese characters as boundary markers

Some thirty years after the Creel–Boodberg debate lapsed into the silence of aggrieved misunderstanding, the *Journal of Asian Studies* initiated a debate on the current state of 'Chinese studies', then a relatively new label which placed the field firmly within the new paradigm of Area studies, a post-World War II devel-opment significantly shaped by the new global-political situation of the Cold War. The debate centred around how this new Chinese studies might – or indeed whether it should – distinguish itself from its predecessor sinology, now seen as a relic of the previous era of European imperialism and colonialism; and was framed in terms of the relationship between 'Chinese studies' and 'the Disciplines', the former including traditional humanities subjects such as literature, history and philosophy, and the latter, by contrast, referring to social science disciplines such as economics, politics, sociology and anthropology. This central issue was char-acterised by one of the participants, anthropologist G. William Skinner in terms of the following self-admitted 'overdrawn comparison':

> In recent years the cry has gone up: Sinology is dead; long live Chinese studies. And in this apothegm, by contrast with its prototype, a fundamen-tal change is implied. Whereas old-time Sinology was given shape by its tools, so that Sinological skills defined the field and became an end in themselves, Chinese studies is shaped by its subject matter and Sinological skills are but means to analytic ends. ... Sinology, a discipline unto itself, is being replaced by Chinese studies, a multidisciplinary endeavour with specific research objectives. ...what is text for the Sinologist becomes, for the disciplinary student of China, evidence.
>
> (*Skinner 1964: 517*)

Another participant, historian Joseph R. Levenson, explained the change as one from what he dubbed an '-ology', a 'self-contained intellectual puzzle', a notion in which the contribution of the 'radical difference in scripts' was particularly influential, to a 'subject', studiable on the same terms as other civilisations:

> China in the round *was* special to Westerners when it was shocking, a new-found land or world without the Greco-Roman heritage, a world that could speak of 'the Classics' without meaning what Europeans meant. The radical difference in scripts doubtless strengthened the diposition to see in China not a subject for history in all its many branches, like France, but an -ology. Egyptology, Sinology – they both suggested not simply chapters in the history of man, as parts of the proper study of mankind, but self-contained intellectual puzzles.
>
> (*Levenson 1964: 507–508*)

When Skinner went on to explain why he regarded the study of Chinese as special, even 'unique' (that word again!), not because of any inherent strangeness it may still possess in the eyes of Westerners but for good objective reasons, it was the nature of its writing system that was brought forward as one of the most significant variables:

> My more significant point can best be stated by recourse to Orwellian grammar: All societies are unique, but some are more unique than others. ... The Chinese case is absolutely essential for an understanding of the development of civilization itself. Civilizations or complex societies presuppose writing systems, and true writing was *invented* only twice – once in the eastern Mediterranean area, culminating in the Greek alphabetic system, and once in the Yellow River valley, culminating in the Chinese ideographic system. If we should count the ways in which Chinese thought and institutions have been shaped by the ineluctable characteristics of its morphemic writing system, we should never have done with it. Chinese society is the decisive test of the thesis ... that an alphabetic writing system gave the Greeks incalculable advantage in civilization building.
>
> (*Skinner 1964: 518–519*)

Skinner even saw the writing system as one of the crucial features explaining why 'what is now China end[ed] up as a single sociopolitical system, whereas Europe did not':

> In terms of cultural diversity and unity, China and Europe have been comparable during many periods of their histories. ... The Sinic tradition ... accomplished a feat of perduring integration which was beyond anything managed in the West. How? It can hardly be said that this question has

been seriously probed, but we know enough to relate it to the cultural homogeneity of a society-wide élite, with its single court language and unitary 'great tradition', perpetuated through a standardized educational system – made possible by a writing system not tied to phonetics – which culminated in national examinations.

(Skinner 1964: 519–520)

Skinner's overall conclusion also stressed the nature of the writing system as one of the 'special features' that 'ensure a long life for Chinese studies *per se*':

But the crux of my case is that there is indeed something very special about Chinese society. … It is precisely the special features – the society's staggering size and complexity, its ideographic writing system, the overwhelming abundance of its documentary record – which … ensure a long life for Chinese studies *per se*.

(Skinner 1964: 522)

From the opposite point of view, looking at 'the disciplines' from the vantage point of 'Chinese studies' allowed the insight that, though claiming to be 'universal', the modern social science disciplines are in fact deeply grounded in the Western context from which they arose:

Social scientists … have been parochial while claiming universality. They studied Western man and spoken of mankind. … Those disciplines which, like sociology, economics, and political science, developed not only *in* the Western world but as studies *of* Western institutions – those disciplines remain essentially rooted in the particular societies, economies, and polities found in the Western world and its outposts.

(Skinner 1964: 517–518)

Or as another participant, historian Mary C. Wright put it more pithily (Wright 1964: 514): 'Some [social scientists] seem under the illusion that to apply their analytic tools to the study of a Chinese problem is narrow, but that to specialize on North American data is somehow universal.'

One further participant, Frederick W. Mote, significantly a Professor of 'Chinese studies' as such rather than like the previous scholars quoted belonging to one of the traditional humanities subjects or social science disciplines, put forward a strong case for the 'integrity' of the field which he characterised using the old label 'sinology'. Using an extended geographical metaphor, he represented what he saw as sinology in terms of the interaction between the inhabitants of the 'Central Plain', the traditional heartland of Chinese civilisation, and the barbarians 'beyond the passes' marking the borders of the Chinese Empire; and simultaneously defined by a pull between a 'provincialism' of their locale or discipline and the larger 'integrity' of the field as a whole:

[I]t is the integrality of the whole realm, or world, of Chinese studies, that I think should define Sinology. ... Sinology ... does admit varying degrees of emphasis, and the distinguished practitioners of 'our science' ... often have defended their personal specializations with vigor and skill. Yet to admit them to the clan, we must be able to assure ourselves that they in fact know and accepted the whole, even when they seemed to defend the building of internal walls. ... However, we should not misjudge and confuse a strong sense of provincial identity ... with true 'kwan-wai' [i.e. 關外 *guānwài* 'beyond the passes'] barbarism. That fragmenting of the culture in the course of its diffusion from the heartland out into the steppes and wilds, where it was often exaggeratedly honoured in the partially-received versions, produced the various forms in which 'Chinese studies' have been wedded to the so-called 'disciplines.' There is a profound difference between that fragmenting, on the one hand, and on the other that superifically manifested provincial loyalty which does not really affect the large integrity.

(*Mote 1964: 531*)

Mote identified only one route into the heartland of Chinese culture, the Central Plains, one via the 'pass' of 'language study':

But to those who decide to accept the native standard of integrity ... there is but one approach route. That is to say, language study is the only pass leading through the Great Wall and into the *chung-yuan* [i.e. 中原 *Zhōngyuán* 'The Central Plains']. Those who fail to enter through this pass must remain more or less tame barbarians basking in the partial glow that is reflected into the outer border regions. But even when that pass is negotiated, one has only begun; the integrity of one's activities is not thereby guaranteed. No matter whether one settles down in the Province of History, or that of Literature, or that of Language Study, or even should he choose to buy his real estate in a treaty port like Economics, he must emulate the native masters in one essential; that is, he must aspire to their sense of the integrity of the realm. Although having, like many of the natives, a strong though superficial provincial loyalty, he must be able to reside in several regions, and to travel without too much discomforture through any of the provinces, noting how the residents of all areas simultaneously display both local color and awareness of the larger integrity.

(*Mote 1964: 533*)

This emphasis on language was supported by one of the commentators on the symposium, Professor Denis Twitchett who described himself as straddling both 'the disciplines' and 'the field' having '[begun] life as a physical geographer, graduated in the high tradition of European Sinology, [and currently] work[ing] in the field of economic history, and administer[ing] a department of languages and literatures'. In his 'plea for the unity of Chinese studies', Twitchett identified 'the traditional discipline of textual criticism and "philology" ' as a *necessary* condition for work in the field:

> Sinology in the narrow sense ... is in the last analysis the traditional discipline of textual criticism and 'philology' applied to Chinese literature, a set of techniques designed to extract the most accurate possible information from a body of data, in this case the written word. In my contention, this discipline is the irreducible essential in the training of a scholar who is to deal professionally with China's past. Without it, the scholar will remain an amateur, however skilled he may be in analysis, since he will never be able adequately to understand or assess his sources.
>
> *(Twitchett 1964: 110)*

The only *sufficient* condition, however, was to combine this 'narrow sense' of sinology as philology with a 'broad understanding' of the whole Chinese world:

> If Sinology in the narrow sense is a prerequisite for serious work on traditional China, Sinology in the broad sense ... should provide us with a broad understanding of Chinese culture and society in all its aspects, to give us the sort of instinctive understanding and orientation which we have of our own society simply by being born and educated in it. Moreover, it should give us the ability to see through the eyes of the Chinese literati who wrote our materials, and thus to enable us to discount their prejudices and preoccupations before reinterpreting what they have written in terms of our own.
>
> *(Twitchett 1964: 111)*

Mote and Twitchett put forward a view of Chinese studies very similar to that recommended in Chapter 1 of this book, and elaborated in Chapter 8 in relation to what might be called the modern descendant of 'philology and textual criticism', i.e. critical discourse analysis. For very much the same reasons, and using very comparable metaphors, these scholars see a lack of direct engagement with the language and with texts as forever shutting the 'barbarian' out 'beyond the passes' and with only limited access to the life of the 'Central Plains'. Conversely, while Skinner's does emphasise the writing system as key in marking out Chinese studies as a separate area – although readers of the previous chapter will no doubt have noted a certain indecision as to whether this supposed 'writing system not tied to phonetics' is best labelled 'ideographic' or 'morphemic' – nevertheless, his point that China provides 'the decisive test of the thesis ... that an alphabetic writing system gave the Greeks incalculable advantage in civilisation building' is undeniably a useful corrective against the sorts of Eurocentric particularistic claims often made in relation to the alphabet (e.g. Logan 1986, 2004).

Conclusion: finding ways of talking across ideological divides

The participants in this second debate examined here, although not agreeing exactly on their definitions of the field, or indeed whether the implied dichotomy between 'Chinese studies' and 'the Disciplines' is in fact a useful one to make at all, do nevertheless share a lot more in common, and manage to come to much more harmonising conclusions, than the head to head opponents of the first debate. In this regard, it may be useful to borrow some wisdom from that great strategist and analyst of human behaviour Madame de Merteuil from the late eighteenth-century French epistolary novel *Les Liaisons dangereuses*:

> No one willingly yields in a dispute: for the simple reason that it is a dispute. By sheer dint of looking for good arguments, we find them and state them; and afterwards hold by them, not because they are good ones, but because we do not wish to contradict ourselves.
>
> (*de Laclos 1782/1961: 79*)

As shown in the previous chapter, and discussed in more detail in Lurie (2006) and McDonald (2009), the sorts of arguments engaged in by Creel and Boodberg continue to bedevil the field of Chinese studies: not only in the discussion of the substantive issues on which, like Creel and Boodberg, the participants commonly fail to agree, thus dooming their debates from the start; but also in terms of the rhetorical strategies, putdowns and rubbishing of the other 'camp' by which they tend to be characterised. In reading through the literature on these issues, there is however one author who, although clearly on the linguistic side, seems to tackle these issues in a way that not only illuminates the substantive issues but does so in the sort of entertaining and light-hearted tone that might perhaps allow both sides to realise their own self-righteousness. This scholar is linguist George A. Kennedy, already quoted a number of times in Chapter 4. A good flavour of his approach can be found in a further extract from his review of one of Creel's textbooks of classical Chinese quoted from in the previous chapter. In this review, as part of his argument against Creel's 'inductive' approach, he takes issue with Creel's explanation of the disyllabic word *huangwang* as used in Mencius, whose two syllables are defined separately by Creel as 'to lose' and 'river', in a way that again re-emphasises the importance of sound in understanding the characters as a writing system:

> If one cares to conjecture the sound of this expression in Mencius' time (and that seems to have some relevance to the reading of Mencius), he will assume something like HWANG-MWANG. Even if he sticks with the Pekingese reading [*huang-wang*], he must be struck by the fact that he has got hold of a 'rhyming compound,' one of a very obtrusive class of dissyllabic expressions. Expressions of this type are analyzable into

syllables of which the second is an echo of the first. A meaning may or may not be attachable to the first. In any case, the second is simply related on the same basis that shows up in English roly-poly, ducky-lucky, henny-penny, – that is, rhyme. ... Everything now becomes quite clear to the student. ... The graph defined [in Creel's textbook] as 'to lose ...' represented the sound MWANG. The element defined as 'river' has been misinterpreted. It is a phonetic H-, found in other graphs. The graph defined as 'an expanse of water', composed of two elements, had the sound HMWANG. ... When the student has reached this point he is ready to see something enormously funny in the text. Sandwiched in between the two occurrences of HMWANG-MWANG is the grave attempt of an early Chinese pedant to define the parts of the expression separately. ... Mencius has warned against frivolity and extravagance, and stated that the early kings had no frivolous pleasures or extravagant pursuits. Into which our unknown pedant, like many a Western sinologue, inserts a comment learnedly and ludicrously: '"Friv" means drifting down-stream; "olous" means drifting upstream; "extrav" means hunting too many wild animals; "agant" means drinking too much wine.' And if this were not funny enough in itself, the definition that he invents for *huang* is additional to the already comprehensive set that Professor Creel has supplied. From this example it will be seen that one's criticism of the present book must be based less on what is included than on what is excluded. And that is unfortunately a whole world of interest, of illumi-nation, and, sometimes, of fun.

(*Kennedy 1953b: 28*)

While I have no doubt Professor Creel would have been hard put to find the humour in this deconstruction of the explanatory practice of his textbook, a cri-tique whose light-hearted tone does not mask its devastating conclusions, I would contend that for the field as a whole, this sort of approach is much more useful than the sort of rigid holding of contrary extremes far more characteristic of par-ticipants in such debates. Kennedy, like Boodberg for whom he expresses consid-erable respect, bases his conclusions on solid linguistic arguments; but, unlike Boodberg, he does not adopt the high-minded superior tone which only nettles his opponents and leaves them very unlikely to acknowledge the force of his arguments.

In conclusion, if I may be forgiven one more literary quotation, it is perhaps through the application of a 'sense of humour' like Kennedy's that such debates can find resolution, or at least a cordial agreement to disagree. This is the nostrum prescribed in a literary context by one of the acknowledged greatest humorists of the twentieth century, perhaps less acknowledged as a deeply reflective thinker, Dorothy Parker. Mrs Parker, in the following extract from her review of a highly self-righteous autobiography by one of the major literary figures of the 1920s and

1930s in the United States, Theodore Dreiser, recommends the leaven of humour in explicit rebuttal of a literary Professor who has belittled the necessity for a sense of it:

> [says the Professor] ... humor may be all very well for those that like it ('Only fools care to see,' said the blind man), but there's no good making a fetish of it. I wouldn't for the world go around making fetishes; yet I am unable to feel that a writer can be complete without humor. And I don't mean by that, and you know it perfectly well, the creation or appreciation of things comic. I mean that the possession of a sense of humor entails the sense of selection, the civilized fear of going too far. A little humour leavens the lump, surely, but it does more than that. It keeps you, from your respect for the humor of others, from making a dull jackass of yourself. Humor, imagination, and manners are pretty fairly interchangeably interwoven.
>
> *(Parker 1931/1973:543)*

Old stuff shop

6

KEEPING CHINESE FOR THE CHINESE

The paradox of nativised orientalism in Chinese linguistics

Introduction: from 'script reform' to 'language modernisation'

It may seem from the discussion in the previous two chapters that language issues have been of concern in Chinese studies only for scholars battling it out amongst themselves for control of the field. On the contrary: questions of language have always been at the forefront in both traditional and modern China, and language *reform*, that is, deliberate and official endeavours to manage and direct language use, has been an essential part of modernisation in China since the early twentieth century. For most of the linguistic and educational heritage that Republican China had inherited from the last imperial dynasty, dramatic modifications were needed to 'equip' the Chinese state to survive a modern international scene on which China was no longer an unquestioned cultural and political first among equals. The political, technological and economic weakness of China, and the encroachments of foreign powers upon Chinese soil and sovereignty lent an urgency to the modernisation process, and a considerable anguish about the degree to which China had fallen from her former pre-eminence. Various 'theories' were put forward as to the best way to accommodate the aggressive impact of the West, to which Japan had already adapted itself so successfully during the Meiji period of reform and modernisation (1868–1912). These ranged from the approach recommended by Zhang Zhidong in his slogan of the late Qing reform period *Zhōngxué wéi tǐ, Xīxué wéi yòng* 中學為體，西學為用 'Chinese learning as essence, Western learning as application', an attempted balancing act which in practice proved unsustainable; to the *quánpán xīhuà* 全盤西化 'full-blown Westernisation' recommended by Chen Xujing of the early Republican May Fourth modernisation period, a goal which also proved unfeasible. In this chapter, we will see how these issues played themselves out in the arena of language reform across a range of competing pressures between tradition and innovation, native learning and imported ideas, particularism and universalism, and humanism and scientism, 'contradictions' which were characteristic of this as of most other areas of modernisation in China.

This chapter will examine modern language reform in China by examining and critiquing developments in two main areas: the reform of the traditional script, and the adoption and adaptation of a framework for describing the grammar of Chinese, the latter being something which had no counterpart in traditional native scholarship. It will give an overview of the main alternative ideologies and points of view with the aim of setting Chinese language reform in its intellectual and historical contexts. It will briefly trace the history of linguistics in China and the main currents in language reform in the last century before going on to examine the key status of Chinese characters in the language reform movement. It will then critique one of the main claims of the 'particularists' in these debates: that the Chinese language is 'unique' (that word again!) and therefore should not be subject to the same standards – or subjected to the same treatment – as other languages. Finally it will examine more recent controversies in Chinese linguistics and language reform, including suggestions by foreign scholars, picking up on earlier ideas from Chinese scholars, to do away with Chinese characters altogether.

We can start by identifying some of the key terms of the discourse of language reform, discourse which of course includes nationalistic and cultural elements as well as strictly linguistic ones, by way of one of the main 'particularists': then young academic, now Professor of Chinese at Fudan University in Shanghai, Shen Xiaolong. Shen had this to say in the foreword to his attempted reopening of the debate about language reform published in that politically significant year of 1989:

> There are many factors holding a nation together, of which one of the most important is the nation's psychological identification with its culture, the main manifestation of this being its language. It is precisely in this regard that the *Book of Changes* says: 'That which stirs up action in the world resides in words'. A nation's language as a whole reflects and determines its worldview (i.e. a particular culture's way of looking at the world) and its mode of thinking.
>
> (*Shen 1989b: Author's Foreword*)

The title of the book from which the above quotation comes, *Humanistic Spirit or Scientism?*, written in the mid-1980s during the first high tide of that still current period of economic reform known as the Open Door, sums up in this stark dichotomy what he sees as a 'crisis' in modern Chinese linguistics, a crisis which also has implications for Chinese language reform. The crux of the problem, as seen by Shen and many others in the then new Chinese Cultural Linguistics movement of which he was a major figure, is the contradiction between the 'humanistic spirit' of the Chinese language and the 'scientism' of modern Chinese linguistics. This contradiction, according to Shen, has divorced the study of the Chinese language from its cultural roots, and thus undercut attempts at language reform based on foreign models. Shen openly called for a complete overhaul of the theory and methodology of linguistics as currently practised in China, and also for the winding back or jettisoning of some of the significant language reforms which had been carried out over the last century.

First we need to clarify some of the main terms that crop up in these debates, terms that cannot be understood without some analysis of their historical roots and contemporary usage. The term 'language reform' is the most commonly used English rendering of the Chinese term *wénzì gǎigé* 文字改革, literally 'script reform'. This part-for-whole usage shows how large issues of the script have loomed in language reform and in modern Chinese history generally. The earliest currents of language reform in the last century were indeed script reform in the strict sense (the Chinese term *wénzì* covering both 'script' and 'writing'), dating from the 1890s and revolving on the one hand around the pros and cons of 'Latinisation', i.e. the use of the Roman alphabet to write Chinese; and on the other around the reform of the standard written language, as represented by the *báihuà* 白話 or 'vernacular language' movement of the 1910s–1930s which sought to replace the traditional classical standard or *wényán* 文言 'written language' with something closer to the modern spoken language. More recently, the term *yǔwén xiàndàihuà* 語文現代化 'language modernisation' has begun to be used, linking the more inclusive term *yǔwén* 'spoken and written language', also the term for 'language/literature' as a school subject, with the *xiàndàihuà* 'modernisation' so pervasive in economic and political discourse since the beginnings of the Open Door period in the late 1970s.

'Humanistic' translates the Chinese *rénwén* 人文, which combines the two morphemes for 'human' and 'writing'. This latter morpheme, *wén*, is in origin 'pattern', and covers not only 'script'and 'written language', but also 'literature', again emphasising the central position of the written language in Chinese culture. Interestingly, the term for 'culture' itself, *wénhuà* 文化, a reverse borrowing from the Japanese in the late nineteenth century, also contains this morpheme in combination with *huà* 'change, transformation': 'culture' in Chinese may therefore be understood literally as 'the transformation of (semiotic) patterns'. 'Spirit' is used to render the Chinese *jīngshén* 精神, which combines the two morphemes for 'essence' and 'spirit'. The former suggests the cultural essentialism which is so much a feature of discourse about Chinese culture and identity, while the latter also figures as part of a poetic designation for China – *shénzhōu* 神州 or 'spirit land' – a term which epitomises the semi-religious fervour felt by many Chinese – and encouraged by their goverments! – towards their homeland.

'Scientism' translates the Chinese *kēxuézhǔyì* 科學主義, literally 'science ideology' or 'science-ism'. The semi-grammaticalised form *zhǔyì* '-ism' is familiar from a host of political terms such as *zīběnzhǔyì* 資本主義 'capital-ism', and *shèhuìzhǔyì* 社會主義 'society-ism i.e. socialism'. Here it carries negative connotations of ideological inflexibility and subjectivity in contrast to the positive objective connotations of *kēxué* 'science', a contrast perhaps more familiar in English as one between the adjectival forms *scientistic* versus *scientific*. Finally the term 'nation', which figures extensively in the extract from Shen's foreword, translates the Chinese *mínzú*民族, a notoriously slippery term which could also be rendered 'ethnicity', 'nationality', or even 'race', in the sense of a group of people who share a similar linguistic and cultural background. In contrast to its largely descriptive use by Shen in the sense 'of the nation, national', the term is also used in China as a label to characterise the different ethnic groupings living within its borders, with the *Hàn(mín)zú*漢(民)族 to which Shen belongs – and to which he almost exclusively refers – making up the largest group, the others collectively known as *shǎoshù mínzú* 少數民族 'minority ethnicities' or 'ethnic minorities'.

A period of stormy weather: from traditional to modern linguistics in China

The 'opening up' of China from the 1840s which proceeded, unlike the later-starting Japanese example, to a growing extent outside the control of the state, was a 'repeated battering' not just militarily and politically, but also economically, culturally and intellectually. The traditional Chinese world view, premised on the notion of the Chinese polity as the centre of *Tiānxià* 天下 or '(All) under Heaven', was no longer plausible, and China's political weakness seemed to many Chinese to have negative implications for the value of Chinese thinking and culture. Below is how Shen describes this 'attack' in the linguistic arena, using appropriately military metaphors:

> Modern Chinese linguistics at the beginning of this century really experienced a period of stormy weather. The late Qing alphabetisation movement led the way, and inspired by the repeated battering of Western phonology, one after another scholars of philology, graphology and phonology 'saw the light'. Ma Jianzhong, 'in the light of existing rules for Western languages … applied a complex series of proofs and inductions in order to determine the scope of the Chinese language', finally sloughing off his old skin to come up with a new Chinese grammar recast in a Western mould – *Mr Ma's Compleat Grammar*. The May Fourth Movement went on to sound the call for the latinisation of Chinese characters, which had become synonymous with old feudal ethics and one of the very things that needed mopping up. On the cover of the *National Language Monthly* of the period, the letters of the National Phonetic Alphabet stood like soldiers of a revolutionary army brandishing their weapons in hot pursuit of the vanquished foe, their swords and guns dripping with blood, slaughtering the green-faced long-toothed Chinese characters so that they fled in panic for their lives and hid here and there. Behind the revolutionary army stood the back-up force in Western-style uniforms with woollen berets, the letters of the National Romanisation.
>
> *(Shen 1989a: 347–348)*

Linguistics in traditional China was known as *xiǎoxué* 小學 'minor learning', usually translated 'philology', because it was linked to the knowledge of the characters which constituted the first stage of the educational process; and because it was seen as preparation for the *dàxué* 大學 or 'major learning' which was the study of the historical, literary and philosophical classics. The sub-branches of this linguistic tradition were directed towards the understanding of the three different ways in which Chinese characters could be viewed – their *xíng* 形 'form', *yīn* 音 'sound', and *yì* 意 'meaning': hence *wénzìxué* 文字學 'graphology', the study of the composition and etymology of the characters; *yīnyùnxué* 音韻學 'phonology', the study of the rhymes in ancient poetry and thus the sound systems of earlier periods of Chinese; and *xùngǔxué* 訓詁學 'exegesis', the study of difficult or archaic words in the ancient texts.

All this scholarly endeavour was directed towards the understanding and interpretation of the Classics that formed the basis of the educational process, leading ultimately to the examination system to recruit scholars for the imperial bureaucracy. While philology, and its related activities such as writing commentaries on texts and compiling rhyme tables and dictionaries, had long played a significant part in the Chinese scholarly tradition, it assumed particular political importance in the late Ming to early Qing period (*c.* 1600–1800) as part of the discipline of 考證 or 'evidential analysis'. Evidential analysis, very similar in spirit to the philological work on the Bible being carried out in Europe at roughly the same period (see discussion in Chapter 9 for more detail), was one of the main tools of the 漢學 'Han Learning' scholars who were determined to recover the original meaning of the classical Confucian texts, which had gained their canonical form during the Han dynasty (*c.* 200 BCE–200 CE), and to remove their later Buddhist- and Taoist-influenced overlay.

In all this scholarly activity, however, there was nothing really comparable to the study of grammar, of the words and structures of the language, which had such a central place in European and Indian tradition. There are good reasons for this. If we compare other great linguistic traditions which produced theories and methods of grammatical analysis, such as the Greek and the Sanskrit, such analysis started from the classification of word endings, in which both Classical Greek and Sanskrit were very rich. It was the search for how these morphological patterns were used that led to the study of syntax, i.e. how words were combined into larger units such as phrases and sentences (see Halliday and McDonald 2005). In classical Chinese, by contrast, there is little or no morphological variation, and syntactic patterns may be understood as conforming to semantic rules, without the need for positing specific rules of grammar, a conception of grammar more recently revived by Shen in his own analyses. The separate study of grammar was therefore not really necessary in the Chinese context and so never developed as a separate sub-branch in the native philological tradition, apart from a basic classification of words into *shízì* 實字 'full words', i.e. notional or lexical words, and *xūzì* 虛字 'empty words', i.e. formal or grammatical words.

By the late nineteenth century, however, an increasing number of grammars were being produced by foreign missionaries, diplomats and scholars based in China (e.g. Gabelentz 1881). By this time also, Chinese scholars and diplomats being trained in

Western languages had come into contact with the richly developed European grammatical tradition and it was not long before they started thinking about applying a similar grammatical framework, basically that of Latin grammar, to their own language. The first to do so was the Shanghai-born diplomat Ma Jianzhong (1845–1900), a protégé of the late Imperial reformist Prime Minister Li Hongzhang, who spent the last decade of his life writing a grammar of classical Chinese which he called *Mǎshì Wéntōng* 馬氏文通 or *Mr Ma's Compleat Grammar*. Ma had studied Western languages, including Latin, first in Shanghai and then in France, and he came to the conclusion that this thing he termed *gēlángmǎ* had a lot to do with the success of Western education in comparison to Chinese, and thus with the superiority of the Western states over a moribund Chinese Empire. His pioneering work was published in 1898, the same year as that dramatic and unsuccessful attempt at political reform, the Hundred Days Constitutional Reform, during which the young Guangxu Emperor promulgated significant modernising reforms, only to have the reforms rescinded and himself placed under house arrest by the more powerful Empress Dowager. This is how Shen describes the context in which Ma's work appeared:

> Before this work, ancient Chinese philology had not produced a systematic grammatical system for Chinese; instead what it focused on was the interpretation of notional and formal words through glosses, the perception of grammatical relations and the appreciation of textual style through reading aloud: it stressed 'personal perception of the spirit'. The author of *Mr Ma's Compleat Grammar* believed that the reason for the underdevelopment of science and technology was that such a teaching approach … made Chinese students unable to grasp the gist of their language. If we taught grammar in school just as in the West, the time for learning Chinese would be greatly reduced, and more time would be left for the study of the natural sciences. The author also maintained that Western people and the Han people 'were all human beings': therefore, they shared the same linguistic mode of thought and grammatical rules. Consequently, *Mr Ma's Compleat Grammar* unhesitatingly modelled itself on the Western grammatical system in order to create a grammatical system for Chinese.
>
> (*Shen 1988a: 40*)

In the modern period, political developments and language reforms have been inextricably linked. Table 6.1, adapted from DeFrancis 1984, shows clearly that language issues have been an integral part of the general process of modernisation in China over the last century. The history of language reform is a fascinating story in itself, particularly for the many dead end attempts at reform and unresolved contradictions that litter this as many other areas of modernisation in modern China (the late John DeFrancis has been one of its main chroniclers in English, see DeFrancis 1950/1972, 1984; see also Zhou 2001). Here I will briefly outline its main developments in the areas of script reform and the development of a framework for grammatical analysis.

TABLE 6.1 Political developments and language reforms in China 1898–1996

Date	Political event	Language reform event
1898	Hundred Days Constitutional Reform	Publication of *Mr Ma's Compleat Grammar*
1912	Establishment of Republic of China	
1918		Promulgation of Phonetic Alphabet 注音字母
1919	Beginning of May Fourth Movement for the modernisation of China	
1927	Reunification of China under the Nationalists (Kuomintang or KMT) with capital at Nanking	
1928		Promulgation of National Language Romanisation 國語羅馬字 *Gwoyeu Romaatzyh*
1930		Name of Phonetic Alphabet changed to Phonetic Symbols 注音符號
1935		Promulgation by Nanking Government of small set of simplified characters (withdrawn the following year)
1935–41		Latinised New Script 拉丁化新文字 *Latinxua Sin Wenz* implemented in Chinese-speaking parts of Soviet Union and various border areas of China
1937	Beginning of Sino-Japanese War	
1938		Renewing Grammar 文法革新 movement
1949	Establishment of People's Republic of China under the Chinese Communist Party (CCP) with capital in Peking; KMT Government flees to Taiwan	
1956		Publication *of Provisional System for Teaching Chinese Grammar*
1958		Promulgation of Chinese Spelling 漢語拼音 *Hànyǔ pīnyīn* and first list of simplified characters
1959	Great Leap Forward	
1964		Promulgation of second list of simplified characters
1966	Beginning of Cultural Revolution	
1974		Promulgation of third list of simplified characters (later withdrawn)
1978	Beginning of Open Door policy and reopening of universities	
1987		Birth of Chinese Cultural Linguistics
1989	Protest Movement	Publication of Shen's *Humanistic Spirit or Scientism?*
1996	Publication of *China Can Say 'No'*	

'If Chinese characters are not destroyed, the Chinese state is lost': attempts at script reform

From his highly critical late twentieth-century vantage point, Shen characterises what he calls 'the phoneticisation of Chinese characters' as the 'historical badge of an outmoded ideal of language revolution'. The issue of writing systems for Chinese, more perhaps than any other problem of language reform, has gone through a series of bewildering turnarounds in the course of the century. During the May Fourth modernisation period of the 1910s and 1920s, many of the most progressive reformers were convinced that Chinese characters were part of the feudal heritage holding China back from joining the modern world (a view more recently revived in the work of one of the Western sinologists critiqued in Chapter 4 – see Jenner 1992) as summed up in the aphorism of famous writer and polemicist Lu Xun: *Hànzì búmiè, Zhōngguó bìwáng* 漢字不滅,中國必亡 'If Chinese characters are not destroyed, the Chinese state is lost' (Lu Xun 1936).

The roots of the three phonemic writing systems officially introduced in the twentieth century lie in the *qièyīnzì* 切音字 or 'alphabetisation' movement of the last decades of the Qing dynasty between about 1890 and 1910, where numbers of attempts were made to devise phonemic writing systems for Chinese: some based, like the Japanese *kana* syllabary, on simplified forms of Chinese characters; others on the Roman alphabet. The first, promulgated by the young Republican government in 1918, only six years after its founding, indeed looks very similar to the *kana* and was initially named *Zhùyīn zìmǔ* 注音字母 or 'Phonetic Alphabet'. This quasi-syllabary, following the analysis of the syllable in traditional Chinese philology, uses separate symbols to represent the *shēngmǔ* 聲母 'sound', i.e. initial consonant, and *yùnmǔ* 韻母 'rhyme', i.e. vowel(s) plus final consonant, of each syllable, along with diacritics to represent tone marks. Still widely used in Taiwan, where it is popularly known after its four initial symbols as the *bo-po-mo-fo*, it is introduced there in the first year of primary education as an aid to learning the characters, and also used as a way of annotating Chinese characters in dictionaries and the like, with the 'letters' written alongside each character, very like the Japanese system of *furigana* used to indicate the pronunciation of rare characters. Although initially intended to function independently, in 1930, just over a decade after its introduction, the official designation of this system was changed from *Zhùyīn zìmǔ* 'Phonetic Alphabet' to *Zhùyīn fúhào* 注音符號 'Phonetic Symbols', in order to stress that it was not intended to be used as an independent writing system.

The second system, *Guóyǔ Luómǎzì* 國語羅馬字 'National Language Romanisation' spelled using its own system as *Gwoyeu Romaatzyh*, uses letters of the Roman alphabet to represent the lexical tones, as well as the vowels and consonants of the standard language. This insistence on including tones was widely attacked at the time, particularly because of the complexity of the ways in which it was indicated, and despite being arguably the most efficient of the three systems from a purely linguistic point of view, the National Language Romanisation was never widely adopted outside scholarly circles; it survives only vestigially in contemporary usage in the distinction between the spelling of the two Chinese provinces Shanxi and Shaanxi, i.e. *Shānxī* 山西 and *Shǎnxī* 陝西, where the doubling of the vowel in the latter indicates the third, or low dipping tone. These first two systems were introduced in the political instability of the Republican era (1912–1949), and for neither was their relationship with the traditional character script thoroughly addressed, nor did either receive the institutional support needed in order to become established as fully fledged writing systems.

However, among non-government organisations during this period, particularly on the left of Chinese politics, calls were widely made for the replacement of Chinese characters by a system that was easier to learn. The best known of these 'unofficial' systems was the script known, using its own spelling, as *Latinxua* 'Latinisation', i.e. *Lādīnghuà* 拉丁化 or *Latinxua Sin Wenz* 'Latinised New Script' i.e. *Lādīnghuà Xīn Wénzì* 拉丁化新文字, a Roman-based script quite similar to the current official romanisation Chinese Spelling, but without indication of tone marks. This system was implemented first in the Chinese-speaking parts of the Soviet Union, and then introduced into various parts of China, particularly the Communist-held areas, in the late 1930s and early 1940s. Typical of progressive thinking of this period was Mao Zedong's 1936 statement to the American journalist Edgar Snow: 'Sooner or later, we believe, we will have to abandon characters altogether if we are to create a new social culture in which the masses fully participate' (DeFrancis 1984: 248). Many on the left strongly supported a gradual phasing out of Chinese characters in favour of a Roman-based script, and such a move was seen as essential for solving the widespread problems of illiteracy in China.

However, in the early 1950s, soon after the establishment of the People's Republic, official policy suddenly started to move in reverse, marked initially by a 1950 statement by Mao that seemed to signal a return to the principles of the earlier Phonetic Alphabet: 'The writing system must be reformed, it should be national in form, the alphabet and system should be elaborated on the basis of the existing Chinese characters' (DeFrancis 1984: 259). Over the next few years, the requirement that it should be 'national in form' was quietly dropped, and the new phonemic system using the Roman alphabet that was eventually adopted, *Hànyǔ pīnyīn* 中文拼音 or 'Chinese Spelling', was downgraded in status from *wénzì* 文字 'script' to *fāng'àn* 方案 'scheme', with the characters retained as the main writing system, this time in a simplified form similar to that originally promulgated by the Nationalist Government in 1935 but withdrawn less than a year later due to conservative opposition (Fei (ed.) 1997: 64).

By the time of the promulgation of this third official writing system in 1958, the official list of 'immediate tasks in writing reform' announced by the Premier, Zhou Enlai, put in first and second place 'simplifying the Chinese characters' and 'spreading the use of the standard vernacular', with 'determining and spreading the use of phonetic spelling of Chinese' coming a distant third. Faced with the necessity of significant reforms in a wide range of other areas, with no consensus on exactly how script reforms should be carried out, and a huge weight of conservative inertia opposing any changes at all, the Government had decided to make some smaller reforms, such as simplifying the characters to make them easier to use, and leave the issue of their long-term viability to a later stage. The Chinese Spelling scheme, far from being envisaged as an autonomous writing system, like in origin at least to its predecessors the National Romanisation and the Latinised New Script, was to be downgraded to the auxiliary role in character learning still performed in Taiwan by the earlier Phonetic Alphabet to this day.

The official use of this 'scheme', commonly known as *pinyin*, is limited in current practice to signs, maps and dictionaries, and in education to only the first year of the primary school system. In the early 1960s, not long after its introduction, one of the older generation of language reformers, novelist Mao Dun, commented ironically on how his granddaughter, having become fully literate in pinyin in the first year of primary education, then became illiterate in Chinese characters for the remaining years of primary school that it took her to learn the requisite number of characters! (DeFrancis 1984: 268). In contrast, in the early 1990s, linguist Shen Xiaolong, from a younger generation but far more conservative, noted with horror that his son was fluent in pinyin but still didn't know enough characters to read a simple text (personal communication). A large amount of the linguistic research and ideological position-taking of the Chinese Cultural Linguistics movement, of which Shen has been a major figure, has centred around the characters and their supposedly deep links with the 'Chinese nation' and 'Chinese culture'. The issue of the status of Chinese characters in language reform and modernisation is one that has much broader implications, not only in the scholarly areas examined in this and previous chapters but in sinophone culture more broadly.

From *gelangma to yufa*: adapting Western frameworks to the Chinese language

Ma's grammar of 1898 sparked a whole series of grammars of Chinese from the 1910s into the 1920s and 1930s, supplementing Ma's description of classical Chinese with analyses of the emerging *báihuàwén* 白話文 or vernacular written standard which had been adopted as part of the reforms of the May Fourth modernisation movement. By the late 1930s when a fair literature on grammar had been built up, a new generation of linguists began to turn a critical eye on what they saw as the Indo-European biases of many of these descriptions of Chinese. A lively debate was carried on in linguistics journals under the banner of *wénfǎ géxīn* or 'renewing grammar', one of the main protagonists being Chen Wangdao from Fudan University in Shanghai (Chen 1939/1987). During the years of the anti-Japanese war (1937–1945), a string of major new descriptions of Chinese grammar were produced by linguists such as Lü Shuxiang (1942/1990) and Wang Li (1944/1985), who both went on to become major institutional figures in the linguistics establishment of the People's Republic, being associated respectively with the two main seats of institutional power, the Chinese Department of Peking University and the Linguistics Institute of the Chinese Academy of Social Sciences.

However, while such descriptions by Chinese linguists within China, including less mainstream approaches like that of Gao Mingkai (1948), as well as work from outside the People's Republic like Chou Fa-Kao on classical Chinese (Chou 1959–1962) and Yuen Ren Chao (1948, 1968) in the United States, did go a long way towards the goal of a description of Chinese grammar on its own terms, the lack of a native grammatical tradition in Chinese linguistics meant that these descriptions were still effectively carried out within Western-derived frameworks. Indeed the main difference between earlier descriptions of Chinese like *Mr Ma's Compleat Grammar* (Ma 1898/1953) and *A New Grammar of the National Language* (Li 1924) with 'renewed' descriptions like *Modern Chinese Grammar* (Wang 1944/1985) was that the latter not only had the advantage of several decades of debate and descriptions seeking to look at Chinese grammar through Chinese eyes, but also drew on a more sophisticated understanding of Western grammatical theory, as well as developments in the still emerging field of Western linguistics in the first half of the twentieth century. The term itself had also undergone evolution over this period, with Ma's sound translation *gēlángmǎ* 葛朗瑪 replaced by the 'calque' (loan translation) *wénfǎ* 文法 'rules of writing', e.g. in Li (1924), and then by *yǔfǎ* 语法 'rules of language', e.g. in Wang (1944/1985) (*wénfǎ* remains standard on Taiwan, *yǔfǎ* on the mainland).

Although various Western theories of language were taken up and applied to Chinese by various Chinese linguists, often after overseas study, the most influential was the brand of American structuralism (Bloomfield 1933) developed by Chao Yuen Ren in his pedagogical work *Mandarin Primer* (Chao 1948). In origin a language textbook developed at Harvard as part of the US war effort, it contained an opening section on grammar which summed up with great conciseness, consistency and elegance the major features of Chinese grammar as Chao saw them. This grammatical section of the book was quickly translated into Chinese (Li 1952) and had an enormous impact, perhaps not least because of Chao's impeccable credentials both as a linguist and a major figure in the language reforms of the 1910s and 1920s.

Just at this time, major educational reforms were being undertaken on the mainland as part of the general reforms of the early period of the People's Republic of China, and a framework very close to Chao's was adopted in the *Zhànnǐ hànyǔ jiàoxué xìtǒng* 暫擬漢語教學系統 *Provisional System for Teaching Chinese Grammar* published in 1956, which became the basis of the grammatical knowledge taught in schools and universities. After the more than a decade-long hiatus in higher education caused by the Cultural Revolution (1966–1978), it was this framework which became fossilised in mainland linguistics and endures essentially unchanged to this day. The type of grammatical knowledge it provides is used largely for the kind of 'parsing and analysis' exercises associated with traditional (Latin) grammar in the West, and it is perhaps doubtful that it has helped to fulfil Ma Jianzhong's original patriotic aim for the teaching of grammar.

The type of linguistics represented by this grammatical system is thus vulnerable on a number of fronts. Practically speaking, it is limited to a basically passive or analytical knowledge of the language which arguably has limited value in solving problems of literacy or language teaching. In Shen's – admittedly biased – summing up of the situation, put forward in an article addressed to language teachers:

> [M]any experienced teachers of Chinese grammar feel, in varying degrees, that students benefit little from the current grammar teaching in terms of their comprehension and use of Chinese. Some teachers propose that our teaching would be much more effective if we asked students to read some literary classics instead of teaching them grammatical rules.
>
> (*Shen 1988a: 40*)

Ideologically speaking, moreover, the history of the development of this system is irredeemably associated with introduced Western concepts and frameworks which successive generations of Chinese linguists have struggled to adapt to the 'reality' of Chinese. The door was thus wide open for an iconoclast and patriot like Shen Xiaolong to take a sledgehammer to the whole edifice.

Foreign versus native: the paradox of reactive relativism

Of all the academic salvos fired over language reform in the last hundred years, Shen's aggressive announcement of the arrival on the scene of Chinese Cultural Linguistics in a 1989 essay must at least be one of the most unconventional. It is hardly a coincidence that it was published, not in a linguistics journal but rather in the literary journal *Shulin*, and in a column devoted to authors writing about their own work, since it reads far more like the manifesto of a literary movement than a serious scholarly statement:

> Almost a hundred years after [the publication of *Mr Ma's Compleat Grammar*], not one of the Western grammatical categories introduced by Ma Jianzhong accords with the linguistic intuition of Chinese speakers. ... On the verge of a new century, Chinese linguistics has fallen into unprecedented bewilderment. In the normal course of things, this bewilderment should have become a turning point, sparking philosophical reflection and a paradigm shift in linguistics. Chen Wangdao, Zhang Shilu, Guo Shaoyu, Qi Gong, Zhang Zhigong, Gao Mingkai and other language scholars have all issued thought-provoking warnings about the 'foreign framework' of modern Chinese linguistics, but these efforts have all been nullified by the wily old gentleman in the capital of Chinese linguistics. Into a Chinese

linguistics beset with crisis he has injected the tranquilliser of 'dealing with facts'.

(Shen 1989a: 347)

Shen contends that, despite all the revising and 'refining' of the system of grammatical categories introduced by Ma Jianzhong, the basic framework is still a 'formalist' Western one and therefore unable to deal with what he dubs the 'humanistic' nature of the Chinese language. Shen characterises the current ideology of grammatical description in China as one of *wùshí* 務實 or 'dealing with facts', whereby the younger generation of linguists are encouraged by their masters, as represented here by the 'wily old gentleman in the capital of Chinese linguistics' (code for Lü Shuxiang, longtime Head of the Linguistics Institute of the Chinese Academy of Social Sciences) to mechanically collect the 'bricks and tiles of linguistics' and not to worry about the reasons for doing so. As Shen sarcastically sums up the supposedly atheoretical current practice (Shen 1989a: 349): '"dealing with facts" means acting according to the blueprints provided by the people who earnestly exhort us to "deal with facts"!'

Shen's earliest work was on classical Chinese (Shen 1988b), and he possesses great familiarity with the traditional methodologies of *xiǎoxué* 'philology'. This background still carries a certain amount of scholarly authority in Chinese linguistics, not yet a hundred years since the classical language ceased to be the official written medium, and features of the classical language such as monosyllabism, lack of morphology and the seeming lack of formal, as opposed to semantically based rules of grammar – all of which are in sharp contrast to the paradigm 'Indo-European' languages like Classical Greek and Sanskrit – seem to set it apart as a special case, at least viewed through European eyes. In fact, the earliest forms of Chinese known to us do contain vestiges of morphological variation in related morphemes, commonly written with the same character, such as the example of 長 *cháng* 'long' and *zhǎng* 'to become long, to grow; senior' that we saw in Chapter 4.

As was also pointed out there, the monosyllabism of Old Chinese is also a general tendency rather than an absolute rule. And as for whether the rules of Chinese grammar are better understood as 'form-based' or 'meaning-based', that would seem to be as much a function of the kind of framework used to describe them as of any supposedly inherent feature of the language itself. In any case, such features are far less evident in the modern language, but with the popular conflation of all historical forms of Chinese as 'the same language', one to which Shen seemingly subscribes, in Shen's eyes neither classical nor modern Chinese should be subject to the so-called 'universal rules' of Western grammar.

Modern Chinese linguistics is in fact unthinkable without Western borrowings. This is not making some sort of imperialistic claim about Western scholarship, which was after all itself heavily influenced by the discovery by European scholars in the eighteenth century of historical links between many European and Indian languages – hence the 'Indo-European' family of languages often invoked by Chinese linguists as an opposite – as well as by the highly developed Indian traditions of syntactic and phonological analysis (Robins 1997: 163). Chinese linguistic scholarship had earlier been profoundly influenced by Indian phonological theories during the period of the introduction of Buddhism from the fourth century CE. However, for many Chinese linguists past and present, one of the prominent members of the latter group being Shen Xiaolong, the current Western-derived framework poses huge practical and ideological problems:

> Once this theory and method have completely discarded the spiritual shackles of (though it may still draw on the experience of) the Western grammatical framework, it will still have two scientific reference points: firstly, the cultural determinism existing between the Chinese language and Chinese philosophy, art, literature, aesthetics, and even way of thinking … secondly, categories and methods used in the ancient Chinese traditions of language analysis. These categories and methods are much closer to the linguistic intuitions of Chinese people, and after scientific systematization and interpretation can be transformed as the basis for the analysis of modern Chinese. To this new linguistic paradigm for Chinese, which takes the humanistic nature of Chinese as its ontology, and the cultural nature of Chinese and the scientific analysis and exegesis deriving from the Chinese linguistic tradition as its methodology, I have given the name of 'Cultural Linguistics'.
>
> (*Shen 1989a: 353–354*)

Shen's manifesto for a 'new linguistic paradigm' shows a significant ambivalence about the Western roots of modern Chinese linguistics, particularly in the area of grammar. Shen's unconscious reliance on Western standards is revealed by such self-contradictory statements as 'Once this theory and method have completely discarded the spiritual shackles of (though it may still draw on the experience of) the Western grammatical framework'. There are good reasons, as pointed out above, for the lack of a native grammatical tradition in China, and the fact that modern Chinese is still a very different language from an Indo-European language like English does not mean that the two are totally incommensurable. The main problem with influence from one linguistic tradition to another is not that it happens at all – after all, how could it be prevented? – but rather that it takes place on far too specific a level (Halliday 1993), such as earlier European attempts to analyse Chinese sentence structure in terms of the traditional noun 'cases' of Latin grammar (e.g. Mullie 1932). Shen's ideologically driven need to *prove* that Chinese is 'different' only ends up trapping him in a superficial and *reactive* type of relativism that cannot deal with the actual similarities and differences between languages.

A good example of this is the claim, continually made by Shen and others in the Chinese Cultural Linguistics movement, that the Chinese language is 'unique' (that word again!), a term that also figures largely in popular discourse about the language. If we take such a claim seriously, that is, if we accept that there is only one language in the whole world quite like Chinese (in itself a rather fuzzy concept), we may seem to be doing nothing but stating a rather obvious truism. On purely linguistic grounds, if we take the Chinese group of languages, commonly referred to as 'dialects' (Chinese *fāngyán* 方言 or 'regional (forms of) speech'), 'regionalects' (DeFrancis 1984), 'topolects' (Mair 1991), or more recently in scholarly circles as 'Sinitic languages' (Chappell 2004), as a whole, it is not difficult to show, despite some obvious links with related languages such as Thai or Burmese on the one hand, and some features shared with neighbouring languages like Vietnamese or Mongolian on the other, that Chinese exhibits a particular mix of phonological, grammatical and semantic features that is not replicated in any other language or language group.

However, once we start looking at it in more detail, and attempt to enumerate the supposedly 'unique' features of Chinese, this claim begins to look a bit shakier. Take, for example, Shen's claim that 'in my Masters thesis, I put forward a uniquely Chinese sentence type – the topic–comment type' (Shen 1989a: 351). Apart from the dubious procedure of implying as his own 'discovery' an analysis of Chinese first suggested, to my knowledge, by Yuen Ren Chao in his *Mandarin Primer* of 1948, explicitly stated in the same author's *Grammar of Spoken Chinese* in 1968, and then developed by Charles Li and Sandra Thompson in their 1976 paper 'Subject and Topic: A New Typology of Language', what exactly does such a claim entail? Chao's understanding of the topic–comment distinction was that it replaced the subject/predicate distinction familiar from the European grammatical tradition. In other words, Chinese sentence structure, rather than being given the actor–action interpretation that seems to work for many European languages, is better understood as consisting of a relationship between a topic for discussion and something said about that topic (Chao 1948: 35, 1968: 69–75). Li and Thompson interpreted this distinction differently, claiming that *both* subject *and* topic were relevant to the analysis of Chinese, with the former understood as identifying the actor, and the latter as setting the framework for discussion. They then classified certain languages like Chinese as 'topic prominent', other languages like English as 'subject prominent', and still others, like Japanese and Korean, as 'both topic prominent and subject prominent' (Li and Thompson 1976).

Shen does not argue for his own analysis in detail, simply stating that 'in the recognition of [the topic–comment sentence type], not only is it impossible to start from form, there is no way of finding it among the categories of Western grammar' (Shen 1989a: 351). The positiveness of this statement is rather staggering, especially as the earliest formulation in the writings of the Greek sophists of the concept which eventually developed into 'subject' was one much closer to 'topic' than to 'actor' (Robins 1951; Halliday 1977); and the related concept of 'theme' has been widely applied in the twentieth century by linguists of the Prague School and other functional schools in linguistics (see Hasan and Fries 1995). A puzzling feature of Shen's claim is that he is in some measure well aware of this. An earlier article of his, 'Topic–Comment Sentences in Chinese and their Typological Significance' (Shen 1984), written in a much more sober style, discusses the origin of what he calls the 'subject–predicate binary' in Greek linguistics; although he is seemingly unaware of its original use by the Sophists, referring only to the actor–action interpretation of Plato and Aristotle, and its application to Chinese philosophy and linguistics from the late nineteenth century. Here too, however, although correctly noting that 'subject and predicate are grammatical categories abstracted from Western language facts' (Shen 1984: 144), he seems determined to prove that such an analysis could not possibly be applicable to Chinese because of the 'essential typological difference between Indo-European languages and Sino-Tibetan languages' (Shen 1984: 145).

This 'essential typological difference' hinges on the supposed lack of morphology in Chinese, as opposed to the rich morphology of 'Western languages' – plausible if we are comparing, say, Old English to Old Chinese but not so obvious for Modern English and Modern Chinese – which he argues calls for a 'humanistic' rather than 'formalised' approach to the description of Chinese. The basis for such a claim is made clear in the following passage from his 1989 'manifesto':

> I believe that all the characteristics of Chinese are a manifestation of its strongly humanistic nature. This is a fundamental difference between Chinese and Western languages. The fact that Western languages are rich in morphological markers means that Western linguistics can easily come up with a set of formalised analytical procedures and theoretical goals and systems compatible with formalisation. However, once a tradition deriving from the scientistic nature of Western descriptive linguistics is applied across the board to the analysis of the facts of a language like Chinese that is non-morphological and strongly humanistic in nature, it will inevitably become intolerably restrictive.
>
> (*Shen 1989a: 353–354*)

This statement reveals some interesting ideological sleights of hand. First there is the semantic slippage from 'formal (i.e. morphological) markers' to 'formalised procedures' which implies that the nature of Western languages makes them supposedly more amenable to either a formal analysis, i.e. concentrating on form rather than meaning, and/or analytical procedures that are formalised, i.e. performable automatically by a computer. Apart from mixing together two very different concepts under (almost) the same label, this implies that the so-called 'Western languages' (a very vague concept in itself) are somehow 'essentially' oriented to form, while 'Chinese' (another vague concept, at least in Shen's usage) is 'essentially' oriented to meaning, ignoring the fact that all languages work by linking form to meaning.

Second, and perhaps more significant from an ideological point of view, is the fact that the supposed 'unique' (that word again!) characteristics of Chinese – non-morphological and humanistic – are both defined *negatively* in contrast to the 'morphological' and 'scientistic' Western languages: in other words, Shen can only say what Chinese *is* by saying how it is *not* like Western languages. Much of the rhetoric of Chinese Cultural Linguistics and other more recent manifestations of

Chinese cultural nationalism fall into this trap of what I have called 'reactive relativism', and these sweeping claims, and the impatience with the details of linguistic analysis which often go hand in hand with it, all seem to stem from the same patriotic compulsion to claim an unassailable status for the Chinese language, like the Chinese state, on the world stage.

Can China say 'no'?: homegrown versus imported solutions to language problems

The sorts of questions agonised over in the language arena are not confined to linguistic problems alone. Perhaps *the* major question faced by Chinese thinkers in the modern era has been: How to modernise? – can we do it in a way that grows out of and respects our own traditions, or do we need to follow the path already blazed by the West? Shen reflects on this situation in his typically high-minded rhetoric:

> The vicissitudes of 20th century Chinese linguistics are a kind of cultural phenomenon which reflects a common failing in the borrowing of Western learning among the human sciences in recent Chinese history: that is, inadequate preparation in thought and cultural theory. We have never had the opportunity to carry out a thorough and profound self-examination in regard to our native cultural traditions. Not only have we been unable to grasp the particular patterns of Chinese culture, we have also been unable to understand the quintessence of Western culture. Gazing from afar on the deep-seated tradition of the West, we see only the harvest and not the sowing; yearning for its surface glories, we have not sought to thoroughly understand it, but merely enjoyed its benefits. Today in researching this cultural faultline we must dissect this morbidity in cultural psychology. This not only relates to a critique of the value of Chinese and Western culture, but also to the self-confidence of the race.
>
> (*Shen 1989b: 282*)

Shen's concluding remarks in his 1989 book come back to the paradox from which he started – the contradiction between the 'humanism' of the Chinese language and the 'scientism' of Chinese linguistics – but broaden his critique from a 'crisis' of a particular discipline to a 'morbidity' of a whole intellectual tradition. Shen's arguments, with all their exaggerations, do represent a serious attempt at the 'thorough and profound self-examination' he calls for. Moreover, the sorts of nationalist sentiments espoused by Shen are not confined to academic or educational spheres but have resonances with nationalistic movements in China and abroad. This development is well represented by the title of a book published in the mid-1990s *Zhōngguó kěyǐ shuō 'bù'* 中國可以說 '不' *China can say 'No'* (Song Qiang *et al.* 1996; a more recent book including one of the same authors has the equally childish-sounding title *Zhōngguó bù gāoxìng* 中國不高興 *China isn't happy* (Song Xiaodong *et al.* 2009).

The tenor of this book, ironically based on a Japanese original written by then current Mayor of Tokyo arguing that Japanese should come out from under the shadow of the United States and 'say no' to a number of other countries, including China, is well summed up by the following slogans from its Foreword:

> America can't be led by anyone, it can only lead itself.
>
> Japan can't be led by anyone, sometimes it can't even lead itself.
>
> China too doesn't want to be led by anyone, it only wants to lead itself.
>
> (*Song et al. 1996: 3*)

The sorts of nationalist political rhetoric put forward in this tract and many other similar ones in recent years is of a piece with the whole edifice of Shen's arguments for the 'uniqueness' of the Chinese language. Both these political and cultural nationalisms argue, in effect, for the need to treat China as a special case, a theme that goes back to official mainland rhetoric of the 1970s and 1980s about *Zhōngguó guóqíng* 中國國情 or 'Chinese characteristics' (Barmé and Jaivin 1992: 366–367; see also McDonald 1995). Both are manifestations of a continuing and uneasy accommodation in Chinese political and intellectual circles to the 'decentring' of China since the incursions beginning with the Opium Wars of the 1840s. The unfinished nature of this accommodation is aptly summed up in a superficially neat division of labour recommended by the late Imperial reform slogan *Zhōngxué wéi tǐ, Xīxué wéi yòng* 'Chinese learning as essence, Western learning as application'.

The problem is that after the huge foreign borrowings of the intervening period, borrowings which have fundamentally transformed Chinese culture, no-one is quite sure any more exactly what the 'Chinese essence' might look like, a paradox reflected in the schizophrenic world view of both Chinese Cultural Linguistics and popular nationalistic rhetoric.

Conclusion: orientalism versus occidentalism in understandings of Chinese

We saw that the kinds of rhetoric explored in Chapters 4 and 5 under the label of 'character fetishisation' also extend beyond the writing system as such into discussions of the grammar of Chinese, and more broadly into characterisations of Chinese society and culture. I noted briefly in Chapter 4 the existence of a similar phenomenon in Japan known as *Nihonjinron*, i.e. 日本人論 or 'Discussions on Japaneseness'. Although in China there is no fixed term for such discourse, we could perhaps follow the Japanese example and coin the term *Zhōngguórénlùn* 中國人論 or 'Discussions on Chineseness'. Both kinds of discourse would, paradoxically perhaps, count as types of 'orientalism' in Said's terms, since although they are being produced by the 'natives' rather than by the 'foreigners', their roots lie in the historical pressures on the native sense of self in these countries, and on the whole East Asian region which long had China at its core, stemming from the incursions – military, economic, social, intellectual and cultural – by the modernising West.

Such examples of *Zhōngguórénlùn* are recurrent best-sellers in China, and sometimes even come from the pens of non-Chinese authors: as witness the work of retired British naval officer Gavin Menzies on the Zheng He naval expeditions of the 1400s to the 1420s, which neatly turns the tables on Da Gama, Columbus and their European imperialistic ilk by proclaiming *1421* as *The Year China Discovered the World* (Menzies 2002 – in the USA the book was published with the subtitle *The Year China Discovered America*, which perhaps made the trumping of Columbus more pointed). Although Zheng He's actual achievements in leading a Chinese fleet as far as East Africa are impressive enough, Menzies' extrapolations from the historical record have about as much historical justification as the stories of Sinbad the Sailor, for which Zheng He, also known as San Bao, was apparently the inspiration. In relation to the kind of evidence Menzies adduces in support of his claim that Chinese explorers 'discovered' parts of the globe well before their European counterparts, a sceptic might note that the famous Piri Reis map which Menzies uses to good effect in his first book was explained by an earlier author as based on a photograph taken by aliens from a spaceship (see von Däniken 1971)!

The sort of historical revisionism and cultural triumphalism characteristic of Menzies and his Chinese counterparts finds its equal and opposite reaction in the highly critical re-evaluations of Chinese history, culture and even national character found in the 1988 mainland TV documentary *River Elegy* (see Barmé and Jaivin 1992: 366–368), or Taiwanese controversialist Bo Yang's book *The Ugly Chinaman* (Bo 1992). The historical roots of such ideas lie in the agonised national self-critique of the May Fourth period, when the fortunes of the Chinese state were almost at their lowest ebb, but enough remains of that lack of self-confidence, even now when China is playing a much more assertive role on the world stage, to give rise to periodic bouts of self-loathing.

In the language sphere, some of the arguments of the 'full-blown Westernisers' of the May Fourth period have been resurrected in a sustained critique directed against Chinese characters and their supposed continuing baleful effects on the whole East Asian region for which characters provided the source and main model for writing systems, a region which hence on cultural and historical grounds could easily be dubbed the 'Chinese character region'. The titles of two books by a major proponent of these arguments, American linguist William C. Hannas – *Asia's Orthographic Dilemma* (1997), *The Writing on the Wall: How Asian Orthography Curbs Creativity* (2003) – give a taste of the importance being laid on the Chinese writing system as a historical deadweight, very similar to the arguments of historian William Jenner examined in Chapter 4. When Hannas goes on to ask the question of whether what he calls 'Sinitic vocabulary', in other words the Chinese terms borrowed into languages within the 'Chinese character region' such as Vietnamese, Korean and Japanese, are proving an intolerable burden on the language because of the extremes of homophony they cause, one has to wonder why this critique is stemming from someone who having presumably grown up with the highly Latinate vocabulary of written English, has, nonetheless, never had to struggle with doubts as to whether to use *accept* or *except*, *affect* or *effect*, *illusion* or *allusion*, and so on with the rest of such doublets. In relation to language reform in China, one might also be led to wonder whether such calls to the Chinese to give up their writing system on the grounds of inefficiency could not with equal justice be directed against the English spelling system with the notorious complexity of its graph to sound relationship.

As for the case of the supposedly pernicious influence of Chinese characters across the Chinese character region, the Japanese writing system shows a very similar blend of two systems to that exhibited by English, and for similar historical reasons: with the mixture of *kanji* and *kana* in Japanese quite comparable to the mix of Anglo-Saxon and Romance spelling conventions in English, despite the fact that the latter pair are both written using the 'same' alphabet. In neither case have strongly felt arguments for replacing the unwieldy current writing system with a more efficient alternative made much headway against a deep-rooted attachment to the inherited system.

In the case of Chinese, it is in fact possible, despite common claims to the contrary, to write the language using an alphabetic system, as shown by the wide if short-lived success of the Latinxua systems in the 1930s and 1940s. However, it soon became clear in that case that the use of such systems required something much closer to the spoken register than was common for written Chinese. Over the millennia of its use, the Chinese written register has developed features of compression and concision which depend on the greater visual distinctiveness of the characters and their role in disambiguating homophones. Any change to an alphabetic writing system would necessitate a move to a register much closer to the spoken one. There are thus practical, as well as ideological, barriers in the way of 'modernising' Chinese in this way (see Chen 1999 for an extended discussion).

In reading discourses of both orientalism and occidentalism in relation to Chinese, it is as if either the 'alphabet' or the 'charactery' are being held up as the villain, as the exotic 'other' which reassures the writer about the essential rightness of his or her own cultural heritage. American psycholinguist Mary Erbaugh, in her aptly titled 'Ideograph as Other in Poststructuralist Literary Theory' (Erbaugh 2002), documents numbers of examples of scholars from outside Chinese studies whose enthusiasm for saddling Chinese characters with, in this case, mostly positive evaluations is matched only by their ignorance of any form of Chinese, or of how writing systems using Chinese characters actually work. Given that numbers of scholars with a profound knowledge of both have also indulged in similar fantasising, such 'outsiders' cannot really be blamed for succumbing to the temptations of casting the characters either as hero or villain, and neglecting many possibly far more mundane factors which would explain the phenomenon without the need for fetishising the characters. The fact that this issue is not at all some quaint myth already long ago relegated to the distant past, but very much a living issue in Chinese studies generally, like the equally extravagant claims made for (Logan 1986, 2004) and to a lesser extent against (e.g. Shlain 1998) the alphabet, only shows what great cultural value is invested by literate cultures in their writing systems, and how easily they became material for a whole industry of mythmaking.

PART C

Getting over the Walls of Discourse

In Part B we went back into the past, in the history of the study of Chinese by the West, in order to understand some of the opposing ideologies that make up the uneasy status quo that is today's Chinese studies. With Part C we come back to the contemporary field from the perspective adopted in Chapter 1 of Part A: the relationship between *texts* and their *contexts*. We will examine this relationship from three distinct viewpoints. The first, in Chapter 7, 'Construing "metrosexual" in Chinese', goes from *context* to text, from the social and cultural environment of the modern globalised developing economy that is mainland China to a certain genre of texts that can give us specific insights into that changing context. As in Chapter 1 we take as our texts something that would have seemed trivial or silly to the traditional sinologist: men's fashion magazines. In fact, in tracing the different ways in which the Anglo-American concept of 'metrosexual' has been adapted into Chinese, and why it was adopted when it was, we can see globalisation – as well as its twin sister, localisation – happening before our eyes in all the particularities of the contemporary Chinese context.

The second, in Chapter 8, 'Reconstruction versus deconstruction', goes from *text* to context, and examines some of the different ways of understanding and analysing texts that are current in Chinese studies. It discusses the roots of the contemporary frameworks for analysing texts that lie in the pre-modern scholarly traditions of both China and Europe, and the different understandings of the relationship between text and context embodied in those frameworks. It suggests that, for all those working within Chinese studies, a complementary focus on text and context – whether the emphasis is on the former, as in the traditional humanities, or on the latter, as in the social sciences – is the fundamental commonality and shared point of reference.

The third, in Chapter 9, 'From "Ed McDonald" to "Ned McHorse"', introduces a point of view not often studied, that of the *individual*. Just as in Chapter 3 we examined the case of a highly influential, though in many ways quite representative, individual as language learner, in this chapter we take a look at the experiences of the author as potential sinophone, and trace the various strands of his background, and the developing experiences with Chinese and China that he brought to that learning process, one which is still ongoing.

The Metrosexuals are here!

7

CONSTRUING 'METROSEXUAL' IN CHINESE

Social and semiotic change in the era of globalisation

Introduction: the age of androgyny

In 2006 in mainland China, two televised talent contests, local versions of the various 'Idol' contests that have been taking place across the world in recent years, captured the attention of the whole country and gave rise to much public debate. The first, with the finals broadcast on Shanghai Dragon TV on August 28, was called *Jiā yóu, hǎo nán'ér* 加油，好男儿, translated on the official website as *My Hero*, but more colloquially, corresponding better to the Aussie message of encouragement 'On ya, guys'. The second, a rerun of the previous year's highly successful competition, whose finals were broadcast on Hunan Satellite TV on September 29, was *Chāojí nǔshēng* 超级女声, or *Chāonǔ* 超女 for short, translated as *Supergirls*, but the full title punning on the homophonous *nǔshēng* 女声 'female voice' and *nǔshēng* 女生, literally 'female student' but often used to mean 'young woman'. These two contests were both ground-breaking for China in that the finalists were significantly determined by public voting in the form of text messages. When the results of the voting emerged, the preferences they exhibited took some people by surprise: in the words of one of the *My Hero* judges, Cao Kefan:

> As far as the kids who took part in the text-message voting are concerned, perhaps their aesthetic criteria tend towards rather 'androgynous' (*zhōngxìnghuà* 中性化) features, just as in choosing 'Supergirls' a lot of people chose the Li Yuchun type: girls displaying a tomboyish style (*nánháiqì* 男孩气) while the boys are rather feminized (*nǔxìnghuà* 女性化). This was probably what all the controversy was about.
>
> (Men's Style, *October 2006, p.57*)

I've started with this example, not only because it gives some insight into the enormous social and cultural changes taking place among young Chinese with regard to gender and sexual identity, but also because it gives a clue to the method we will be following in this chapter to explore a related area of social change: the rise of the so-called 'metrosexual' in China. I emphasise the 'so-called' in the first instance because the term and the identities it refers to have been through a process of evolution since it was first picked up by Chinese men's magazines around mid-2004. The magazine which reported the comment above, and had exclusive magazine rights to covering the competition, *Men's Style*, headed its special edition on *My Hero* with the headline 'Metrosexual 来了！' ' 'The Metrosexuals are here!'. However, as we will see in this paper, the *Men's Style* late-2006 'metrosexual' shows some significant differences from even the same magazine's early 2005 'metrosexual', not to mention the *Men's Health* late-2004 'metrosexual', or the *MENBOX* mid-2004 'metrosexual'.

But I also stress 'so-called' because it is crucial to the current approach to attend very closely to particular 'ways of saying' – 'discourses' in the strictly linguistic sense – as well as to the 'ways of living' – 'discourses' in the Foucauldian sense of complexes of social framing – in which they make sense. My approach here is to look at *texts*, the products of semiosis or meaning-making processes, in relation to their varied *contexts*: in technical terms, an approach that is both *semiotic* and *social*. The approach known as social semiotics was introduced by Bob Hodge and Gunther Kress in their 1988 book of that name (Hodge and Kress 1988), and grew out of a confluence of the close socially informed analysis of discourse shown in functional linguistics (e.g. Halliday 1978) and the growing academic interest in uncovering the ideological underpinning of discourses later dubbed critical discourse analysis (e.g. Fairclough 1989, 1992, 1995 – see discussion in Chapter 8).

From this viewpoint, what we are looking at in this chapter is not simply the *translating* of 'metrosexual' into Chinese, though that does of course form part of what happens, but rather a more dynamic process we could call *construing*. The implication of this term, etymologically linked to 'construct', is that the semiotic and social aspects of the process are 'co-constructed', i.e. mutually influencing and mutually creating. As we will see, although 'metrosexual' was taken up widely by Chinese men's magazines as a useful and indeed strategic notion, it was adopted only when the economic and social conditions were ripe for the kind of lifestyle it represents, and its use in Chinese contexts shows significant adaptations to local conditions and needs.

The archaeology of 'metrosexual' in China

To start our exploration of these processes of social and semiotic change, it would be useful to carry out what, borrowing a notion from Foucault, we could call an 'archaeology' (Foucault 1969/2002) of the term 'metrosexual', tracing the process by which it was adopted into the mainland Chinese context and progressively adapted to local conditions. What I will do here is note the different ways the term has been used in three local men's magazines (the reasons for choosing these particular magazines will become clearer below), both with the direct borrowing of the English term and in its various Chinese translations, commenting particularly on the connotations of the renderings and the contexts in which they are used. For convenience I have divided the different adaptations of the term into three chronological 'phases' largely characterised by a particular semantic 'theme', although the order of appearance does not directly match the kind of rendering.

The term 'metrosexual' was originally coined by British social commentator Mark Simpson as early as 1994, in the context of what he called the 'men's style press', to characterise the appearance in British and American magazines of 'narcissistic young men sporting fashionable clothes and accessories', whose interest in their own appearance, in an Anglo-American context at least, made their sexuality rather dubious. The term was defined in more detail in an article by the same author in 2002 as 'a young man with money to spend, living in or within easy reach of a metropolis – because that's where all the best shops, clubs, gyms and hairdressers are' (thus explaining the 'metro' part of the term), and nicely summed up the intersection of consumption and sexuality in this label by characterising a metrosexual as someone who 'has clearly taken himself as his own love object and pleasure as his sexual preference'. The following year, the American Dialect Society voted Simpson's coinage the 'most influential word of 2003', and it was this that brought it to the attention of the international media (for Simpson's own sardonic account of how this term 'went global' see Simpson 2003), including the Chinese.

Decorative male

TABLE 7.1 Stage 1: Decorative male

Date	Source	Term	Rendering
August 2003	sina.com trans. of *International Herald Tribune*	metrosexual 都市玉男 *dūshì yùnán*	metropolitan jade male ~exquisite
April 2004	*Men's Health*	花样男子 *huāyàng nánzǐ*	decorative male
May 2004	*MENBOX*	型男 *xíngnán*	model male

The first trajectory of translating 'metrosexual' in Chinese is one which I have dubbed the 'decorative male'. The earliest mention of the term in the Chinese media that I have been able to trace is a translation of a piece originally published in the *International Herald Tribune* which appeared on the popular Chinese website sina.com on 8 August 2003. In this translation, the etymology of the English term is correctly indicated as deriving from *dūshì* 都市 'metropolis' and *xìngbié* 性别 'sexual distinction', but the actual Chinese rendering is *dūshì yùnán* or 'metropolitan jade male', which I have provisionally translated as 'metropolitan exquisite'. In this rendering, the most obvious change is the disappearance of '-sexual' as an explicit element of the term, and this is in fact the case with all of the translations I have seen: no-one, as far as I am aware, has taken the route of putting beside *yìxìngliàn* 异性恋 'different sex love – heterosexual', and *tóngxìngliàn* 同性恋 'same sex love – homosexual', the third term *dūxìngliàn* 都性恋 'metro sex love – metrosexual'.

However, many of the terms that are used do have a sexual connotation: for example in relation to 'jade male', the more usual combination would be *yùnǚ* 玉女 'jade female', most commonly in the names of attendants of Daoist immortals *Jīntóng Yùnǚ* 金童玉女 'the Golden Boy and the Jade Maiden'; so there is an implied gender reversal here, one which we will see below comes into greater prominence in more recent uses of the term.

In the following year, while not actually yet mentioning the term 'metrosexual', a couple of the men's fashion magazines analysed here dealt with the sort of phenomenon Simpson had identified a decade before. In April 2004, *Men's Health* ran a feature on male health and beauty products, featuring the two well-known male models Song Ning and Zheng Dapeng, titled *huāyàng nánzǐ* or 'decorative male'. Around the same time, *MENBOX* in its 8th issue included an editorial on what it called the *xíngnán* or 'model male', that referring to 'model' as in model of car or model of phone (see the Introduction to Chapter 9 in relation to these kinds of 'models'), and singled out Korean actor/model Won Bin as its perfect 'model male'.

Updated yuppie

TABLE 7.2 Stage 2: Updated yuppie

Date	Source	Term	Rendering
July 2004	*MENBOX*	metrosexual male 都市质男 *dūshì zhìnán*	metropolitan quality male
August 2004	*MENBOX*	metrosexual 城市新男人 *chéngshì xīn nánrén*	new urban male
August 2004	*Men's Health*	metrosexual 花色男人 *huāsè nánrén*	variegated man
		后雅痞 *hòu yǎpǐ*	post-yuppie

The first explicit appearance of the term 'metrosexual' in one of the magazines examined here was in the 9th issue of *MENBOX* in an unsigned editorial titled *Nánrén àiměi wúzuì* 男人爱美无罪 'It's no crime for men to love beauty'. This editorial takes a commercial orientation, discussing the growing phenomenon of men's beauty and health products, and when it introduces the English term 'metrosexual male' – interestingly enough in the light of the discussion of the significance of 'quality' in Chinese society discussed in Chapter 1 – renders it as *dūshì zhìnán* 'metropolitan quality male'. A month and two issues later, after *MENBOX* had undergone a change of editorship, the new senior editor took a more generally lifestyle-related approach to the idea of metrosexual in the context of the pressures on the modern urban male to conform to numerous standards and expectations. For this editor, then, the 'metrosexual' was a type of updated yuppie, and so she rendered the term as *chéngshì xīn nánrén* 'new urban male'.

At about the same time, the August 2004 issue of *Men's Health* ran a special feature on the metrosexual, or what it termed the *huāsè nánrén* 'variegated man', harking back to its earlier use of the term *huāyàng nánzǐ* 'decorative male'. Introducing the feature with a cartoon-like illustration of languid dandies, it argued that men beautifying themselves is a type of 'animal instinct, like the rooster's comb or the peacock's tail', and the main change in this age of the 'variegated male' was that 'we've begun to face up to the fact'. In the same issue, a more formal essay entitled 'The new age of male beauty' while arguing for the use of the term 'variegated male' mentioned other previous renderings such as the 'jade male' *dūshì yùnán* 'metropolitan exquisite' and a variation on the 'model man' *dūshì měi xíngnán* 'metropolitan beauty model male'. It also added a new one which recalls the *MENBOX* editor's 'new urban male' – *hòu yǎpǐ* 'post-yuppie' – significantly choosing for the sound rendering of the English term not the usual characters *yǎpí* 雅皮 'elegant skin' but the almost homophonous *yǎpǐ* 雅痞 'elegant ruffian', recalling the term *pǐ.zi* 痞子 used for the cynical anti-establishment dropouts of the 1980s as made famous in the fiction of Beijing author Wáng Shuò 王朔.

From mensch to Johnny's boy

TABLE 7.3 Stage 3: From mensch to Johnny's boy

Date	Source	Term	Rendering
January 2005	*Men's Style*	metrosexual 闷士 *mènshì*	sulky scholar ~ mensch
October 2005	*Men's Style*	metrosexual 魅力先生 *mèilì xiānshēng*	Mr Charming
October 2006	*Men's Style*	metrosexual 都市美型男 *dūshì měi xíngnán* 杰尼斯型男 *Jiénísī xíngnán*	metropolitan beauty model male Johnny's model male

At the beginning of 2005, the just-launched *Men's Style* took the term in quite a different direction. Editor Wang Yipeng decided to take on the 'exquisite' connotations of the previous Chinese renderings of the term metrosexual, and in

a closely argued editorial rejecting the 'jade male – exquisite' label as too femi-
nised, he coined a completely new term of his own, *mènshì*, which when
expanded translates literally as 'sulky gentry' (*mènsāo shēnshì*). The first part of
this term was justified as an approximation – albeit very partial – of the sound of
'me(tro)' and as referencing the 'sulkiness' (sense of superiority, individuality) of
the fashion-conscious male; with the 'gentry' element referencing the 'adequate
income and taste' of the traditional Chinese elite; the term as a whole also perhaps
recalling the Yiddish term for a 'real man' *mensch*. Despite this confident
opening, the magazine did not take up the term itself, replacing it with its own
title *Mèilì Xiānshēng* 'Charming Gentleman', and following the metrosexual
theme throughout the year, choosing a monthly 'charming gentleman' with
models ranging from the slighter build and more boyish types like Leica model
Song Ning, Taiwanese popstar Jed Lee/Li Xueqing, and hot young mainland actor
Liu Ye; through the more mature masculine types such as self-proclaimed
supermodel Hu Bing, Hongkong actor Francis Ng and martial arts star Zhen
Zidan; with popular actors/clothes-horses Taiwanese-Japanese Takeshi Kaneshiro/
Jin Chengwu and even the English Jude Law coming somewhere in between.

Leaping almost a full year ahead, we come back to where we started with the
Hero talent competition, proclaimed by *Men's Style* as the 'coming of the metrosexual'. The magazine has now reverted to one of the earlier mentioned terms,
dūshì mĕixíngnán 'metropolitan beauty model man', which is perhaps the least
loaded in terms of gender connotations; but the competitors to which it is applied
are mostly much younger than the earlier models, around twenty years of age on
average, and are specifically identified by a feature on the competition as belonging to the *Jiénísī xíngnán* or 'Johnny's Men' type of image. This term refers to the
Japanese talent agency *Johnny's*, whose most famous product is popstar/actor
Kimura Takuya, and which promotes men of a type described by the magazine as
having a 'frail, slight, physique' and being 'pure as a virgin, gentle as Venus'.

This brief overview of the rendering of 'metrosexual' into Chinese raises some
interesting questions. The most obvious one is that despite the lack of a direct
translation of the '–sexual' element of 'metrosexual', questions of gender identity
are never far from the surface in the process of adaptation and use of this label.
In order to understand the meaning of these changes, and why the term was taken
up in the first place, we need to go back to the socio-economic context of mainland China in the early 2000s and understand the conditions that opened up a
space for the adoption of this foreign concept in the mainland market.

The rise of men's magazines in China: social and economic background

The men's magazine, defined here as a glossy magazine mainly directed towards
male consumers and with generally lifestyle-related content, has made only a
relatively recent appearance in the People's Republic of China. *T.O.M.* (The
Outlook Magazine), the published offshoot of the T.O.M website set up by Hong

Kong tycoon Li Kashing, was launched on the mainland market in early 2002; the international staple *Men's Health* started its Chinese edition at the beginning of 2003; the locally devised *MENBOX* started in mid-2003, and its competitor *Men's Style* came onto the market in early 2004.

The economic and social conditions that have made such magazines viable are also fairly recent. Although China has been 'opening up to the West' and developing 'socialism with Chinese characteristics' since the late 1970s, it is only since the mid-1990s, with the economy growing at more than 10 per cent a year, that the urban population has begun to see the real benefits of increased prosperity. So for urban professionals, who make up a tiny proportion of the overall population, but given China's huge population amount to a large and viable market, there is now both the money to spend and an increasing range of products to spend it on: real estate, cars, fashion, food, travel – the staples of the lifestyle magazine.

The appearance of such magazines was no doubt preceded by market research. This can be seen very clearly in the case of *T.O.M / The Outlook Magazine*, pitched towards the top end of the market, with its target readership the very specific and no doubt lucrative one of 'successful male business executives'. The case of the more broadly aimed *Men's Health* is more complex and interesting, particularly since there are many different editions of this title designed specifically for different countries. The original American version of *Men's Health* is aimed at a readership that is large but presumably reasonably well-defined in marketing terms: 'today's educated and active men'. When a Singaporean edition of *Men's Health* was launched in 2003, the target market was very similar: 'the sophisticated and active man'. It seems clear that in the original Western setting of the USA, or the highly westernised country of Singapore, or the assumed to be highly westernised class of Chinese 'successful male business executives' at whom *T.O.M.* is aimed, the existence of these markets, and thus the motivation for buying the magazine, could be almost taken for granted.

However when in the same year a Chinese edition of *Men's Health* was launched, the Chinese editor obviously felt that rather more 'semiotic work' needed to be done in order to justify its existence and actively create a market for itself. The editor, identified by a curiously un-*Men's Health*-like photo and by the snappy nickname *Shou Ma* 'Thin Horse', starts with the obvious facts about the mature man's social identity as defined by his *zhèng(jiàn)* or identification cards (in Chinese all the types of ID quoted below end with this element *zhèng*):

> Once a man's reached 30, he's basically got the following types of certificate: ID card, educational record, work ID, marriage certificate, driver's license, club member's cards. And these are often asked to be shown, made copies of, filed, and of course may also be cancelled: from different points of view and at different times, they define and describe the holder.

He then extends the image to take in an area not normally regarded as part of someone's identity, but which is ostensibly the main business of his magazine – health:

> In daily experience the 'head of the household' often deliberately omits one important type of certificate – a health certificate. Some people use a very significant phrase for it: health passport. Most of the time this passport is a mere formality.

Moving on, the editor begins to 'leverage' – using an appropriate marketing metaphor – the potentially fatal gap between the pressure of 'public opinion' and the realities of 'men's health':

> In public opinion, the name of man is in itself a kind of permit. As time goes by, men become so dizzy with success that they ignore a major fact: they don't in fact possess this permit, and the false power passed on to them by public opinion only covers up their inner fear and unease. To put it simply, men's fear and sense of infallibility makes them turn down the health passport. Subconsciously their fear is still being 'extended': as soon as the passport is granted, they have to go for a visa, and men feel that a visa isn't just a hassle, it's humiliating. Surely the word *Man* is already *certified*, and it's a lifelong visa!

By the time we reach the end of this harangue, it would be an extremely secure man indeed who could reject its arguments out of hand: 'After their power has been totally withdrawn, and there's no more clamour, and material desires have weakened, as far as men are concerned, the last card that's left to them is their own health.'

What this goes to show is that it is not enough simply for the economic conditions of disposable income to be present: there needs to be a social value attached to the practice of consumption that will justify it in the eyes of its practitioners, and of course of the wider society. In going on to examine the two locally initiated magazines, *MENBOX* and *Men's Style*, we will see that they have to work even harder to create their market, and that they do so by taking over a convenient label from the West, the 'metrosexual', which as we saw above combines consumer status and sexual identity – there's more than one kind of social engineering going on here! – but that in borrowing the term, they significantly adapt it to local contexts and local needs.

Adopting and adapting a foreign identity label: the 'metrosexual'

The term 'metrosexual' was originally coined by gay British social commentator Mark Simpson in 1994 to reflect a very specific phenomenon: that of straight men adopting aspects of gay fashion as well as a concern with beauty-care traditionally associated with women. The term was taken up in China almost exactly a decade later, and very quickly became one of the latest buzz words. According to one editor of a Chinese men's magazine writing in 2005 'in the summer just passed [i.e. mid-2004], paying attention to these new urban males was the main game of many magazines'. Why has this label proved such an attractive one in the relatively new market of men's magazines in China?

We can begin to explore this question by looking in more detail at the original and adapted definitions of the term. This is how Simpson originally introduced the term 'metrosexual' in 1994, in the context of men's magazines in the United Kingdom and the United States whose description transfers almost exactly to the China of ten years later:

> The promotion of metrosexuality was left to the men's style press, magazines such as *The Face, GQ, Esquire, Arena* and *FHM*, the new media which took off in the Eighties and is still growing. They filled their magazines with images of narcissistic young men sporting fashionable clothes and accessories. And they persuaded other young men to study them with a mixture of envy and desire. Some people said unkind things. American *GQ*, for example, was popularly dubbed 'Gay Quarterly'. Little wonder all these magazines, with the possible exception of *The Face*, address their metrosexual readership as if none of them were homosexual or even bisexual.
>
> (*Mark Simpson, 'Here Come the Mirror Men',* The Independent,
> *November 15, 1994*)

A more formal definition was given in a 2002 piece by the same writer:

> The typical metrosexual is a young man with money to spend, living in or within easy reach of a metropolis — because that's where all the best shops, clubs, gyms and hairdressers are. He might be officially gay, straight or bisexual, but this is utterly immaterial because he has clearly taken himself as his own love object and pleasure as his sexual preference. Particular professions, such as modelling, waiting tables, media, pop music and, nowadays, sport, seem to attract them but, truth be told, like male vanity products and herpes, they're pretty much everywhere.
>
> (*Mark Simpson, 'Meet the Metrosexual,'* Salon.com, *July 22, 2002*)

When this definition is transposed to a Chinese context, we can note some very interesting changes. *MENBOX* senior editor Yang Lin, in her *From the Editor* column, makes some highly significant modifications to Simpson's 2002 definition:

> Famous author Mark Simpson coined a new noun 'new urban male' – metrosexual, they're *a nucleus of 25 to 40 year olds* who love fashion, beauty-care, *and have received a good education*. They live in big cities, because big cities provide the best eating and entertainment venues, including boutiques, bars, gyms, beauty salons etc. They *love life, beautiful women, games, risk-taking, enjoyment, cars, having fun …*
>
> (MENBOX, *Issue 171, 2005, changes highlighted in italics*)

Basically what Yang Lin's additions do is recast the notion of metrosexual into something much more like the traditional Chinese *shēnshì* or 'gentry'. We will come back to this term in a minute, but for the time being, we can note the stress on 'education' *jiàoyù*, which in spoken Chinese is commonly referred to using the broader term *wénhuà* 'culture'; on the fact that the age range is more specifically delimited, perhaps to fit with the pre-married rather than married age range; and the fact that there is no mention of what to a Chinese readership would come across as socially demeaning service professions such as 'modelling' or 'waiting tables'. The Chinese 'metrosexual' is quite obviously being recast as an updated form of 'yuppie' (Chinese *yǎpíshì* 雅皮士 – this earlier term also includes the element *shì* 士 'gentry'), in the term used by Yang Lin, *chéngshì xīn nánrén* 'new urban male'.

Moving on to another men's magazine, the more recent arrival on the scene, *Men's Style*, we find the editor here very self-consciously playing with both traditional Chinese and borrowed Western concepts and social identities:

> The term <u>metrosexual</u> invented by the English is generally translated *dūshì yùnán* [metropolitan exquisite], referring to straight men who like shopping, are crazy about fashion, and have highly developed tastes. Calling someone an 'exquisite' implies that they lack masculine strength – that's roughly my intuitive impression – as though men should all be rugged, and so I think it's better to call <u>metrosexuals</u> *mènshì*. The word *mèn* can be explained as a phonetic rendering of <u>metrosexual,</u> and at the same time understood as implying how sulky (*mènsāo*) fashion-loving metrosexuals tend to be. The word *shì* ['scholar, gentry'] can be used to emphasise the group included under this term: those with an adequate income and sense of taste who can correctly spend their ever-increasing spare <u>money</u>.
>
> (*Wang Yipeng,* Men's Style, *4 January 2005*)

Executive editor-in-chief Wang Yipeng develops an argument for the social value of his magazine, and therefore the motivation for his readers to buy it, based squarely on a close linguistic analysis of the term 'metrosexual' that defines a new social class. First he cites its most common rendering as *dūshì yùnán*, 'metropolitan dandy'. He takes exception to the term *yùnán*, literally 'jade male', as carrying connotations of femininity which he believes are unsuitable for the type of masculinity he is promoting in his magazine, one in which masculine strength and cultivated tastes are not contradictory. He then boldly coins a new term of his own, *mènshì*, and gives some very sophisticated arguments for this choice.

The first half of the term is justified first as a 'sound rendering', something to which Chinese very easily lends itself (the fact that it is only the beginnings of *mèn* and *metro* that are similar is largely determined by the limited possible combinations of sounds in Mandarin). Something the language also lends itself to is the choice from a range of meaningful elements with similar sounds, and Wang Yipeng here paradoxically chooses an element with an *un*favourable connotation, *mèn,* standing for *mènsāo* 'sulky' which, according to Dr Bruce Doar of the University of Sydney, dates back to the anti-establishment heroes of the traditional novel *Shuǐhǔzhuàn* 'The Water Margin', and refers here to 'a self-assertive loner who has inner qualities reflected by his cool demeanour' (personal communication) – the image that comes to mind is that superior sneer on the face of a fashion model who knows he's far better looking and better dressed than anyone around him! The second half, *shì*, is the old term for the most highly regarded class in imperial China, the *shēnshì* or scholar-official, the traditional repository of cultivation and learning and at the same time belonging to a kind of landed gentry, a fitting precedent for the 'adequate income and … taste' of the modern metrosexual. The term as a whole, *mènshì*, may also recall the Yiddish term of approval for a 'real man', *mensch*, fitting in with Wang's project to 'remasculinise' the *yùnán* or 'exquisite'.

So both magazines adapt the metrosexual label in order to define their ideal reader, and in doing so, they unashamedly take a very directive role in actually *creating* an ideal reader. This social role is explained by the editor of *Men's Style* in another editorial on the purpose of his magazine which is to help men create for themselves a 'self-confident' identity covering everything from clothes and cleanliness to personal interaction:

> *Men's Style* hopes to become a 'dummy' (*shǎguā*) handbook for the working man in dressing and spending – not an easy task. But we're making an effort, at least in this issue, which looks a bit more 'dummy' than the previous issue. Our rationale is as simple as this: if after reading our magazine, a reader can dress according to the recommendations in it and gain self-confidence, then we've succeeded. … The article 'General and not so general knowledge about shirts' provides everyone with 15 principles for wearing shirts, and tells you when and where to break out of the ordinary and wear something individual. … 'The way to successfully manage personal interactions' is aimed at encouraging our readers to be more proactive in personal interactions. In everything it's the beginning that's hard, so daring to say the first thing in a personal interaction is halfway to success.
>
> (Men's Style, *6 March 2005*)

The *Men's Style* editor summed up this aim more colloquially when I interviewed him about his magazine in Beijing in June 2006: 'we're here to give men more cultural ways to spend their money'. And when you reflect that such magazines cost around 20 yuan, more than ten times the price of an ordinary newspaper, it is clear that the ideal metrosexual reader of these magazines belongs to a kind of elite defined by income level. In the new China, as in the old West, it is really money that maketh the man, with manners – helped by these magazines – following close behind. As the editor of *MENBOX*, whom I also interviewed in June 2006, explained it: her readers form not so much a *qúntǐ* 'community' as a *quān.zi* 'circle'. This distinction, at least as I interpret it, plays down the notion of a socially stratified, occupationally differentiated community – though there would of course be such aspects to the magazine's readership – in favour of a group of consumers with varying proximity to the 'centre of things'. As the editor went on to elaborate, a small proportion of this *quān.zi* or 'circle' are the highly educated, high-earning *yùnán* 'exquisites' i.e. metrosexuals, and this identity is something that the large proportion of *MENBOX* readers aspire to.

The social reality behind the label

But the social reality behind the glossy exterior is a great deal more complex, and more fraught. The current media environment in mainland China, despite a superfical impression of free-market 'anything goes' pluralism, underneath is still tightly controlled. Where such magazines are completely in line with official government policy is in their desire to encourage consumption. The creation of a socially valued class of consumers under the label of 'metrosexual' fits perfectly with official government policy for China to become a *xiǎokāng shèhuì* 小康社会 or 'moderately well-off society' by 2020. Metrosexuals can be seen as aspirational for the population as a whole, and the emphasis on the good life has of course positive implications for the Chinese economy. Where formerly such a concentration on material affluence would have been seen as characteristic of the *xiǎozī* 小资 or 'petit bourgeois', one of the most socially despised classes in the old socialist China, now in former leader Deng Xiaoping's terms, 'to get rich is glorious', and to consume is equally encouraged.

But an aspirational consumer is not the only social reality hiding behind this label. You will recall that Mark Simpson's original definition of 'metrosexual' – as the name would suggest – included the idea of sexual identity: basically straight men, such as the classic metrosexuals David Beckham or Brad Pitt, adopting aspects of gay fashion and beauty-care. In this original definition, Simpson tended to take an ironic even parodic approach to the issue of sexual orientation, pointing out that the magazines' emphasis on the body beautiful instantly made their readership sexually dubious in the eyes of the wider society; and in his later definition Simpson cheekily dismissed sex altogether on the grounds that the metrosexual 'has clearly taken himself as his own love object and pleasure as his sexual preference'.

The adopted–adapted Chinese metrosexual label also relates to sexual identity, though in a very different way from its original Western use, and in a way that is not admitted, verbally at least, by the magazines. When the official English-language daily newspaper caught up with the development of this new identity in mid-2005, it took a very firm line on the issue of sexual orientation, stating bluntly: 'He's not gay' – perish the thought! – 'He's metrosexual'; and driving home the point even more strongly: 'He may not be your father's idea of a macho man, but nevertheless, he loves women.':

FIGURE 7.1   Magazine 'proper'

He's religious about moisturizer. He knows what colors he looks good in. He knows his Zegna from his Armani. He's not gay. … He's metrosexual. … He goes to hairdressers rather than barbers and avoids using soap because it's too harsh for the skin. A subtle hint of cologne glorifies his body. He drapes himself in a sharp outfit before hitting an evening hotspot. He has a discretionary income to keep up with the latest hairstyles and the right shoes. He's a fan of GQ magazine and not ashamed of it. He may not be your father's idea of a macho man, but nevertheless, he loves women.

(*A new breed of man, the 'metrosexual',* China Daily, *12 May 2005*)

However a quick look at the men's magazines quoted from above tells a very different story. When you hand over your 20 yuan to the news-stall seller to buy a copy of *MENBOX* or *Men's Style*, the magazine 'proper' is not all you receive. What you get, carefully packaged together in a plastic bag, are *two* magazines, the *zhŭkān* 主刊 or 'main issue', which concentrates on the accoutrements of the metrosexual existence: clothes, accessories, lifestyles, and so on; and a thinner *fùkān* 副刊 or 'supplement' – the magazine 'improper' if you like – which is full of glossy pictures of more or less naked men! (Figures 7.1 and 7.2.)

What is going on here? Well, for a start, these developments do not mean that 'ideological correctness' has completely disappeared. According to the editor of *MENBOX*, the magazine, both main issue and supplement, come under the eye of

FIGURE 7.2   Magazine 'improper'

an official 'censor' around twice a year. Given the stress on the need – indeed the virtue – of making money in contemporary China, the censor is obviously willing to countenance the presence of homoerotic images, particularly in the supplement, as long as there is no direct mention of gay identity, an issue which is still very sensitive in China. And there are of course restrictions on the nature of the images shown in these supplements – no full nudity, models 'artistically' posed, only ever single figures in any one image, and so on. If we track the changes in images through different issues of the magazine, they veer from the highly erotic 'flesh shots' to the mildly sexual 'clothes shots', no doubt in response to pressure from these occasional bouts of what in Chinese is called *jiāndū* 监督 or 'supervision'.

   In the 'open' market economy of the contemporary Chinese media, as opposed to the more 'closed' socialist command economy of the previous media system, it is the commercial imperative, in terms of both *readership* and *advertising* that largely determines content. During the period being studied here, mainly 2003–2006 (*MENBOX* actually ceased publication in mid-2006 for financial reasons), the two locally launched magazines chose different strategies in relation to these two sources of income. With its more homoerotic images, *MENBOX* depended more largely on sales, which according to the editor peaked at about 10,000 per monthly issue, a very respectable number given the relatively high price of the magazine in the local market; but as a side-effect of the more 'daring' content, advertisers – except for underwear companies! – tended to shy away from it. The case of *Men's Style* was exactly the opposite: with less homoerotic images, it gained a much greater proportion of its income from advertising, of which it carries a much wider range. The *Men's Style* editor described his magazine to me as *zhōngxìng* 中性, literally 'middle sex' – i.e. neutral or androgynous; and characterised its readership as 50 per cent gay men, 35 per cent (presumably straight) women, and interestingly enough, 10–15 per cent straight men. The magazine needs to keep its gay readership, since they make up half of sales, but can't risk turning off its other readers, or more importantly its advertisers, by containing images that are too openly homoerotic. Starting from 2005, however, it initiated what seems like an attempt to get the best of both worlds, by including with each issue a video compact disc with about an hour's worth of video of the 'fashion' shots being done – in most of these the models start off clothed, but very soon lose most of their covering.

Overall, comparing what can be read and what can be viewed, the main issue and the supplement of these magazines seem to operate in two separate universes. And so we come to the paradox that, despite the official Chinese media's loud protests to the contrary, the Chinese metrosexual as defined by these magazines is to most intents and purposes gay: almost the exact opposite of the way the term was originally applied by Mark Simpson. Simpson saw the direction of influence as operating from a certain group of gay men, identified as leaders and makers of fashion trends, out to a certain segment of straight men. For these magazines, the direction of influence is in the first instance stemming from the ultra-modern West, and then to the young urban male with the requisite disposable income who *as likely as not is gay*. Of course these magazines are not trying to promote a specifically *gay identity* – even if the political and ideological situation in contemporary China allowed such a thing – they are catering for a particular market, whose significantly gay identity is, as it were, sneaked past the censors in the perfectly respectable guise of a metrosexual.

Reworking a local identity label: the Chinese *Men's Health* and 'men's looks'

Another perspective on the adaptation of this Western identity concept to a Chinese context can be seen in the gradually increasing 'localisation' of the international staple *Men's Health*. We saw earlier that when the Chinese edition of *Men's Health* was launched in 2003, it went to some trouble to justify its existence and therefore create a market of people willing to buy it, and this process of self-justification and market creation was a continuing one. For its first twelve months, the Chinese *Men's Health*, renamed *Shíshàng Jiànkāng* or 'Fashionable Health', looked outwardly very like its American counterpart, with most of the visual content directly borrowed and much of its verbal content obviously translated directly from that source. Just after the beginning of its second year,

FIGURE 7.3   Unusual suspect

however, it suddenly took quite a different direction, with the cover featuring hot – in Chinese *hóng* or 'red' – young, but not particularly muscular actor Liu Ye, followed over that year not just by the kinds of figures you might expect as cover types, such as footballers Zheng Zhi and Liu Yunfei, and model Hu Bing, but also by public figures like entrepreneur Zhang Chaoyang, founder of the successful Sohu search engine (Figures 7.3 and 7.4.). In a retrospective article at the end of 2004, the magazine described what it was doing:

> In 2004, *Men's Health* invited many famous male stars to be photographed as topless models: this was a first for the Chinese media. To keen appreciation and wild abuse, to support and questioning, the cover of every issue became a hot topic on the web.
>
> (Men's Health, *December 2004: 54*)

But it was not just the fact that the men were topless – which although completely normal for the American *Men's Health*, and even for foreign models on the cover of the Chinese *Men's Health*, was obviously shocking when using Chinese men – it was the unconventional choice of subjects. The magazine went on to call on Marx for support:

FIGURE 7.4 Usual suspects

> Marx said 'A person is the sum of their social relationships', and reflecting this philosophy of human nature, our 'men's looks' will certainly not just be the F4 [Taiwanese boyband] kind of handsome men. They have their own identities: entrepreneur, athlete, actor, singer, model; they have their own possessions: different genders, different orientations, different professions, different tastes …

The above quotation uses the term 'men's looks', in Chinese *nánsè*, a new and very significant coinage. *Sè* is a very old concept in Chinese: literally 'colour', it also covers physical appearance, physical attractiveness, and sex – as we saw in Chapter 1, Confucius famously remarked 'I have never met anyone who was more interested in virtue than in looks'. However, when referring to a specific gender, the usual term is *nǔsè*, quaintly translated by my dictionary as 'women's charms', showing that physical attractiveness was traditionally seen in China as a women's prerogative. So *nánsè* 'men's looks' is not only a new term, it is a new concept of masculinity for China – as the article puts it, a 'revolution in gender roles'.

In explaining what it means by 'men's looks', the article carries out a short historical analysis which fits well within the sort of social semiotic framework used here:

> Since the existence of written records, it is women's looks that have always been a commodity and an object of consumption for people (mainly men). Men have had power and control of money, so their values have been the values of the whole society, and their aesthetic trends have determined women's aesthetic trends. But the rapid development of socio-economic culture in the present age has also shifted men and women's gender roles. More and more women have begun to have more and more power and money, they have mastered the discourse, and are increasingly influencing social culture and roles.

As the article goes on to explain, these changes, along with the rise of feminism, have brought about a concomitant 'movement for male liberation', and lo and behold – it turns out that the motive force for this is *consumption*:

> Sex becoming a consumer item is no longer something disgraceful: mutual appreciation and pleasure between the sexes is one of the important driving forces of historical development. It's only when men also become a consumer item that the consumption of women will be revealed as equitable, no longer a type of sexual exploitation.

It is under this completely respectable ideological banner that *Men's Health* goes in to fight the good fight:

> The age of men's looks has arrived. Whether it's F4 or male beauty pageants, the boom in male beauty parlours or indeed the male covers of *Men's Health*, they're all doing the same thing: making men's looks into a commodity for people to appreciate, buy, use and consume.

And on this new level playing field, there is no longer any sexual discrimination – all individuals are equal in the new age of the consumer: 'The consumers are men, and they're also women. They set out from their own latitude to find their own goal and direction.'

It's easy to laugh at the crudity of all of this. But it only sounds crude because it's so direct, and it's only direct because social and economic developments that have taken decades in the West are being squeezed into a few years in China. What is clear from the case of this magazine, and the others examined above, is that the popular media in China, just as more obviously the State media, are concerned with putting forward a particular world view. Of course the need to sell copy, both to readers and to advertisers, lies at the bottom of all this discourse. But if we examine the case of foreign magazines being adapted to the local market, and local magazines starting up completely new markets, we can see that along with the encouragement of consumption – indeed inseparable from it – is the creation of new social identities and new social values. And in mainland China, both consumption and culture come under the overall direction of a media system that deliberately sets out to 'mould' its readers into various socially sanctioned roles, at the same time as allowing more problematic and ambiguous identities to be read between the lines.

Cyborg metrosexual

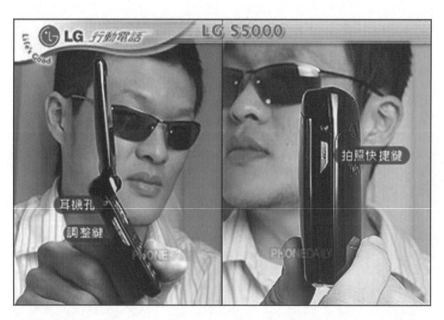

Mafioso metrosexual

8

RECONSTRUCTION VERSUS DECONSTRUCTION

Textual criticism, social semiotics and New Sinology

Introduction: relating text and context – applying a social semiotic framework

In this chapter, we start with similar sorts of analyses to those we saw in the previous chapter, and then go on to discuss the kinds of theoretical concepts needed in examining such verbal and visual 'texts'. As we will see, 'theory' is far from being some sort of optional added extra: it is rather a question of making explicit the kinds of understandings we bring to our analyses, and how we ground them in evidence from the texts. Let's start by looking at two different Chinese advertisements for mobile phones, which play in interestingly different ways on the Chinese 'metrosexual' discussed in the previous chapter, and see what can be revealed here by a *social semiotic* analysis, i.e. one that relates the semiotic *text* to its social *context*.

This first image is very clearly 'Western', both from the appearance of the model and the brand of the phone – Motorola, which has a large presence in China. The model exhibits the sculpted body and casually elegant clothes we expect from this kind of image, plus a blatantly sexualised positioning of hand, phone and crotch which recalls Simpson's crack quoted in the previous chapter about the metrosexual having 'clearly taken himself as his own love object'. The Chinese text adds an interesting play on words: *motuo*, the first two syllables of the Chinese version of the brand name *Motuoluola*, are close to the term *mótè'r* or 'model' thus neatly conflating the model of man and the brand of phone; and the two advertised qualities which play with this abbreviation of the brand name could also equally well apply to both: *Duōzhì* MOTO 'Multi-intelligence Model', and MOTO *Mírén* 'Model Charms People'. The very model of a modern metrosexual, as you might say, quasi-cyborg status and all.

The 'Eastern' advertisement, for the Korean firm LG (Life's Good) which also has a strong Chinese presence, is significantly different and plays on the knowledge of quite a different cultural universe. Back in the early days of mobile phones in China, when they were clunky things almost the size of a walkie-talkie, they were very expensive and so were sported only by gangsters who could afford them on the proceeds of their life of crime and use them to impress both their clients and their victims. Back then these phones were therefore known as *dàgēdà*, literally 'big brother big', one of the terms for a gangster boss. The model in this advertisement, despite the headline attached to it by the newspaper editor, and the slogan which is reportedly being used to market the phone, couldn't be further away from the image of a metrosexual: he is in fact the very model of a modern (Chinese) mafioso, with the aggressively jutting square jaw, the dark glasses, and the phone being held out threateningly, almost as if daring the viewer *not* to buy. The positioning of the phone in relation to the model makes it seem relatively large, and the way he is holding it seems to imply the 'threat' of two new features: being able to save your number if you're foolish enough to ring him, and to take your photo if you're unfortunate enough to run across him.

The analysis I've just done, like that of the taxi-driver conversation in Chapter 1, may seem on the surface merely like culturally informed commonsense, not owing much, if anything, to any theory. In a university context, 'theory' tends to be regarded by many students – and even by some academics – as some sort of superfluous add-on to 'the facts', merely a confusing and difficult jargon obscuring the 'real meaning'. The following quotation, from British classical scholar Peter Green, may be taken as representative of this attitude:

> Like the systems of Freud or Marx, those of the structuralists and their successors can be raided for useful insights; but to adopt any such ideological stance *in toto* puts the free critical intelligence into blinkers, and leaves its owner a mere exponent of whatever creeping theological monadism he may have chosen to embrace.
>
> (*Green 1989: 9*)

Although Green would no doubt resist this claim, in the approach taken here, the 'free critical intelligence' is just as much an 'ideological stance' – a 'theory', if you like – as any other. A *theory* – to draw on the metaphor which is the basis of the original Greek term *theoria* 'contemplation' – is a 'point of view', a way of looking at something. Of course those viewpoints commonly deemed worthy of the explicit title of 'theory' are those which have been set up and argued for as frameworks, and part of that process is defining a technical vocabulary. But *any* point of view, even the most natural-seeming 'commonsense', is a theory, a particular understanding of reality (see Ellis 1993). The obvious advantage of an *explicit* theory is that it can be explicitly critiqued, improved, argued about, rejected, replaced and all the things that academics do; whereas the sort of 'commonsense' that is presented as *not* open to critique is usually hiding some – often conservative – social agenda, which masquerades as 'the facts' precisely because it hopes to escape critique or challenge.

But there *are* no such things as 'pure facts': as the German polymath J.W. von Goethe pointed out almost two centuries ago: *Alles Faktische schon Theorie ist* 'Everything factual is already (part of a) theory' (quoted in Ellis 1993: 127). In other words, as soon as you distinguish, classify, and identify aspects of your reality, which you then recognise as 'facts', you are doing so in accordance with some sort of understanding of what it is you are seeing – in other words, a theory.

The supposedly 'informal' analysis I just went through, like the analyses in previous chapters, is in fact deeply 'informed' by the general theoretical approach known as 'critical discourse analysis' (cf. Fairclough 1995), and more specifically by the subtype of it known as 'social semiotics' (Hodge and Kress 1988; Hodge and Louie 1998). This kind of approach examines the *text*, the semiotic patterning – above including both verbal and visual 'texts' – for evidence of the *context*, the social order. And it is this two-way approach that allows us not just to *describe* the nature of people's meaningful behaviour in terms of the texts they produce – a basic precondition for any type of social semiotic analysis – but also to *explain* why they produce the texts they do. Furthermore it opens up a space for this kind of semiotic analysis – a 'close reading' in the sense of literary theory, or even a type of *kǎozhèng* 考证 'evidential analysis' in terms of the Chinese philological tradition – to link in with the other concerns of Chinese studies such as the historical, political and economic trends which make up the complex weave of the social, as well as the traditions of philosophy, poetics, political economy and historiography that attempt to pick apart the tangled threads of the semiotic.

'Text' and 'context'

What I would argue should be the common ground for all people working in Chinese studies is the notion of *text*. The Latin-derived term 'text' used in English is in origin a metaphor taken from the production of cloth. *Textum* in Latin means 'woven', applied literally first to cloth, as in *textiles*, and then to the physical form of a written document. From this extended meaning was derived the notion of *context*, literally the 'with text', the text physically around the part of the text being focused on, a term that finds its exact equivalent in the Chinese term *shàngxiàwén* 上下文, literally the 'above and below text' (see Halliday 1985: 5). The traditional method of interpreting texts in European scholarship, which became formalised in the seventeenth and eighteenth centuries under the label of *philology* (see von Wilamovitz-Moellendorf 1921/1982), was first to place a particular word, phrase, sentence, etc., in its context, and then use the evidence of the text to draw conclusions about the historical and cultural background from which it derived. A crucial part of this project was to critically examine the text itself for evidence of its own authenticity, to identify possible later additions or interpolations, and to determine what German scholars called the *Urtext*, or original form of the text.

This methodology can be called one of *textual reconstruction*, and along with its historical contemporary, the methodologically comparable Chinese *kǎozhèng* or 'evidential analysis', forms the first strand, to call on our Latin metaphor once again, in the textual tradition of Chinese studies. The ideology implicit in such an approach is summed up in a pithy, if rather caustic, manner by the British translator of a recent edition of the Roman poet Catullus:

> Yeats in his well-known poem *The Scholars*, which might more reasonably be called *The Pedants*, imagines how horrified those 'old, learned, respectable bald heads' would be if they could meet the real Catullus. In fact Catullus would have been far more horrified could he have seen the state of his text at the beginning of the fourteenth century [when a complete manuscript of his poems was rediscovered EMcD], some 1350 years after his death. [D]own the centuries Yeats's despised Scholars have gradually purified the text of Catullus and brought it ever nearer to what its author intended. ... Yeats's poem: amusing as it may be, ... is hardly fair to the Scholars, for despite baldness, respectability, coughing in ink, and wearing out the carpet, it is to them that we owe the text of Catullus; were it not for them there would be no Catullus to read.
>
> (*Lee 1990: ix–xi*)

Such an approach to texts depends very strongly on being able to regard them, in effect, as archaeological records which, once the depredations of time and wear have been cleared away, will 'speak' to us just like their original creator. A similar reconstructional ideology animated evidential analysis in seventeenth and eighteenth century China, as described by Benjamin Elman in his sociological and historical study *From Philosophy to Philology* (Elman 1984), which describes the intellectual project of the so-called *Hànxué* 汉学 or 'Han Learning' scholars in the late Ming and early Qing period, who sought to return to the Han dynasty forms and interpretations of the canonical texts as a better guide to what Confucius had originally meant.

This tradition of textual reconstruction in the West suffered its first major challenge at the hands of anthropologists and ethnographers coming into contact with 'primitive' non-European cultures, by which they meant cultures without writing, in Africa, the Americas, Asia and the Pacific. One of the pioneering figures here was the Polish anthropologist Bronislaw Malinowski, who eventually became Professor of Anthropology at the University of London in the significantly named School of Oriental and African Studies (the following account is adapted from Halliday 1985: 5–6). While still a student, Malinowski was caught in Australia by the outbreak of World War II, and though as an Austrian citizen liable to internment as an enemy alien, he was generously allowed by the Australian Government to pursue his ethnographic fieldwork in the Trobriand Islands off Northeast New Guinea, then under Australian administration. A gifted natural linguist, he quickly became fluent in the local language, gained a comprehensive understanding of the local culture, and transcribed many spoken texts collected from a range of everyday situations. However when it came to analysing the texts he had collected, he found himself at somewhat of a loss.

In the European written text-based tradition, words were assumed to have more or less fixed meanings which could be listed in a dictionary and consulted during the process of interpretation. The meaning of a text, then, at a first rough approximation, could be understood as the combination of the meanings of all the words in it. But such an approach depended on the fact that written texts were already separated from any immediate situation, and thus to a large extent 'created' their own situation. When Malinowski glossed his spoken texts using this method he found they made absolutely no sense to someone who was not familiar with the original situation in which they had been used – which of course included most of his European readers.

Below is an example of a text taken from his fieldwork, glossed by 'giving under each word its nearest English equivalent' in a way very similar to the texts analysed in Chapter 1:

Tasakaulo	*kaymatana*	*yakida;*	
We run	front-wood	ourselves;	
tawoulo	*ovanu;*	*tasivila*	*tagine*
we paddle	in place;	we turn	we see
soda;	*isakaulo*	*ka'u'uya*	
companion ours;	he runs	rear-wood	
oluvieki	*similaveta*	*Pilolu*	
behind	their sea-arm	Pilolu	

(*Malinowski 1923: 300–301 – formatting adapted*)

As Malinowski remarks, '[t]he verbatim English translation of this utterance sounds at first like a riddle or a meaningless jumble of words', and even a listener 'acquainted with the language, but unacquainted with the culture of the natives' would need 'to be informed about the situation in which these words were spoken' and 'to have them placed in their proper setting of the native culture'. So in order to understand this utterance, what was needed, as he argues in terms very close to those put forward in Chapter 1, was not simply 'translating', in the sense of 'inserting ... an English word for a native one', but rather 'a long and not altogether simple process of describing wide fields of custom, of social psychology and of tribal organisation' (pp.301–302).

Having done this, and having grasped the crucial point that this utterance is 'not a mere statement of fact' but rather 'a boast, a piece of self-glorification', something 'very characteristic of the Trobrianders' culture in general' (p.301), we can gain an understanding of the text as summed up by Malinowski in the following 'free commentary or paraphrase':

> A number of natives sit together. One of them, who has just come back from an overseas expedition, gives an account of the sailing and boasts about the superiority of his canoe. He tells his audience how, in crossing the sea-arm of Pilolu (between the Trobriands and the Amphletts), his canoe sailed far ahead of all the others. When nearing their destination, the leading sailors looked back and saw their comrades far behind, still on the sea-arm of Pilolu.
>
> *(Malinowski 1923: 305)*

In characterising the process of explanation he has just carried out, Malinowksi identifies at least two explanatory stages, each of which requires calling on a different conception of *context*. The first stage involves the familiar operation of working out 'the meaning of an expression' by relating it to 'the context of the whole utterance'– in this case 'context' has something close to its historical meaning. But when dealing not with the traditional type of written *text* from which this sense of context derives, but rather with the spoken *utterances* of a non-written language, Malinowski sees that this first stage of explanation needs to be supplemented by another conception of 'context' for which he transforms the traditional term:

> [T]he context of the whole utterance ... becomes only intelligible when it is placed within its *context of situation*, if I may be allowed to coin an expression which indicates on the one hand that the conception of context has to be broadened and on the other that the *situation* in which words are uttered can never be passed over as irrelevant to the linguistic expression.
>
> *(Malinowski 1923: 306, original emphasis)*

Although this may already have seemed sufficiently radical for his readers, Malinowski does not stop there, but goes on to question the whole bedrock of the traditional philological approach to *meaning*, and to show how his new notion of *context of situation* actually subsumes the traditional notion of the linguistic context of the text itself:

> [T]he conception of meaning as being *contained* in an utterance is false and futile. A statement, spoken in real life, is never detached from the situation in which it has been uttered ... utterance and situation are bound up inextricably with each other and the context of situation is indispensible for the understanding of the words. Exactly as in the reality of spoken or written languages, a word without *linguistic context* is a mere figment and stands for nothing by itself, so in the reality of a spoken living tongue, the utterance has no meaning except in the *context of situation*.
>
> *(Malinowski 1923: 307, original emphasis)*

With the notion of 'context' having thus become detached from its original exclusive application to writing, the notion of 'text' was also transformed, and has come in linguistic scholarship to refer not merely to a written document but to spoken utterances as well, on the recognition that spoken language is not formless, but like written language has its own 'texture' or principles of organisation (Hasan 1985: Ch.5). The term 'text' is also now commonly applied beyond linguistics to characterise other semiotic modes like visual image (Kress and van Leeuwen 1990, 1996), sound (van Leeuwen 1999) and so forth. The question for the analyst then becomes, having reworked the notions of text and context, and made both of them much more open-ended categories, how then do we understand the relationship between them?

The first step in this direction was taken by the English linguist J.R. Firth, a colleague of Malinowski's at the University of London, who developed Malinowski's notion of 'context of situation' into a much more rigorous theoretical framework. Firth characterised the context of situation as follows:

- the PARTICIPANTS in the situation ... corresponding ... to what sociologists would regard as the statuses and roles of the participants;
- the ACTION of the participants: what they are doing, including both their VERBAL ACTION and their NON-VERBAL ACTION;
- OTHER RELEVANT FEATURES OF THE SITUATION: the surrounding objects and events, insofar as they have some bearing on what is going on;
- the EFFECTS of the verbal action: what changes were brought about by what the participants in the situation had to say.

(Firth 1956/1968, quoted in modified form in Halliday 1985: 8)

It was one of Firth's students, T.F. Mitchell, who made the first detailed application of this framework in his classic 1958 study 'The Language of Buying and Selling in Cyrenaica' (reprinted in Mitchell 1975), which constituted a pioneering example of discourse analysis within an explicit linguistic framework almost two decades before this became acknowledged as an independent field of study within and beyond linguistics. And it was another of Firth's students, M.A.K. Halliday, who, having in his doctoral research carried out a complete description – phonological, grammatical and lexical – of the language of a text, the early Modern Chinese version of *The Secret History of the Mongols* (Halliday 1959), went on in conjunction with other scholars to characterise the context of situation in a more detailed way through the concept of *registers*, that is, functional varieties of language use in context (Halliday *et al.* 1964; Gregory 1967; Ure 1971).

These scholars argued that the notion of register could most usefully be broken down into three concurrent aspects – in shorthand, the *what*, *who* and *how* of language use:

1   field: *what* is going on – the social processes in which language is involved;
2   tenor: *who* is taking part – the social roles created through language;
3   mode: *how* communication is taking place – the means by which language is being exchanged.

Thus to take the example analysed by Malinowski above of the narrative about canoe racing told by the successful competitor after the fact, the three aspects of the register of this narrative might be summarised as follows:

1   field: a group of men taking part in canoe racing at sea;
2   tenor: fellow tribesmen well known to each other and of roughly equal status;
3   mode: spoken to small group.

Thus the particular features of this situation as reflected in the language (what in Chinese is called the *yǔjìng* or 'language-situation', see below) could be comprehensively explained in terms of this three-part framework: field – the telling of a narrative about an activity of great significance in the society; tenor – told by a member of a group in order to consolidate or even raise his status in that group; and, mode – spoken in a context where the verbal would be emphasised or filled out by other communicative modalities such as facial expression and gesture.

However, even with this more detailed conception of context, the question remained of how the actual forms of language used could be related to the situation. Halliday made the crucial link between language and context here in attempting to map out the grammar, first of Chinese (Halliday 1956) and then of English (Halliday 1961, 1967–1968), not in the traditional approach in terms of its 'structures' or possible combinations, but in terms of its 'systems', or meaningful options. From this point of view, Halliday saw that the wordings of a language, including both its words and structures, could be grouped into three sets which corresponded to three types of meanings:

1   ideational: how language is used to represent experience;
2   interpersonal: how language is used to negotiate social relationships;
3   textual: the organisation of language in context.

Halliday termed these three types of meanings *metafunctions*, that is, generalised abstract functions of language, and showed that the language of every text, every instance of language use, whether spoken or written, needed to be understood as simultaneously expressing these three types of meaning.

Although the notions of register and of metafunction were arrived at independently, it became clear that the two could be systematically related: ideational to field; interpersonal to tenor; and textual to mode. To take the same example from Malinowski analysed above, we can distinguish the wordings of the language by metafunction here in a way which relates them to the three aspects of the context of situation:

1   ideational: specific vocabulary for actions and objects to do with racing canoes at sea, along with the structures indicating relations of cause and effect between them and the actors;

2   interpersonal: systematic contrast between 'us' and 'them', with solidarity created by listeners being encouraged to identify with speaker;

3   textual: the narrator as actor taking himself as the reference point for the place of action, and simultaneously making clear its relation to the place of narration.

Such a model (see Halliday and Hasan 1985 for an accessible introduction) provides a principled way of linking semiotic texts of any kind, not just linguistic, to their social contexts. To summarise the key concepts of this model, it would be useful to set out its basic terminology side by side with its Chinese equivalents (Hu *et al.* 2005), since these tend to be more semantically transparent than the Latin- and Greek-derived English originals. The semiotic aspect of the theory recognises that any semiotic system (*fúhào xìtŏng* 符号系统 'sign system') or system of meaning, can be analysed according to the three generalised *metafunctions* (*yuángōngnéng* 元功能 'fundamental function') of *ideational* (*gàiniàn* 概念 'concept'), *interpersonal* (*rénjì* 人际 'human relation'), and *textual* (*yŭpiān* 语篇 'text'). The social aspect of the theory takes explicit account of the relationship between the *text* (*yŭpiān* 语篇, literally 'language-text'), or unified instance of meaning-making, and the social *context* (*yŭjìng* 语境 'language-environment') from which it emerges, and in which it functions, through the concept of *register* (*yŭyù* 语域 'language-region') which shows the three simultaneous variables of *field* (*yŭchăng* 语场 'language-ground'), *tenor* (*yŭzhĭ* 语旨 'language-aim') and *mode* (*yŭshì* 语式 'language style').

Once this broad model of text and context was opened up, the first major publication being Halliday's 1978 study with its significant title *Language as Social Semiotic*, it wasn't long before this theoretical understanding of the relationship between text and context was being applied to other semiotic systems. Some of the earliest scholars to take up this challenge were two academics then resident in Australia, Bob Hodge and Gunther Kress, first in their 1979 work, *Language as Ideology* (Kress and Hodge 1979), and then in a 1988 work which was indeed called *Social Semiotics* (Hodge and Kress 1988). These books dealt with a number of verbal texts, not from an exclusively linguistic point of view, but extending their analytical gaze out to the social and ideological currents of the culture which produced them. In a later collaboration with Theo van Leeuwen, Kress went on to extend the purview of social semiotics to visual texts as well in a 1996 work whose title reflects its linguistic derivation, *Reading Images – the Grammar of Visual Design* (Kress and van Leeuwen 1996); while Hodge further collaborated with a Chinese studies colleague, Kam Louie, on *The Politics of Chinese Language and Culture* (Hodge and Louie 1998, already referred to in Chapter 4 above; see further discussion below) which, despite the title, examines not just linguistic texts but also visual and filmic ones.

From this broader point of view, the metaphor embodied in the traditional Chinese term for 'text', 文 *wén*, might perhaps serve us better than its Latin-derived equivalent 'text'. *Wén* referred originally to visual 'pattern, mark', later generalised to written markings or 'script', then 'language'; and from there to a number of semiotic systems that are mainly or significantly expressed through language, whose names in modern Chinese, borrowed via Japanese, contain the term *wén*, such as *wénxué* 文学 'literature' and *wénhuà* 文化 'culture' (see Louie 2002 for a fascinating study of its wider cultural implications in traditional China, with *wén* as 'cultural attainment' as opposed to *wǔ* 武 as 'martial valour', or as we might say here, for those whose power derived from semiotic as opposed to material action). The ordinary Chinese term for the humanities or human sciences, *rénwén kēxué* 人文科学, neatly includes both the social – *rén* 'people', and the semiotic – *wén* 'pattern', and a social semiotic approach, as hinted by Hodge and Louie in their application of the model to Chinese (Hodge and Louie 1998: 8), may therefore find itself more readily accepted in Chinese academic contexts.

Metatheoretical stocktaking: different approaches to text in Chinese studies

We now need to consider how such a social semiotic approach might fit into Chinese studies as currently constituted. So far we have identified two main 'strands' in approaches to texts in Chinese studies: the *reconstructional* approach, which attempts to recover the original form of the author's text, and – more problematically – the author's 'intention' or 'original meaning'; and what we might term the *deconstructional* approach which takes the text apart for evidence of the social and ideological pressures that produced it. These two approaches may seem to be contradictory, and indeed tend to be used by different groups of scholars within Chinese studies who, just as in the example of the European classi-cists quoted above, tend to be dismissive of or even hostile to each other's concerns.

A more useful way of understanding this distinction, and one which has the potential to reconcile these two approaches, has been put forward by American sinologist Chad Hansen in the context of his reinterpretation of Mohist texts on logic. Hansen contrasts an imagined extreme which he calls the 'spiritualist' method of gaining access to the past – as represented in the deliberately absurd scenario of a séance where the spirit of a dead author talks through a medium – with a more realistic 'interpretative' method which 'deals directly with a text, not a mind' (Hansen 1983: 2). Hansen goes on to characterise this latter method in a way very similar to the approach to theory taken above, using the context of working on texts such as the *Analects* of Confucius:

> An interpretation … is a theory. Like other scientific theories, we judge the interpretation by how well it fits the facts to be explained. There is no exhaustive and definitive criteria of the 'best fit' of a theory to a body of

data. ... The test of an interpretative theory ... is not a matter of comparing that theory with either the 'original' or the psychological facts (what
Confucius actually believed). We have no access to either fact *except* via
the theories.

(*Hansen 1983: 6*)

When you look closely at how the 'reconstructionist' Lee describes the way he
actually deals with texts, it fits very well with this interpretative characterisation.
And although textual deconstructionists normally deal with contemporary texts
that do not require the same 'archaeological' work to be carried out before they
can be interpreted, they can also benefit from the rigorous methodology of reconstructional textual criticism in understanding the internal logic of a text as a
semiotic artefact. (The term 'textual criticism' here refers to the process of comparing different transmitted versions of a text, identifying and judging variant
readings, and so on; it is not equivalent to the more recent use of this term in
literary theory which refers to something more like the 'close reading' mentioned
earlier.)

So if it is the text that provides the site where different sorts of interpretative
methodologies in Chinese studies can meet on relatively common ground, how
can we characterise those methodologies in ways that make them complementary,
not contradictory, approaches? In this regard, a mixture of object lesson and cau-
tionary tale is provided by the first extended attempt to apply the methodologies
of critical discourse analysis, and specifically social semiotics, to the field of
Chinese studies: Bob Hodge and Kam Louie's *The Politics of Chinese Language
and Culture* (Hodge and Louie 1998).

Hodge and Louie start their book, just as I started this chapter, with an examination of two visual texts, in their case the very obviously Chinese image of a
dragon, in two different forms: the first embroidered on a silk robe from the Qing
dynasty and intended for the Imperial Court; the other reproduced on a cheap
coffee mug (Hodge and Louie 1998: 4–5). The authors use their analysis of these
two images to raise some very pertinent issues about the priorities of traditional
Chinese studies or sinology and how well those priorities meet the needs of
current-day students and researchers of Chinese and China. They go on to carry
out some very insightful interpretations of Chinese texts – visual, verbal (popular
as well as literary) and filmic – using an interpretative practice they call 'symptomatic reading', which functions to 'uncover suppressed truths or insinuate new
meanings or both' (Hodge and Louie 1998: 18).

To give an idea of their approach, I will briefly examine their second chapter,
'Reading Style: Interacting the Chinese way', which juxtaposes the bare,
unproblematic interpersonal encounters characteristic of many Chinese language textbooks (as we saw in Chapter 2) with the highly nuanced treatment in
literary texts of this sensitive area of human interaction. To exemplify this area
of social meaning, they examine extracts from the 1980s novels of writer Ah
Cheng, which 'provide suggestive insights into style as social practice, and the

role that judgments on style play in everyday social life' (Hodge and Louie 1998: 25).

I have singled out this particular chapter because it is, in the main, an exemplary instance of the benefits of a social semiotic analysis, but also a subtle warning of some of its dangers. The analysis of Ah Cheng's novel *Chess King* is masterly in its careful coordination of the details of a semiotic close reading with a well-argued social contextualisation of the fraught nature of the meeting and greeting between the hero, the 'Chess King' Wang Yisheng and the socially superior but gaffe-prone Ni Bin. However, Hodge and Louie make a few 'gaffes' of their own that point to some of the dangers of a social semiotic approach for Chinese studies and more generally. These hinge on their analyses of the differences between Northern and Southern Mandarin as represented by the speech of Wang Yisheng and Ni Bin respectively.

Hodge and Louie accurately *describe* as characteristic of southern dialects of Mandarin Ni Bin's use of the degree marker *mán* 蛮 'very' as in *mán hǎo* 蛮好 'very good'. However when they then go to *explain* this in terms of the supposed 'original' meaning of 蛮 *mán* as '"barbaric", "wild", or "southern"' (Hodge and Louie 1998: 32), they go beyond what the linguistic evidence can support. In fact, such 'degree markers' across languages tend to be semantically bleached versions of descriptive words expressive of high degree – compare a similar metaphorical use of *wild* as a colloquial term of approval in some dialects of English. It is unnecessary to go any further than this widely recognised tendency in explaining the *linguistic* meaning of this term as a grammaticalised use of *mán* 'wild'. In this use it is exactly comparable to its standard equivalent *hěn* 很 'very', derived from *hěn* 狠 'fierce'; or the northern variant *tǐng* 挺 'very', from 挺 *tǐng* 'upright'; or for that matter its standard English equivalent *very*, from medieval English via French *verray* 'true'. The fact that the choice of character used to write *mán* implicates southernness or barbarism may well be *ideologically* significant at some level (cf. the characters for the traditional 'barbarians' surrounding the Chinese heartland, of which *mán* 蛮 is one, all of which include semantic elements related to animals or insects); but this does not mean that hearers and users of this expression – including the author Ah Cheng – will necessarily think 'wild southerner' whenever someone uses it.

This kind of argumentation reveals the ideological logic identified in Chapter 4 as 'character fetishisation': that is, 'an inordinate status given to Chinese characters in the interpretation of Chinese language, thought and culture'. As I pointed out in one of the few reviews of *The Politics of Chinese Language and Culture* from a linguist's viewpoint (McDonald 2000), in carrying out such analyses Hodge and Louie were in effect hoist by their own petard, openly critiquing the notion that Chinese characters represent the ultimate reality of the Chinese language, but in their own analyses again and again treating the characters as the basic 'semantic primes' according to which all varieties of the language can be understood. A similar kind of 'character fetishisation' rhetoric also shows up in their characterisation of the northern features of Wang Yisheng's speech, revealing itself this time in a passing and what seems almost subconscious manner.

Hodge and Louie again correctly note the significance of Wang's 'reversion' to his northern childhood speech at the end of the novel where he refers to himself as *ér* 儿 'son' rather than using the more normal adult pronoun 我 *wǒ* 'I', and to his mother as *mā* 妈 'mum'. However in the very next breath they go on to make a rather confused analysis of Wang's use of *érhuà* 儿化 or 'rhotacisation', that feature of many northern accents that 'appends' an 'r'-sound to the end of many words, the 'r' being written with the same character 儿 used for *ér* 'son'. First they quote the relevant passage with an interestingly emphasised transcription:

> 'Mum, I've understood now. People have got to have something before they can really live. Mum …'
>
> [*Ma, er jintian mingbai shier le, ren hai yao you dianer dongxi, cai jiao huozhe, ma …*]
>
> > (*Hodge and Louie 1998: 33*)

Next they analyse the passage in a way that seems to confuse two different levels of analysis:

> In this context we can see the significance of his use of the northern *er*, which we have underlined. This marks the language as dialect, the more prestigious northern dialect. But in this instance its use is associated with the low-status Wang, as he remembers his own lowly origins and the wisdom of his low-status mother.
>
> > (*Hodge and Louie 1998: 33–34*)

Hodge and Louie's social exegesis here is unexceptionable. But their framing phrase *in this context* takes on a strange ambiguity. On the one hand, a 'straight' or 'surface' reading would have it referring simply to the social context; on the other hand, a 'deep' or 'symptomatic' reading – in Hodge and Louie's own terms – would see it as referring to a supposed comparability between Wang's use of *ér* 'son' to refer to himself and his use of *érhuà* as reflecting his northern origins, since both *ér*'s are written with the same character.

Part of the problem here is the same as identified previously in the case of *mán*: it is not necessarily the case that a lexical and a grammatical use of a word, even if the two can be seen to be historically or *diachronically* related, are therefore contemporaneously or *synchronically* comparable, to call on another one of Saussure's complementarities (1916/1957: 81). *Mán* 'wild' and *mán* 'very' are two completely different words in the contemporary language, and so too are *ér* (*zi*) 'son' and (*e*)*r* '[word ending]'. (Hodge and Louie subsequently (p. 36) fall into another similar confusion in relation to the word ending *zi*, historically derived in a similar way from *zǐ* 'son'.) But in the second case, we do not even have the identity of pronunciation we saw in the *mán* 'wild'/*mán* 'very' case. The words Hodge and Louie write as *shier* 'matter' and *dianer* 'bit', exactly transcribing the pronunciation in isolation of the separate characters 事儿，点儿, are not in fact pronounced that way at all: *shì* plus *ér* is *shèr* (pronounced to rhyme with American English *fir*), i.e. with a different main vowel from its 'r-less' variant *shì*, and *diǎn* plus *ér* is *diǎr* (rhyming with American English *tar*), with a different variant of the 'a' vowel as well as lacking the nasal ending of its 'r-less' variant *diǎn* (rhyming with *den*). The only feature that joins them is their written form; and Hodge and Louie's analysis thus, casually and, it seems, almost by accident, reinforces the ideological primacy of the character-based written form as against the spoken language.

But it would be unfair to completely blame Hodge and Louie for falling into this trap, since not only is this discursive practice common among sinologists across the whole range of disciplines in Chinese studies, as we saw in the discussion of character fetishisation in Chapter 4, but because the original English social semiotics of Hodge and Kress and van Leeuwen unwittingly provides a model for a similar blurring between the linguistic and the ideological in analysing texts. The nature of the analytical method developed in social semiotics works by a kind of analogy: taking over and adapting originally linguistic terms and concepts, but detaching them from their direct connection with the analysis of linguistic form.

A good example of this is the formulation for characterising real-world events, where a distinction is made among others between 'transactive', in which 'the action is seen as passing from the *actor* across to the *affected*', and 'non-transactive', which is 'vague about precise causal and affected status' (Kress and Hodge 1979/1993: 8). Although this distinction is avowedly based on the traditional grammatical distinction between 'transitive' and 'intransitive' verbs, Hodge and Kress make it quite clear that the two sets of terms are not equivalent:

> Transitive and intransitive are labels for structures with a particular form; transactive and non-transactive are labels for structures with a particular meaning ... one is about meaning, semantics, the other is about surface form, order. The two are rarely in a one-for-one relation.
>
> (*Kress and Hodge 1979/1993: 8–9*)

This argumentation suffers from a number of problems. First it seems to assume that distinctions like 'transitive' and 'intransitive' are somehow meaningless, mere 'labels' for differences in 'surface form', dead metaphors which can only be revived by separating them from their direct relationship to grammatical form (the original metaphor here derives from the Greek *diábasis* 'passing across' via the Latin *transītus* of the same meaning, with the action of the verb either extending to an object – *transitive* 'passed across', or being confined to the subject – *intransitive* 'not passed across' (see McDonald 2008: Ch. 7)). But even once we have 'revived' them, and separated them from a direct relationship to their formal expression, how then do we recognise the difference between them in the analysis of texts? Such a methodology, which seems to recommend an almost 'intuitive' approach to analysis, is problematic enough when applied to linguistic texts by Hodge and Kress, but when Kress and van Leeuwen, and following them Hodge and Louie, go on to apply a similar framework to visual as well as verbal texts, not to mention texts in languages other than English, the refusal to pin these categories down to objective criteria seems to leave them dangerously floating in air.

This kind of 'transferral' also has implications for the basic arguability or falsifiability of the theory. In Halliday's original social semiotic analysis of language (e.g. Halliday 1973, 1978), the features of the social context are explicitly linked to features of the semiotic text, not in a straightforward one-to-one fashion, since that is typically not how social semiotic systems like language work; but nevertheless according to a 'line of evidence' that can be explicitly traced and thus explicitly critiqued. But if analytical categories are not linked, however indirectly, to objectively identifiable criteria, then analysis becomes a kind of free-floating interpretation, which may be very revealing, but cannot easily be critiqued. Hodge and Kress's work, as well as the later collaborations with van Leeuwen and Louie, does provide a number of insightful angles on the relationship between texts and their social and cultural contexts, but it does so in a way that tends to shut down the range of possible interpretations rather than opening them up. Either, it seems, you accept such analyses on their own terms, or else you reject them altogether; and unfortunately such an either/or reaction seems to have been typical of the published reviews of Hodge and Louie's work by other sinologists (e.g. Keane 1999; Goodman 2000; Sun 2001).

Conclusion: text and the 'New Sinology'

As already mentioned earlier in this book, Australian scholar Geremie Barmé has argued for a 'New Sinology' that will incorporate the advantages of both traditional sinology and newer approaches. Barmé calls for a 'robust engagement with contemporary China and … with the Sinophone world in all of its complexity, be it local, regional or global' and recommends 'strong scholastic underpinnings in both the classical and modern Chinese language and studies' alongside an 'ecumenical attitude in relation to a rich variety of approaches and disciplines' (Barmé 2005: 1). He reaffirms one of the emphases of traditional sinology, also stressed by many of the participants in the debate covered in Chapter 5, by warning that 'if we fail to insist on linguistic competence in Chinese as a necessary requirement for precise and rigorous engagement with Sinophone texts and images, our students may ultimately fail to make their *own* sense of what it means to be studying Chinese' (Barmé 2005: 2, original emphasis).

Hodge and Louie specifically critique this as one of the gatekeeping 'assumptions of Sinologism' that 'language is an either-or issue that absolutely divides the curriculum and separates students into the sheep and the goats' (Hodge and Louie 1998: 22). However, although an insistence on Chinese literacy may seem excluding in the short term, in the long run, as I argued in Chapter 1, it is the only way to make students into independent thinkers and researchers about China. By the same logic, I suspect that in the long run, there are some aspects of Hodge and Louie's approach that will end up shutting students out from a genuine and nuanced understanding of Chinese language and culture, particularly their analysis of the writing system and the grammar, since while it ostensibly *critiques* the 'hegemony' of the characters, it ends up in effect using the characters to *reinforce* claims of exclusivity for the Chinese situation, claims which we saw in Chapter 6 provide the ideological underpinnings for character fetishisation.

Barmé's call for a New Sinology has not gone uncritiqued itself. The first critique I am aware of derives, rather paradoxically, from the commissioning editor for the *Chinese Studies Association of Australia Newsletter* where it first appeared, historian John Fitzgerald, then at the Australian National University (Fitzgerald 2005). Fitzgerald characterises the China Heritage Project at the same university, for which the New Sinology essay provides a sort of theoretical manifesto, as 'a kind of historical practice that supplies translations and heritage news from the front lines', and sees this approach as 'consistent with that of an older Sinology that specialised in translation and interpretation, two arts at the heart of the New'. He provides a variation on Hodge and Louie's critique of old sinology by claiming that it 'exclud[ed] people of Chinese descent from the art of Sinological interpretation' and contends that a 'New Sinology would truly earn its name if it could cultivate Sinology among people of Chinese descent'. Such an argument seems to transpose to an academic context arguments like those of Lee Kuan Yew examined in Chapter 3 that those of Chinese heritage without access to Chinese language and culture are somehow not really Chinese (see Chapter 9 for a discussion of these issues in the context of becoming sinophone).

Fitzgerald's critique contains several strands which are not, I believe, clearly separated in his own discussion, but which do relate to some long-term concerns of Chinese studies since it emerged out of a confluence of Old Sinology and Area studies at the hands of scholars like historian John Fairbank in the 1940s and 1950s (see discussion in Chapter 5 above). Fitzgerald starts by accusing the New Sinology of disciplinary eclecticism. He carries out a little thought experiment in which he imagines the 'advent of a new school of Anglostudies' among 'an eminent group of scholars in China', describing it, in terms obviously intended to be applicable to the New Sinology, as:

> characterized by eclectic borrowing from the insights of sociology, art history, literature, political science, demography, literary studies and so on without claiming allegiance to any discipline other than cross-cultural translation itself, which at the end of the day is grounded in an intimate

knowledge of the language in all its forms and the cultures embedded in its various dialects.

(*Fitzgerald 2005*)

This 'ecumenical attitude to the disciplines', according to Fitzgerald, seems to downgrade 'research methods' in favour of 'fluency' in 'cultural idioms'. He dismisses this as '[a]ll to the good – but hardly history', for him a more demo-cratic field in the sense that it 'assumes ... that anyone anywhere can participate, in any language, if they have the requisite discipline skills-set'.

In context, this reads like not just an attack on the New Sinology, but an *ad hominem* jibe at Barmé himself, whose own research, as contained most acces-sibly in a series of 'readers' of contemporary China starting with the collabora-tion with John Minford on *Seeds of Fire* (Barmé and Minford 1986), continued with Linda Jaivin in *New Ghosts, Old Dreams* (Barmé and Jaivin 1992) and carried on by himself in *In the Red* (Barmé 1999), encompasses the broad range of disciplines listed by Fitzgerald, and to some extent derives its authority from Barmé's continuing close engagement with and understanding of contemporary China since his student days in the Northeast in the 1970s (see Barmé's own account of this background in the 'Introduction' to *In the Red* (Barmé 1999: x–xiii)). The implication is not only that Barmé floats across disciplines with-out being grounded in any single one, like the caricature of a modern day Cultural studies practitioner, but that his type of sinology is fundamentally elit-ist, accessible only to a small coterie of latter-day 'Great Souls'.

Fitzgerald compares his own theoretically grounded discipline of history with the apparently untheorised practices of New Sinology in a passage which deserves quoting at length:

Nor do historical studies operate on the assumption that their work is done when they adequately translate and interpret one cultural-linguistic past into another. This is properly the business of translation studies, a business best confined to a few experts ... who can faithfully master the nuances of the relevant languages and dialects, and provide comparative annotations on the translated materials. ... Chinese historical studies were practiced and carried beyond the ANU [Australian National University] not by Sinologists but by historians trained in the Far Eastern and later East Asian history programs. Graduate students in the history program were expected to be fluent in Chinese languages and studies, and they were expected to learn, practice and study history in the program. The New Sinology differs from the old in assuming that it can displace historical studies of this kind – something the old Sinology would never have presumed to do – by inflecting language studies with references to heritage and *kaozheng* research, once the preserve of Chinese language and literature departments.

(*Fitzgerald 2005*)

In defending history here from the supposed incursions of the New Sinology, Fitzgerald shows a fundamental misunderstanding of the nature of the Chinese scholarly tradition of *kǎozhèng* or 'evidential analysis' on which Barmé lays such stress. This analytical tradition, which as Elman's study (1984) shows was at the heart of philosophical, historical and scientific endeavour in the early to mid Qing dynasty, was *both* internally text-based in its aim of restoring the 'original' forms of the classical texts, *and* externally focused on the historical and philosophical implications of the resulting reinterpretations of these texts: in the terms of the current study, *both* social *and* semiotic. There is no sense in trying to separate the two: they are two sides of the same coin.

In relation to contemporary historical studies, Fitzgerald does in fact seem to be recommending a separation of the social from the semiotic in analytic practice; and furthermore implying a conflation of the social with the theoretical, and the semiotic with the 'merely' descriptive, in a way that lays itself open to accusations of being elitist and anglocentric, given that it is overwhelmingly the 'people of Chinese descent' who make up the ranks of the 'language side' in Chinese studies. Such a critique of the New, and by implication also the Old Sinology, hardly seems consonant with the original aims of Area studies as articulated by its founding 'dean', John Fairbank, in a joint paper with long-term collaborator, Japan specialist Edwin Reischauer:

> The very lack of disciplinary specialization on the part of the old-fashioned sinologist was tacit recognition of the futility of over-specialization until a solid foundation had been laid in general linguistic and 'area' fields. What is new in Area Studies is not the idea of breadth so much as the broadening of the actual approach to an area. This is done by adding some of the techniques of the anthropologist, sociologist, economist, and political scientist to the more familiar techniques of the historian, linguist, archaeologist, art historian or student of literature which were the usual approaches of the sinologist.
>
> (*Reischauer and Fairbank 1948: 121*)

As in the distinction between 'humanities' and 'social sciences' defining the debate described in Chapter 5, Reischauer and Fairbank here group the 'historian' like Fitzgerald on the same side with the 'archaeologist, art historian or student of literature' like Barmé, both emerging from the ranks of the 'old-fashioned sinologist[s]', rather than from the newer 'area' fields. Reischauer and Fairbank go on to critique the very division Fitzgerald invokes between 'language' and 'area' study (in Fitzgerald's narrower characterisation 'translation' and 'disciplinary') aspects of the field:

> Although it is common practice to divide Area Studies into the two aspects of language study and 'area' study, the two are in a sense really

one, for language is not only a necessary tool in the study of human society but also a major element of the whole social complex, intimately bound up with all other aspects of it.

(*Reischauer and Fairbank 1948: 121–123*)

Rather than getting embroiled in what are obviously deep methodological and ideological differences about how Chinese studies should be carried out, which in part at least seem to derive from the entrenched mindsets of different disciplinary 'homes', we need to step back and understand these 'contradictions' from a broader point of view. The first point to make is that it is characteristic of academic polemics generally to take two concepts or approaches that can easily be seen as complementary and turn them into dichotomies. Fitzgerald's 'historiography' and Barmé's 'poetics', to use what is perhaps the most inclusive characterisation of the latter's practice, are equally ways of dealing with the semiotic, and equally depend on linking semiotic patterns to their social contexts, with 'social' being understood in its broadest sense as covering historical, economic, political, cultural and ideological contexts.

But if the historian Fitzgerald mistakenly interprets Barmé's eclectism as lack of a disciplinary base, since it does not conform to the criteria he takes as central to his own historical methodology, Barmé also does himself a disservice by in effect claiming to operate *without* an explicit theoretical framework, as articulated in the introduction to his most recent collection *In the Red*:

Despite the theoretical concerns in these pages, rather than pursuing an argument in one of the many dialects of hoch-po-mo, I prefer to use platt-English. By so doing and avoiding the obvious deployment of disciplinary strategies – whether they be the paradigms of race and queer theory, sociology of youth, psychoanalysis, media studies, or literary criticism – it is inevitable that my work will be judged by some to be intellectually too flabby, a non-starter in the development of what Matt ffytche so aptly terms '"neurobics" for intellectual fitness freaks.' In steering a treacherous course in the two-line struggle between theory and empiricism I am guilty of too little of the former (being 'undertheorized' is, after all, the cardinal sin of modern academe) and too much of the latter.

(*Barmé 1999: xvi–xvii*)

There are two extremes to avoid here. Barmé, in what we have seen as a common misconception, equates being 'free of theory' with being 'free of jargon', comparing his own approach favourably in comparison to the jargon-encrusted products of Cultural studies, among which he would perhaps include Hodge and Louie's *The Politics of Chinese Language and Culture*. Such a prejudice is unfair to both the Barmés and the Louies of Chinese studies: with the former by no means being 'free of theory' or merely 'speaking commonsense'; and the latter being able to make positive use of their theoretical categories to make sense out of complex semiotic patterns, even if that 'sense' is sometimes over-determined by simple theoretical dichotomies.

So Barmé is being a bit too glib in ironically patting himself on the back for being 'undertheorised': his work is of course highly theorised, and might perhaps benefit from that theory being more explicit, in a way that does not necessarily involve 'jargonisation'. And from the viewpoint taken here, Hodge and Louie's main problems do in fact stem from their work being 'undertheorised' in the area of Chinese linguistics; as well as more generally in the crucial understanding of what 'language' is and how we understand the relationship between its spoken and written forms, as discussed in Chapter 5.

So where do we find common ground here? Perhaps where the three areas mentioned in the title of this chapter – textual criticism, social semiotics and the New Sinology – meet, and in the domain in which the methodology recommended and demonstrated here operates: *between* the semiotic and the social. It makes no sense, as I said before, to talk about one without the other. Semiotics by itself, in what has unfortunately been characteristic of far too much academic work going under that title in the last century or so, degenerates into mere structure-building, abstract frameworks which are often very insightful in themselves but fail to show how semiotic distinctions are realised in actual social practice. The social sciences by themselves too easily veer into ungrounded generalisations and essentialism: over-simplified interpretations of complex social conditions which are unable to show how social structures and values are dynamically construed through semiosis, or processes of meaning-making.

In fact what we should be aiming for is summed up in the seminal passage from Saussure, when he sketches the wider field of *semiology*, more commonly known in English-speaking circles as *semiotics*, in which he sees linguistics taking its place:

> *A science which studies the role of signs as part of social life* is conceivable; it would be part of social psychology, and consequently of general psychology; I shall call it *semiology* (from the Greek *semeion*, 'sign'). Semiology would show what constitutes signs, what laws govern them. Since the science does not yet exist, no-one can say for certain what it would be; but it has a right to exist, a place staked out in advance. Linguistics is only a part of the general science of semiology; the laws discovered by semiology will be laws applicable to linguistics, the latter will circumscribe a well-defined area within the mass of anthropological facts.
>
> (*Saussure 1916/1957: 16, original emphasis*)

So if the New Sinology is to build on the strengths of the Old Sinology as well as grounding its interpretations in clear and explicit disciplinary frameworks, it will need to be constantly attentive to the inextricable links between the social and the semiotic. What we need is *more*, not less, theories in Chinese studies; more ways of explictly understanding what it is we are doing, and thus of being able to both *improve* our descriptive practice and *prove* the facts that we derive through it.

Dr McHorse does discourse

9

FROM 'ED McDONALD' TO 'NED McHORSE'

Negotiating multiple identities in a globalised world

Introduction: language learning and the potential sinophone

In Chapter 3 we took the point of view of one particular learner in order to look at the process of *learning Chinese*. In this final chapter, we revisit many of the concerns of the book as a whole from the point of view of the particular sinophone who is the author himself by looking at the process of *becoming sinophone*. These two different formulations of what may superficially seem like much the same process reflect, in the latter case, a much broader view of the process of learning language in context, and open up a number of issues beyond language learning as such.

If we recall Lee's views, despite his own rich multilingual and multicultural background, the boy who 'looked very Chinese [but] seemed more Malayan in his ways' grew up into the adult – or, perhaps more pertinently, the politician – who took one thing as absolutely categorical in determining his language-linked identity: his ethnic background as Chinese. We also saw that Lee's understanding of his 'Chineseness' put great stress on mastering the writing system and its related standard spoken language. Although for political reasons, in an episode of his linguistic autobiography not covered in Chapter 3, he did also become fluent in the majority local Chinese dialect of Hokkien, at no stage did he attempt, or even raise the possibility of learning his own ancestral dialect of Hakka, although he quite clearly regards himself as Hakka in affiliation.

Lee's experiences raise many questions that are relevant to you as potential sinophone in becoming sinophone, the main ones of which could be summarised as follows:

- What is the relationship between your 'mother tongue' and Chinese?
- What sort of 'Chinese' are you setting out to learn, and how much is this choice affected by the practical and/or political contexts of your learning?
- What is the relationship between your mother tongue identity and your sinophone identity: in other words, to what extent do you do different things, behave differently, and therefore in a sense become a different person in a sinophone context?

For some preliminary answers to these questions, it would be useful to put a potted biography of the sinophone Lee beside a similar treatment of my own sinophone history, which will be the main subject of this chapter, and see what differences emerge. As can be seen from Table 9.1, from our common starting point of knowing no Chinese, Lee and I exhibit significant differences in our motivations for becoming sinophone and in the uses to which we have put this skill. The path that led Lee to his current sinophone status should be already quite familiar from the discussion in Chapter 3, so from the same point of view, we will now go on to examine the trajectory of my own process of becoming sinophone. In both of these histories, of course, you may find many commonalities with your own experience as potential sinophone.

First I'll give a quick sketch of my relevant background and then explore in more detail the nature of sinophone identity and of language-based identity more generally. In investigating the process of becoming sinophone through an account of my own experiences in 'learning Chinese', I will at the same time be describing the process of 'turning Chinese': in other words, how I managed to build up a sinophone identity.

Edward James McDonald: a sociolinguistic autobiography

Social background

I was born, shortly before the assassination of President Kennedy, in a maternity hospital in the inner west of Sydney, the third child of a doctor and a social worker, the latter having been for the almost three years since the arrival of her first child a full-time homemaker. Three weeks after my birth, my father and mother moved their three young children from their small cottage in the Eastern suburbs to a larger house on the more affordable lower North Shore, where they would stay for the next forty years, bringing three more children into the world, and seeing all six through primary, secondary and tertiary education.

Early education

Normally known within the family as Edward, I was, like my sisters, first sent to a local preschool at the age of four, then in the following year to the lowest grade, or kindergarten, of the local public school, where I stayed until the end of third

TABLE 9.1 Anglophone and sinophone contexts: Lee Kuan Yew and Edward McDonald

Anglophone contexts		
Full name	Harry Lee Kuan Yew	Edward James McDonald
Known familiarly as	Harry	Edward, Ed
Known professionally as	Lee Kuan Yew, Mr Lee, PM/	Mr McDonald, Dr McDonald
	SM/MM Lee	
Sinophone contexts		
Full name	李光耀 Lǐ Guāngyào	马爱德 Mǎ Àidé
Known familiarly as	?	老马Lǎo Mǎ 'Old Ma'
Known professionally as	李总理 Lǐ Zǒnglǐ,	马老师 Mǎ Lǎoshī
	'Premier …'/国务资政	'Teacher Ma'
	Guówù Zīzhèng	马爱德先生 Mǎ
	'Domestic Affairs Mentor	Xiānsheng 'Mr Ma'
	…'/内阁资政 Nèigé Zīzhèng	
	'Cabinet Mentor …' '… Lee'	
Reasons for learning	Political utility, remedying	Interest, gaining professional skill
Chinese	cultural deprivation	
Uses for Chinese	Political speeches, public	Living skills and social
	delegations, private tutoring,	intercourse, professional skills
	personal interactions	(editing and translating), teaching
		and researching Chinese language
		and culture

grade, not long after my eighth birthday. Here I was commonly known to my schoolmates as 'Eddie' or 'Horse', the latter moniker inevitable given the existence of a popular American series shown on local television called 'Mr Ed the Talking Horse'. Moving into fourth grade at the Jesuit-run Catholic school where I stayed till the end of high school, I had to get used to an all-male environment, the most obvious linguistic marker of which was being called by my surname, 'McDonald', by both teachers and students, a practice that persisted among my school fellows into early high school.

Early language learning experiences

I gained my first exposure to languages other than my native English in my first year of high school, when I began the study of Latin and French, the latter being then the default foreign language for Australian schools, while the former was still a marker of the traditional 'grammar school' education which had survived in the private system and to a limited extent in the public system. Encouraged by my father, who had studied both Latin and Classical Greek at school in the 1930s and 1940s – a process I once heard him characteristically describe to a dinner guest as 'a very *sophisticating* experience' ('Don't you mean sophistica*ted*?' was her puzzled response) – and by the existence of a copy of *Teach Yourself Greek* lying around the house, I began to take the latter advice literally. Then from the second year of high school, through the generosity of an English teacher who had also taught classics, I studied Greek more formally, as well as continuing my study of Latin and French, the three languages taking up three out of the five subjects I sat for the Higher School Certificate at the end of my sixth and final year. The teaching of all three languages concentrated on mastering the written form, most naturally in the case of the classical languages Latin and Greek. By the time I got to university, I had become interested in learning an Asian language; and it was probably the fact that a neighbour a couple of years older was already studying Chinese, and the presence of some older family friends who had grown up in pre-1949 China, that steered me towards studying Chinese.

Learning Chinese

The Chinese program that I entered in the significantly named Department of Oriental Studies at the University of Sydney (a name long since replaced by a more modern-sounding title) was still essentially a reading program, conducted on similar lines to the classical languages I had studied at high school, and so I naturally found its teaching methods both familiar and reasonable. Although at least half of the first year of the program was devoted to an initial exposure to the modern spoken language in the form of a weekly two hours of class-time with a grammar-translation textbook and one hour with a conversation textbook, both of them newly written by members of the department, the main emphasis was really on mastering a sufficient number of characters to read simple written texts. As a beginner student I spent hours writing characters over and over again in order to memorise them, something that, as an amateur calligrapher, I quite enjoyed, and further hours copying out characters, their associated pronunciations, and what seemed like their almost endless series of meanings, in order to interpret the assigned written texts. From the second year onwards, apart from an hour of conversation and an hour devoted to history, the bulk of the six-hour weekly program was devoted to the study of literature, ancient (i.e. in classical Chinese) and modern.

The normal process followed in class consisted of going through a segment of text we students would have prepared for beforehand by looking up the characters in a dictionary and trying, often unsuccessfully if it was a classical text, to work out what words they corresponded to. In class, one student at a time would be chosen to read out a sentence, or the equivalent, and attempt to translate it, the translation then being corrected by the teacher. This was assessed by the simple process of providing selected 'seen' texts, and 'unseen' texts with some vocabulary attached, to be translated into English. In fact the whole teaching process was based around translation from Chinese into English, and since the class was made up roughly half of Asian students – Japanese, Korean and some Chinese or of Chinese background – and half of native English speakers, whatever advantage the East Asians gained from greater knowledge of Chinese characters and/or the Chinese language was pretty much matched by the English speakers' advantage in the language of translation.

In my second year, a fellow student who had become friendly with one of our Chinese lecturers took me round to the lecturer's place for what I discovered were regular Friday night 'at homes'. At this time, the early 1980s, there were actually not very many Mandarin speakers in town, but the first wave of mainland students were just beginning to arrive, and it seemed as if most of them at one stage or another turned up at these Friday night dinners. My spoken Chinese, after a little more than a year of the program described above, was still pretty basic, but regularly meeting numbers of Chinese speakers fresh off the plane whose English was not up to the standard of even my meagre Chinese meant that our most convenient language of communication was Chinese. Over the next six years these sorts of contacts gradually helped me improve my grasp of the language to the point that, by the time I first went to China in the early 1990s as a postgraduate student, I was able, albeit sometimes rather slowly and painfully, to make my needs understood and negotiate the bureaucratic processes that were an inevitable part of life at a Chinese educational institution.

In the meantime, however, that same lecturer had helped me choose a Chinese name for myself. There were, as it happened, standard 'sound translations' for both my surname and given name, and I could conceivably have made my first arrival in China under the imposing label of *Àidéhuádé Màikètángnā*. However, apart from being in the un-Chinese order of given name + surname, such a polysyllabic monstrosity would have been awkward to work with in a sinophone context, where the full name is normally from two to four syllables. I chose to take the first two syllables of my sinicised given name – thus *Àidé* – which also happened to be a reasonable approximation, to a Chinese ear, of the shortened form *Ed* which had become my usual label outside the family. For a surname beginning with Mc/Mac, *Mai* 麦 would have been a common Chinese equivalent, particularly since in Cantonese, the most common dialect in use in Australia at the time, it comes out as *Mak*; and another Australian student with the same surname whom I met later in China, and who also spoke Cantonese, had indeed chosen this as his Chinese surname. My lecturer had, however, also mentioned *Mǎ* 马 as a possible Chinese surname for a Mc (or indeed for a 'Mick' – see below), and since its regular meaning 'horse' inevitably recalled the 'Mr Ed the Talking Horse' of my schooldays, it seemed a fated choice.

Adjusting to a sinophone context

My arrival in Beijing in the early 1990s as a foreign student or *liúxuéshēng* 留学生 – a very clearly defined role in sinophone culture – marked the beginning of my first experience of immersion in a Chinese-speaking context. The first six months of what turned out to be a two and a half year stay, in which time I completed a Masters degree at Peking University – the old spelling denoting its pre-1949 status – I found to be a highly disorienting experience. Unlike most of the foreign students, who were either straight out of high school, like many of the Japanese, or in the middle of a bachelor's degree, like the bulk of the Europeans and North Americans, I was several years beyond an already prolonged BA. In contrast to the majority of foreign students, who were taking language classes together, I went into classes 'on my own' with Chinese students right from the beginning, and had to cope not only with a range of non-standard accents on the part of my lecturers, but also a cursive style of writing on the blackboard which I found at first almost impossible to decipher.

Already in my mid-twenties, unlike the late teens or early twenties of the majority of *liúxuéshēng*, I also found the process of building up a new network of friends and learning to live in a strange country and operate in a foreign language quite daunting, though perhaps more in the anticipation than the reality. Having learned French all through high school and taught myself Italian from books and tapes in my early undergraduate years, I'd learned to operate quite confidently in both languages. And what's more – the proof of the pudding – when I took a three-month European holiday in the middle of my degree, I'd found myself able to make my way round Italy and France with only minor problems. But learning to cope with China in the early 1990s seemed a much more daunting prospect – something a couple of short anecdotes should make clear.

Peking University, in the days when almost all students and staff lived on campus, was almost like a self-contained small town, with shops, restaurants, and even a bar for us foreign students, as well as the expected canteens, bath houses, bookshops and library. A small shop that in an Australian context I would have called a 'grocery store' sold soap, detergent, washing powder, stationery, etc., as well as fruit and some other food items. However, unlike an Australian grocery store, all the goods were placed out of reach behind glass-fronted counters, and even more strangely, as I discovered in my first forays there, I would often be left standing before the counter for a good ten minutes while Chinese customers casually pushed their way in front of me. It took me some time to realise that *I* was the one who had to initiate the transaction, not the shop assistant as would have been normal in Australia; and that a simple 'give me two of those' was perfectly civil, indeed expected, in a Chinese context, with none of the polite openers like 'Would you mind …' and 'Could I have …' that would be expected in a comparable Australian context.

The other occasion – which incidentally brought home to me some of the inadequacies of my classical-style Chinese education for functioning in the modern world – involved, appropriately enough for China, trying to buy some rice. Although the student dormitories where we were obliged to live didn't provide cooking facilities, many of the students did nevertheless cook on a simple electric ring which could be easily bought nearby. Although I normally took the path of least resistance by eating at the foreign students' canteen a couple of minutes walk from my dorm room, one day I decided I was going to cook myself a simple meal of rice and one dish, and so sallied forth to buy the ingredients.

When it came to buying the rice, I realised that not only didn't I know where rice was sold, I actually had no idea what uncooked rice was called! Hoping that if I could see it somewhere, I wouldn't actually need to ask for it, I tried out my usual 'grocery store', with no success. Next, rather doubtfully using the only term I knew, I asked for *mǐfàn* at a local restaurant, where, as I expected, they brought me a bowl of cooked rice. Then I tried something like a dry goods store, thinking surely there must be rice there, but no such luck. Finally, through a combination of questioning Chinese who must have thought I was simple – 'No, I want cooked-rice that hasn't been cooked' (for the record, this is known as *dàmǐ*, literally 'big rice' – a combination, incidentally, you'd be unlikely to find in a dictionary if you were looking under the headword *mǐ* 'rice') – and simply wandering the streets, I eventually found rice, with the other grains, in a corner of what was then known as the *zìyóu shìchǎng* or 'free market', a large covered market where peasants brought in their fruit and vegetables from the countryside to sell direct to their customers outside the state-run system which was then the norm – hence 'free'.

After many of these kinds of encounters, I gradually began to feel at home in this very different environment, to the extent that when I first went back to Australia after eighteen months to attend the wedding of one of my sisters it was the *Australian* way of life I found bizarre! In the meantime, though, I had been through another ordeal of sorts that would prove to be equally significant: I had acquired a Chinese by-name. Although I had carefully chosen my Chinese name as conforming to cultural norms, and after arriving in China had discovered that the use of the full surname + given name was much more common than in anglophone Australia, I did notice that many Chinese seemed to have another more casual label used by friends or colleagues. I had made friends with some students at the nearby Languages Institute, now the Languages University, and when one of them suggested I join them for some extracurricular classes in taichi – specifically the type known as *tàijí jiàn*, with a sword – I willingly went along. We had two teachers, a younger woman who was aggressively fit and confident and laughed at my stumbling attempts to coordinate my four limbs and the sword, and an older man, a jovial kind of fellow, who early on in the classes started calling me *Lǎo Mǎ*, 'Old Ma'.

In contrast to the custom in southern China where it is common to use part or all of the given name for these more informal labels, often with the ubiquitous prefix *Ā*, in northern China, it is more normally the surname plus some sort of prefix – the two most common here being *Xiǎo* 'young' and *Lǎo* 'old'. My age – mid-twenties – and my student status would normally have suggested I should be called *Xiǎo Mǎ*, 'Young Ma', but for some reason, whether it was my status as a foreigner, or my height – over six feet – the teacher dubbed me *Lǎo Mǎ*, this label stuck, and Lǎo Mǎ I remain to this day to most of my Chinese friends and colleagues.

Living 'Lǎo Mǎ'

Becoming 'Lǎo Mǎ' may have happened almost instantaneously, when the tai chi teacher bestowed this label on me, but learning how to *live* as Lǎo Mǎ, exploring the potentialities of this new identity, was a somewhat longer and more complicated process. In order to understand how this happened, we need to know something more about the implications of the label itself – its semiotic aspects, as well as about the contexts in which it was usable – its social aspects (the two of course being ultimately inseparable, as will become clear in the discussion below). We will also see that, although my adoption of this identity did on the whole conform to sinophone norms, there were also differences from the local norms that emerged based on my status as a foreigner.

To start with the *semiotic* aspect, the key features of a term of address like Lǎo Mǎ can be summed up as: other-bestowed, reciprocal, intimate and respectful. Let's look at each of these in turn and then see how they may have been modified somewhat in my case. A term like Lǎo Mǎ is *other-bestowed*: in other words, it is not one you give yourself, nor one you use in reference to yourself, it is assigned to you by another person in recognition of a certain relationship between yourself and that person. You would not normally use it to identify yourself: for example, if I rang a friend up on the phone, I might open by saying *Wǒ .shì Mǎ Àidé* 'It's Ed McDonald here', to which my friend might respond *Èi Lǎo Mǎ, nǐ hǎo!* 'Hey Lǎo Mǎ, how are you?'.

The nature of that relationship is commonly a *reciprocal* one: in the simplest case, people who call you *Lǎo* X_1 (X = *xìng* 'surname'), you would also call *Lǎo* X_2 in return. So another version of that phone conversation might go: *Wèi, Lǎo Gāo, wǒ .shì Mǎ Àidé* 'Hi Lǎo Gāo, it's Ed McDonald here' – *Èi Lǎo Mǎ, nǐ hǎo!* 'Hey Lǎo Mǎ, how are you?'. The term of address need not be exactly the same, but it would normally be of the same level of formality: for example, a term of address using *Xiǎo* 'young'. In a work situation, however, this reciprocation may not be observed: for example, in one of my jobs in a Chinese company, I would call my immediate superior X_1 *Lǎoshī* 'teacher', the latter term used here not in its literal sense but as a respectful term for an educated superior, and he would call me Lǎo Mǎ. However, when *his* superior rang for him, he would address my superior as *Xiǎo* X_1 'young', while being addressed as X_2 *Zhǔrèn* 'boss' in return. In an actual educational context, by contrast, my colleagues would normally address me as *Mǎ Lǎoshī* and I would address them in turn as X *Lǎoshī*, with the proviso that I would also address educated colleages as *Lǎoshī* even if they weren't teachers: for example, a departmental secretary.

The third main feature of a term like Lǎo Mǎ is that it is *both intimate and respectful*. The flavour of it can best be understood by comparing it with its opposite *Xiǎo* X which, while intimate and in no way *dis*respectful, does not carry the same deference as *Lǎo* X, age being traditionally a revered quality in sinophone societies. The work driver at one workplace commented on this two-way connotation once when he rang for me in the office and heard my colleagues calling me *Lǎo Mǎ*: he obviously thought this was both a comfortable term to use, without the formality of a mostly 'foreign-addressee' term like *Mǎ Xiān.shēng* 'Mr Ma', but at the same time respectful of my status as a (Chinese-speaking?) foreigner.

To sum up the semiotic force of a label like Lǎo Mǎ, we could place it on a cline of formality, from most formal on the left to most intimate on the right:

Mǎ Xiān.shēng   *Mǎ Lǎoshī*   *Lǎo Mǎ*   *Mǎ Àidé*   *Àidé*

From this cline, we can see that a term like Lǎo Mǎ sits around the middle in terms of a balance between intimacy and respectfulness. The most formal term *Mǎ Xiān.shēng* 'Mr Ma' is normally used for foreigners, or in an educational context as a highly respectful term for a 'great Master' (male or female) – one of the original meanings of *Xiān.shēng* being 'teacher' as in its Japanese *on* equivalent *Sensei* 先生. *Mǎ Lǎoshī* 'Teacher Ma' is still respectful but used by colleagues or students who know me in or from an educational context, not normally by strangers. *Mǎ Àidé* would also commonly be used in an educational context, by teacher to student, but without the 'scolding' tone the use of full given name + surname often carries in English. *Àidé* is the most intimate, as well as the most unlikely, form of address. Although the use of given name as a term of address seems to be coming in among younger Chinese, possibly due to influence from English, its use in sinophone societies has traditionally been reserved for parents to child – something obviously not relevant in my case, or from partner to partner (husband to wife, boyfriend to girlfriend and vice versa). Many younger Chinese, particularly those who live overseas or work in a foreign company in China itself, do in fact take on an *English* given name in order to have access to the informal connotations of this form of address in English without the intimate overtones it carries in Chinese.

Moving on to the *social* aspect of this label, without giving a full sociolinguistic account of this or similar terms of address, which indeed would be a book in itself, we can sum up its social uses according to the general cline of professional to personal. In a *professional* context, as noted above, a term like Lǎo Mǎ is in contrast to an obviously professional label like *Mǎ Lǎoshī* 'Teacher Ma', a term which largely takes the place of what in an anglophone context would be its most likely equivalent 'Dr McDonald', in Chinese *Mǎ Bóshì*. Although the latter term does also appear in very restricted academic contexts, it is often in the kind of abbreviated form, i.e. *Mǎ Bó* 'Doc Ma', that is much more common in corporate contexts: cf. *Dèng Zǒng* 'Gen Deng' for *Dèng Zǒngjīnglǐ* 'General Manager Deng'. In my earlier days as a student, my full Chinese name *Mǎ Àidé* would also have been possible here, but this would be relatively unlikely with my current more senior status, except coming from someone like a former teacher – whom I would continue to address as X *Lǎoshī*, the initial status difference being permanently observed. Likewise, in a professional context, whether educational or not, to senior colleagues I would either use the generally respectful X *Lǎoshī* or a more specifically occupational label like X *Zhǔrèn* or X *Dǎobó* 'Director'; while to junior colleagues I could use their whole given name + surname, or a more intimate term like *Xiǎo* X, or even a doubled form of (part of) their given name (perhaps more likely to a female addressee) such as *Xiǎo.xiǎo* for *Xiāonán*.

Evidence that Lǎo Mǎ has become more than just a marker of relationship and now functions almost as an identifying label can be seen from an anecdote from my time as a Masters student at Peking University, a story which also reveals some of the complexities of the use of a Chinese label when applied to foreigners. I happened to be attending a conference in my department at which, apart from a couple of Hong Kong and Taiwan attendees, I was the only overseas participant. One of my *tóngxué* or 'classmates' (see Chapter 1), herself also a postgraduate student in that department, was reading through an academic paper on behalf of someone who hadn't been able to attend when to emphasise a particular point, she said *Wǒ.men dōu .shi Zhōngguórén, zhǐyǒu Lǎo Mǎ cái .shi wàiguórén* 'We're all Chinese, only Lǎo Mǎ is a foreigner'. This combination of a unambiguously foreign status with a clearly Chinese label obviously struck the company as rather humorous: my neighbour promptly turned to me and said *O, nǐ jiù.shi Lǎo Mǎ?* 'Oh, *you're* Lǎo Mǎ?', and for the rest of the conference I became 'Lǎo Mǎ' to all and sundry, even to my Masters supervisor, coming from whom I found it a little awkward, since it implied a reciprocity and equality of status that did not really exist.

In *personal* contexts, Lǎo Mǎ has become almost my exclusive label when I am operating in sinophone settings, in a way that departs somewhat from its normal usage. Thus I will in fact often use Lǎo Mǎ rather than Mǎ Àidé to identify myself on the phone, and will suggest this label to others – *Nǐ jiào wǒ Lǎo Mǎ jiù xíng .le* 'Just call me Lǎo Mǎ' – rather than waiting to have it bestowed by others. With younger Chinese friends, a similarly respectful but more intimate label that *is* bestowed on me is *Mǎ Dàgē* 'Big Brother Ma'; the use of such family terms being quite common in personal and professional contexts between Chinese.

The fact that Lǎo Mǎ has become a kind of alternative name for me rather than just a term of address, strictly speaking, raises the question of just *how Chinese* this person called Lǎo Mǎ can be regarded as being. This question can be illuminated by another anecdote, the context here being a regular gathering of what is called, to use a characteristically modern Chinese term, a *shālóng*沙龙, from the French *salon*, i.e. an informal meeting for discussion of intellectual and/ or topical issues, in this case, one organised by postgraduate students of linguistics at Peking University. One of the members, a professor from a nearby university, had just come back from the latest annual meeting of a linguistics association abroad and was describing it to us. I don't remember exactly how the issue arose, but at one point she drew a distinction between 'Chinese' and 'foreigners', whereupon one of the other members asked where I fitted in this dichotomy. She immediately answered in a half-joking tone: *O, Lǎo Mǎ suàn .shì Zhōngguórén .ba* 'Oh, Lǎo Mǎ counts as Chinese'.

It's worthwhile reflecting on exactly what these two little words *suàn .shì* 'counts as' imply here. From memory, the contrast the speaker was setting up was between the anglophone academic sphere that was the norm for these particular conferences and its sinophone counterpart to which all those present belonged. Even though I originally came from anglophone academia, I had at that point been operating in sinophone academia for about two years, and was still based at a Chinese institution. Under these fairly limited terms, then, I could 'count as' Chinese. Although there was also an emotional aspect to the identification being made here by the speaker – I counted as 'one of us' rather than 'one of them' – in any case it was mainly the professional context that made this possible.

Taking on a new name

In recounting the formative experiences that gave rise to the sinophone Mǎ Àidé, I placed great emphasis on naming practices, and how they related to different kinds of interactions in sinophone society. Looking at these issues from a broader point of view, we can see that they relate to the nature of sinophone *identity*, and of ethnic and cultural identity in general. So what *is* in a name? Or a nationality? And how do these relate to identity? And how might my ethnic identity as a *McDonald* affect my attitudes towards my sinophone identity as a *Mǎ*?

We can explore these issues in the first place by taking a look at an interesting puzzle in my own McDonald family history, one which has only recently come to light. When I was growing up, although the received family history had us as having come from Inverness, on the borders of the Scottish Highlands where the McDonalds have traditionally been a major clan, we knew little if anything about our Scottish heritage. Practically the only things I remember being told by my father about our McDonald ancestry were: first, 'Hate all Campbells', the traditional clan foes of the McDonalds (my father, having married a Burns, a Lowland family associated with Clan Campbell, once proclaimed dramatically that if he'd known about my mother's background he never would have married her!); the second, another joke by my father, which as a child I took absolutely literally, to the effect that the reason for the difference between 'Mac' and 'Mc' in the spelling of Highland surnames was that the Highlanders were so uneducated they didn't even know how to spell their own names!

Although paradoxically these jokes reflect the historically unflattering image of Highland Scots in the rest of Britain as violent and illiterate, an even greater paradox emerged when about ten years ago some of my cousins took it upon themselves to research the family history. When tracing back our forebears through birth records, ships' registers and the like, they discovered that not only did the initial ancestor to sail to Australia come from Limerick, County Cork, in the southeast of Ireland, about as far away from the Scottish Highlands as you could get at the time and remain within the United Kingdom, but when he arrived in Australia in 1855, it was under the label of *McDaniel*! While this is a reasonable approximation of the original Gaelic *MacDhomhnaill* (whether or not he was actually a Gaelic speaker is not known), interestingly enough when he brought his wife and children out to join him just over a decade later, they travelled under the unambiguously Scottish label of *McDonald*.

In order to understand what was going on here we need to know something about the social divisions in Australia which were in operation at the time of my ancestor's arrival there, divisions which were religious as well as ethnic and which lasted well into the twentieth century, with the Protestant English and the Catholic Irish as the two poles of the social divide. As summed up in an historian's account of a fascinating instance of sectarian strife in the 1920s:

> in early twentieth century Australia … Catholics were mostly Irish by birth or descent, the Irish were mostly Catholics, and Irish Catholics were mostly on the lowest rungs of the socio-economic ladder. This three-fold identification of religion, ethnicity and class had been a feature of Australian society since the nineteenth century, and from the earliest days of European colonisation Irish Catholics had perceived themselves as a persecuted minority.
>
> (*Kildea 2006: 31*)

The McDonalds were one of the clans who had remained Catholic at the time of the Reformation starting from the sixteenth century when most of the rest of Scotland had turned Protestant, and it is likely that my original McDonald forebears had fled at that time across the Irish Sea to southern Ireland, which though under English control had remained largely Catholic. When some centuries later, my McDaniel ancestor made the decision to emigrate to Australia, he would have found himself in danger of falling into the same status of persecuted minority that *his* ancestors had fled from in Scotland. Although his religious identity as Catholic was something he was obviously unwilling to give up, his 'renaming' himself McDonald, and whether from his own or the next generation, 'assuming' a Scottish ethnicity, clearly made the way easier for his family in the Australian society of the time.

Some further evidence from the other side of the family showing that such social attitudes were very real and persisted well into the twentieth century, comes from my Burns mother, who, reflecting on her childhood in the 1930s growing up Catholic in a small country town where her father was the town doctor, once commented that his high status led to the whole family being regarded as 'honorary Protestants'! From this point of view, the situation of the Irish Catholic McDaniel arriving in Australia and 'deciding' to be Scottish shows a keen awareness of the pluses and minuses of ethnic identity and a strategic approach to making the best use of it that he could. The fact that such issues are also live ones in the sinophone sphere can be seen from some similar histories in relation to people of Chinese descent that we will now go on to examine.

'On not speaking Chinese'

The title of this section is taken from a fascinating book by Cultural studies academic Ien Ang, which explores the implications of being ethnically Chinese and *not* sinophone. Ang describes the genesis of her book as stemming from an invitation to speak at a conference in Taiwan:

The conference organizers said it was up to me what I wanted to talk about. I was elated, of course, for I had never been to Taiwan before, but when I started to prepare for the event I was suddenly faced with an insurmountable difficulty. Imagining my Taiwanese audience, I felt I couldn't open my mouth in front of them without explaining why I, a person with stereo-typically Chinese physical characteristics, could not speak to them in Chinese.

(*Ang 2001: vii*)

Ang describes herself as coming from a background very similar to that of Lee Kuan Yew:

I was born in postcolonial Indonesia into a middle class, *peranakan* Chinese family. The *peranakans* are people of Chinese descent who are born and bred in South-East Asia [dating from the sixteenth century onwards], in contrast to the *totok* Chinese, who arrived from China [beginning from the nineteenth century]. … Having settled as traders and craftsmen in South-East Asia long before the Europeans did … [the *peranakans*] tended to have lost many of the cultural features attributed to the Chinese, including everyday practices related to food, dress and language. Most *peranakans* lost their command over the Chinese language a long time ago and actually spoke their own brand of Malay, a sign of their intensive mixing, at least partially, with the locals.

(*Ang 2001: 26*)

As Ang explains, the distinction between the two kinds of 'Chinese', 'local' *peranakans* and 'immigrant' *totoks*, relates to the differing political situation of the Chinese Empire at the time they left China: the outward-going Ming dynasty which actively established trading networks with South-East Asia and beyond, the most famous example being the voyages of Zheng He in the early fifteenth century referred to in Chapter 6; as opposed to the more inward-looking Qing dynasty, which from the early eighteenth century actually forbade Chinese subjects to go abroad, and if they did so and then tried to return to China, punished them with the death penalty! This division between *totok* and *peranakan* Chinese remained strong even after the collapse of the Qing dynasty in the face of the 'pan-Chinese nationalist movement which emerged in the early decades of the twentieth century', where '*peranakans* only partly responded to calls for their resinification, predominantly in the form of education in Chinese language, values and customs', a reluctance which 'made the *totoks* regard the *peranakan* Chinese as "unpatriotic" and their behaviour as "non-Chinese"'(Ang 2001: 26–27).

Because of their more attenuated links with the Chinese homeland, *per-anakans* such as Ang's grandfather, who briefly took his family 'back' to China in the late 1920s, found himself regarded as 'no longer … "one of them"', and on his return from China sent his two daughters to study in Holland; while Ang's mother, although having as a result of this China sojourn become fluent in spoken and written Chinese 'carefully avoided passing this knowledge' on to her daughter. Ang herself grew up speaking Indonesian and regarding herself as Indonesian, something which, nevertheless, in the context of the troubled ethnic politics of the time, did not prevent her from being 'yelled at' by local kids: '"Why don't you go back to your own country?"' – 'a remark', she notes 'all too familiar to members of immigrant minorities anywhere in the world'. As she comments further on the huge distance of the very idea of China from her own Indonesian experience:

> to be told ... that I actually didn't belong there but in a faraway, abstract, and somewhat frightening place called China, was terribly confusing, disturbing and utterly unacceptable. I silently rebelled, I didn't *want* to be Chinese. ... Chineseness ... at that time ... was an imposed identity, one that I desperately wanted to get rid of.
>
> (*Ang 2001: 28*)

A similar sense of being 'trapped' by his Chineseness was also the experience of third-generation Chinese-Australian, professional photographer and raconteur William Yang, as he tells in his inimitable style:

> One day, when I was about six years old, one of the kids at school called at me 'Ching Chong Chinaman, Born in a jar, Christened in a teapot, Ha ha ha.' I had no idea what he meant although I knew from his expression that he was being horrible. I went home to my mother and I said to her, 'Mum, I'm not Chinese, am I?' My mother looked at me very sternly and said, 'Yes, you are'. Her tone was hard and I knew in that moment that being Chinese was some terrible curse and I could not rely on my mother for help. Or my brother, who was four years older than me, and much more experienced in the world. He said, 'And you'd better get used to it.'
>
> (*Yang 1996: 65, quoted in Ang 2001: 37*)

A further dilemma, experienced not only by peranakans like Ang herself and of course Lee Kuan Yew, emerges from another peranakan history quoted by Ang, that of Malaysian woman Ruth Ho 'who grew up in Malacca before World War Two'. Despite being inescapably identified as Chinese, not being able to speak any form of Chinese seemed to condemn her and others like her to being judged as somehow 'not really Chinese':

> [W]hen I was young there was no motivation to study Chinese. ... [but] today we are described by one English writer as belonging to 'the sad band of English-educated who cannot speak their own language'. This seems unfair to me. Must we know the language of our forefathers when we have lived in another country (Malaysia) for many years? ... Are the

descendants of Italian and Greek immigrants to Australia expected to study Italian and Greek? Of course not, and yet overseas Chinese are always expected to know Chinese or else they are despised not only by their fellow Chinese but also by non-Chinese!

(Ho 1975: 97–99 quoted in Ang 2001: 33)

Such a rigid identification of ethnicity and language in the case of 'Chinese', although quite common within and beyond the sinophone sphere, can be psychologically very destructive for those who experience it, as well as imposing an impossible burden on those, like Ang, who see no need in their personal and professional trajectories for knowledge of Chinese, or even for those, like many potential sinophones from a Chinese background, who do. The converse of this identification, that those who are not ethnically Chinese are somehow 'not entitled' to 'full sinophone status' and will forever be locked out from a productive and meaningful engagement with sinophone language and culture, an attitude we saw being played out in some of the textbooks examined in Chapter 2, is equally unhelpful for the potential sinophone.

Playing with identity

What such individual histories suggest is that official classifications of ethnicity, which lock people into a particular category from birth, don't leave space for the kinds of shifting identities associated with being part of more than one linguistic-cultural grouping from birth, like Harry Lee Kuan Yew; or taking on another language and culture later in life, like Ed McDonald/Lǎo Mǎ; or living with what others may regard as a permanent disjunction between your assigned ethnicity and your sociolinguistic repertoire, like Ien Ang or William Yang or Ruth Ho. In the case of someone born a 'Lee' and classified ethnically as 'Chinese', the process of becoming sinophone was seen as the reinforcement of a pre-existing ethnic identity – 'a person who gets deculturalised ... feel[s] a sense of deprivation'; while conversely the fact of being a native English speaker was regarded as ultimately never able to give Lee an anglophone identity – 'I'll never be an Englishman in a thousand generations'.

From this point of view, someone born a 'McDonald', who would normally be classified ethnically as 'Scottish' (however tenuously in my own case), should surely feel deprived unless able to have access to his 'ancestral language', Scottish Gaelic, as well as feeling equally unable ever to 'be an Englishman'. While this latter 'deprivation' was certainly relevant in the early history of colonies like Australia, and still exists to a certain extent in the form of the 'cultural cringe' – i.e. the expectation that cultural 'products' of the previous British Empire or the current American one are inherently superior to Australian ones, what is far more prominent for me as a sixth-generation Australian in my own self-identity is my *nationality*. In fact I think of myself as first and foremost as *Australian* – and similarly we saw in Chapter 3 that, at least at certain points in his career, Lee took pains to stress that he and his ethnically Chinese compatriots were first and foremost *Singaporeans*. Nevertheless, while it has been religious adherence that has figured more prominently in my own family history, ethnic background can be also an important part of our identity, even if only as a means whereby others in our society will classify us. This holds even for those in many anglophone societies from geographically and linguistically 'English' or 'Anglo' backgrounds who, being the majority, are commonly denied the status of being or having an 'ethnicity' at all!

In my own case, quite some time after having developed a complex and fluent sinophone identity, I did set out to explore my ethnic roots by taking an Adult Education course in Scottish Gaelic, and was met in the first class by something I could represent as follows:

> 'Morning good! Welcome to class Gaelic Scottish! Came people galore today on who be good names Gaelic – wrote me them on the paper this. Listen to me while read me them:
>
> *Eadairt Seumas MacDhomhnaill'*

As is probably obvious, this is not really English at all, but an 'Englished' version of Gaelic which shows significant differences from English in word order, apart from the enormous differences in pronunciation disguised by this process of Englishing. Included here is 'my Gaelic name', consisting of an original Scottish surname *MacDhomhnaill*, literally 'son of Donald', with conventional 'translations' of the two English names Edward = *Eadairt* and James = *Seumas*. How might this differ from the – by now far more familiar – *Mǎ Àidé* found in the following document, dating from the midpoint of my MA at Peking University?:

> Australia foreign-student *Mǎ Àidé* (Edward Mcdonald) now at apply 1991 to 1992 year Chin-Aust agreement fixed's by China government towards Australia student provide's scholarship, in order to complete he's study. Aust-side already accept he's apply, seek towards our country government recommend, now our country EduCom thus require our school about he's number two year's study express agreement, only-then can work out decide.

The process of Englishing in this case, a more informal version of the glossing used in Chapter 1, interestingly enough shows a language that sounds in some ways far more English than the 'Gaelic-English' above. The context of this short text is clearly a formal educational one, and shows my supervisor and myself, who were jointly responsible for its composition, negotiating with the educational bureaucracies of both China and Australia in order to obtain the resources to finish my studies. What this text *doesn't* show, of course, is the previous experience of sinophone contexts that allowed me to function at such a high level in sinophone society in the first place, something which I have so far not been able to achieve to anything like a comparable level in the case of Gaelic, which remains at the level of a personal and partly professional hobby (anything is grist to a linguist's mill – cf. McDonald 2008).

Interestingly enough, my grandfather, grandson himself of the Irish McDaniel who reinvented himself in Australia as a freshly minted Scottish McDonald, on at least one occasion made use of his supposedly Scottish identity in a context that can only be called a playful one. During World War II when on military service in the Middle East, he received an invitation to New Year's Eve celebrations from a colleague of the 66th British General Hospital by the name of Campbell, the traditional clan foes of the McDonalds. Both the invitation and the effusion it evoked in response are very instructive:

From a verra guid Scot to a possible bad ain:

Hast heard o' Hogmanay when the Pixies and Goblins hunt for such as ye: and when the Brose is drunk and the Haggis piped? If a true McDonald you be, the above you'll know and your footsteps this way will go. A Campbell (not black) will expect you to cross swords in Eightsome Reels, Strip the Willow, Petronella and such in the Sisters' Mess of the 66th B.G.H. on the 31st as ever was at 20.30 hours.

Reply from Lt-Col C.G. McDonald

I dinna like Campbells. When my sire dangled me on his knee he wud speak of sich as they and he wud spit oot for, said he, the wurrd left a nasty tang on the tongue. Better, said he, the worst Sassenach from ower the borrder than a trait'rous Campbell. For though, said he, the voice of a Campbell be sleekit, there is black murrder in his heart. Mind ye, said he, till the day ye dee, that accursed night in the vale o' Glencoe, when our fathers lay sleepin' and the Campbells joined with the sodgers o' the foreign King to cut the throats o' them. A murrain on the Campbells, said he, and my spittle on their hands! Do ye likewise!

This McDonald hasnae mickle desire to sort with a Campbell on Hogmanay. But perchance ye has some honest blood in ye, if your mither be a Cameron or such like. I shall accept your invitation and I thank you for it. Let it niver be said that a McDONALD showed no courtesy to a foe, e'en though it be a Campbell.

Some useful context to this grandiloquent rejoinder by my grandfather, whose very exaggerations reveal its fundamentally jovial nature, is supplied by one of his sons, my late uncle, himself a veteran of the Pacific theatre in the same war, in a letter to me:

It is wartime and the troops are largely thrown on their own resources to provide whatever light relief is available. Do you think CG penned those idiomatic phrases without help? I don't know but I doubt it. I imagine he had great fun seeking out 'experts' who could fashion the language with the authentic touch. I am not aware that back in civvy life he did anything to explore Scottish ancestry until [much later in his life].

It is clear from the above exchange that both 'Campbell' and 'McDonald' are enjoying using the ancient feud as a pretext for some mutual mock abuse – if the British officer's jibe in the title of his message, in standard English 'From a very good Scot to a possible bad one', is not simply referring to the Australian's distance from his ethnic roots – a joke which as my uncle notes probably also provided others in the camp with some 'light relief' in the harshness of the wartime context. More generally, what this exchange suggests is that ethnicity is to a certain extent 'created', just as my great-great-grandfather 'created' himself as a Scot soon after arriving in Australia.

This kind of situation seems miles away from that of the overseas Chinese described in the previous section whose ethnicity is 'forced' on them whether they like it or not, and whose lack of the linguistic marker of ethnicity is seen as undercutting the genuineness of their ethnic identity. In discussing the paradoxes of Chinese ethnicity, Ang herself places great stress on the role of '"racial" markers for Chineseness', the stereotypical '"yellow skin" and "slanty eyes"' (Ang 2001: 49), but from the histories related above, it is political and economic conditions in both the (original) 'homeland' and (new) 'home' countries that prove just as significant in determining the status of the 'ethnic'. However significant such physical markers may be in many societies, they are not in any case something over which the individual has any control. A more flexible conceptualisation of ethnicity and identity which pays greater attention to linguistic repertoire seems not only more realistic in our increasingly globalised world, but more suited to the concerns of the potential sinophone who is the focus of this book. The easiest way to explore this is to take a hint from my grandfather and do so *playfully*, to show the power of language in both building up an identity and in revealing its fundamentally relative and contingent nature.

'Dr McHorse does discourse': the discursive creation of identity

The first lesson we can draw from these individual histories of accommodation to their respective societies is that ethnicity is to a certain extent, *instrumental*: in other words, it allows people to do certain things – as well as shutting them out from other things – in their societies. In the case of my McDaniel-McDonald ancestor, his own forebears, finding their original society no longer congenial, had fled to somewhere that would accommodate their religious beliefs, one aspect of their identity they were obviously not prepared to give up. He himself, while equally attached to the old religion, found his Irish identity quite dispensable, even while culturally he and his descendants remained very much part of the Irish

Australian community, his descendants happily marrying into other Catholic and mostly Irish families.

The second lesson is that ethnicity is fundamentally *contingent*, not something set in stone for all time according to *where you have come from*, but adjustable in the light of changing circumstances according to *where you are headed*. In my own home context of an anglophone multicultural society like Australia or New Zealand, the starting point is to acknowledge that, contrary to popular under-standings and government policy alike, *everyone* is 'ethnic' of some sort, and has the right to a knowledge of and pride in their own ethnic background. While it was no doubt considerations of this sort, as well as my personal linguistic bent, that led me to explore my own Scottish heritage by taking up the study of Gaelic, I would never have felt *deprived* by not being Gaelic-speaking, and likewise, there is no reason why people of Chinese background should be made to feel guilty for not being sinophone.

At the same time, however, it needs to be acknowledged that of equal impor-tance to your native socio-cultural background, which is to a large extent given, are *the new areas you move into by choice or circumstance*. For many citizens in migrant societies such as Australia or New Zealand, these new areas are quite literally the new countries they moved to as children or adults, and the whole new repertoire of linguistic and cultural skills they have developed in order to adjust to this new context. But equally for those, of whatever background, who have chosen to become 'at home' – to use an interesting metaphor – in the language and society of another culture like the potential sinophones who are the target of this book, that process should not be regarded as a threat to, or a replacement of, your original cultural repertoire or sense of identity as much as an *extension* of it (Gao 2001). An important part of this process, again in contrast to the understand-ings of what is officially promoted as 'multiculturalism' in Australia and New Zealand, is acknowledging the existence and value of your own ethnic identity – or indeed identities – an acknowledgment that should help give you the flexibility to adjust to the different cultural choices embodied in sinophone societies.

To finish up this long journey through the building up of a sinophone identity as examined in this chapter, and as well through the construction of the whole edifice of Chinese studies as examined in this book, I would like to give a brief introduction to a sort of alter-ego of myself, developed partly in order to explore in a performative context some of the issues of identity examined here. Allow me to introduce: Dr Ned McHorse!

> Ned McHorse, born Ma Naide in the Chinese province of Henan, has a BA in Chinese literature from Yanjing University, a Masters in Communication Studies from the Sinny Uni of Scitech, and a PhD in Intercultural Studies from the University of National Importance in Cambra. Dr McHorse recently took up a position in the newly created Professional Institute for Sociological Semantics in Theorising and Actioning the Knowledge Economy where he offers courses in cross-cultural bluffing, analytical obfuscation, and

sensitive deconstruction. Dr McHorse is also currently pursuing research interests into the role of the horse in history and into ethnic identities and strategic masquerade, as well as undertaking performance interventions in academic and corporate contexts.

It should be clear that both Dr McHorse's name and his biography are a sort of distorted mirror version of my own. The details of his 'CV' are quite recognisably garbled versions of real places and institutions, and his parodic identity as *the* most Cultural studies of Cultural studies academics – an academic area in which questions of identity are part of the very definition of the field and those working within it – underline how all such details are, in the formulation of Benedict Anderson in relation to national identity, *imagined*. As human beings we 'make up' identities for ourselves from the socio-cultural mix around us, a process which in childhood in the case of our mother tongue is largely unconscious and beyond our control, but as we move into adulthood, and if and when we choose to take on another sociolinguistic repertoire such as becoming sinophone, certain elements of that identity are, or at least can be, deliberately chosen.

Of course, we don't do this in isolation from the pressures and power relations of our social context, and perhaps the best way to demonstrate this is to take one final text, Dr McHorse's 'theme song' which despite its rather aggressive tone, in its emphasis on the inextricable combination of the social and the semiotic does nevertheless sum up much of the approach put forward in this book as a whole:

McHorse the Knife (with apologies to Bert Brecht and Kurt Weill)
Now the strong ones like their power, dear
And they flaunt it, full of fight
A fine scalpel wields McHorse, dear
But he keeps it out of sight

Now the strong ones *write* their power, dear
And its discourse shakes their stick
But that tool is double-edged, dear
Ned is up to every trick.

Comes some big man, parading postures
Right to rule and all that stuff
Our friend Ned knows well his weakness
In a flash falls pomp and bluff

Power woman, so maternal
'Ma knows best' her soothing cry
Ned's keen vision tears the veil off
Her real meaning – no lullaby

Prating pollies, jingling journos
Media moguls, CEOs
Ned McHorse dissects their discourse
It's so clear they're on the nose

And so who is Ned's next victim?
Power punctured in its course?
Will *your* discourse get dissected?
Who is safe from Ned McHorse?
Your own discourse gets dissected –
No-one's safe from Ned McHorse.

I hope this little 'sermon' from Dr McHorse doesn't leave you, as it were, trembling in your sinophone boots: quite the opposite, it should give you as potential sinophone a sense of your own agency, your own ability to intervene in the discourses of the sinophone sphere. The fact that *all* discourses are constructed, that *all* identities are imagined, may initially be disconcerting for those of us who through the very working of these processes have come to accept them as natural, as givens which cannot be changed. But just like my great-great-grandfather reinventing himself in a new country, or my grandfather taking on a parodic Scottish identity in order to playfully berate an old clan foe, or myself accepting the moniker of 'Old Horse' and all the possibilities that opened up as well as the restrictions it imposed, you always retain the ability to *choose* as you make your own unique journey into the sinophone sphere. The range of competing discourses introduced in this book may seem at times to approach the level of a Babel of nonsense, or a pandemonium of demonic discord. But as the Irish anglophone–francophone author Samuel Becket commented in another context (quoted in Liu 1988: 55), acknowledging that discourse was central to human life and could not be escaped from: *Que voulez-vous, Monsieur? C'est les mots – on n'a rien d'autre.* 'What do you expect, sir? They're words – we don't have anything else.'

PRIMARY SOURCES

Primary sources already listed under References are listed here with only author, year, and title: for full publication details see References.

Chapter 1   Arguing semantics with a Beijing taxi-driver

《漫画详解三字经——千古一奇书》自如绘画，胡晓林注释，中国国际广播出版社，北京1991年

Dark Horse (2005) *Saddam, SARS, Sex*《250演播室》黑马著, unpublished MS supplied by author.

Editor's Note 卷首语，空也？色也？杨林《时尚君子》*MENBOX* 总第188期, p. 10.

Chapter 2   Gateways to becoming sinophone

Lee, Philip Yung-Kin (1993) *You Can Speak Mandarin Vol. 1.*

Xing, Janet Zhiqun (2006) *Teaching and Learning Chinese as a Foreign Language: A Pedagogical Grammar.*

National Office for Teaching Chinese as a Foreign Language/Beijing Organizing Committee for the Games of the XXIX Olympiad (2004) *Basic Chinese 100 for Beijing 2008 Olympic Games/100 phrases de chinois pour les J.O. de Beijing*, Beijing: People's Education Press. 《奥运汉语100句》中国国家对外汉语教学领导小组办公室、第29届奥林匹克运动会组织委员会合编，人民教育出版社，北京 2004 年

Chapter 3   Learning Chinese the Lee Kuan Yew way

Chua, Chee Lay (ed.) (2005) *Keeping my Mandarin Alive: Lee Kuan Yew's Language Learning Experience.*

Chapter 4   Character fetishisation

Bacon, Francis (1605/1998) *The Advancement of Learning.*

Watters, T. (1889) *Essays on the Chinese Language.*

Gilbert, Rodney (1926) *What's Wrong with China.*
Kennedy, George A. (1953a) *ZH Guide: An Introduction to Sinology.*
Hansen, Chad (1983) *Language and Logic in Ancient China.*
Liu, James J.Y. (1988) *Language – Paradox – Poetics: A Chinese Perspective.*
Graham, A.C. (1989) 'The Relation of Chinese Thought to the Chinese Language'.
Booth, Alan (1991) *Tuttle's Illustrated Guide to Japan.*
Jenner, William J.F. (1992) *The Tyranny of History: The Roots of China's Crisis.*
Boltz, William G. (1994) *The Origin and Early Development of the Chinese Writing System.*
Hodge, Bob and Kam Louie (1998) *The Politics of Chinese Language and Culture: The Art of Reading Dragons.*
Ames, Roger T. and Henry Rosemont, Jr. (1999) *The Analects of Confucius: A Philosophical Translation.*
Shen, Xiaolong (2001) 《汉语语法学：写21世纪的第一部"汉语语法学"》[Chinese Grammar: The First "Chinese Grammar" written for the 21st Century].
Chow, Rey (2001) 'How (the) Inscrutable Chinese Led to Globalized Theory'.

Chapter 5   Ideolatry versus phonolatry?

The debates

Ideography versus phonology

Creel, Herrlee Glessner (1936) 'On the Nature of Chinese Ideography'.
Pelliot, Paul (1936) 'Brèves remarques sur le phonétisme dans l'écriture Chinoise' [Brief remarks on the phonetic principle in Chinese writing], *T'oung Pao*, xxxii, 162–166.
Boodberg, Peter A. (1937) 'Some Proleptical Remarks on the Evolution of Archaic Chinese'.
Creel, Herrlee Glessner (1938) 'On the Ideographic Element in Ancient Chinese'.
Boodberg, Peter A. (1940) '"Ideography" or Iconolatry?'.

Chinese studies and the Disciplines

(a) Symposium in Chinese studies and the Disciplines

The Journal of Asian Studies, 23.4 (Aug. 1964).
Levenson, Joseph R. (1964) 'The Humanistic Disciplines: Will Sinology Do?', 507–512.
Wright, Mary C. (1964) 'Chinese History and the Historical Vocation', 513–516.
Skinner, G. William (1964) 'What the Study of China Can Do for Social Science', 517–522.
Freedman, Maurice (1964) 'What Social Science Can Do for Chinese Studies', 523–529.
Mote, Frederick W. (1964) 'The Case for the Integrity of Sinology', 531–534.
Murphey, Rhoads (1964) 'Discussant Remarks', 535–536.
'Comments by Benjamin Schwartz. The Fetish of the "Disciplines"', 537–538.

(b) Comments on the 'Chinese studies and the Disciplines' Symposium

The Journal of Asian Studies, 24.1 (Nov. 1964).
Twitchett, Denis (1964) 'A Lone Cheer for Sinology', 109–112.
Hsiao, Kung-Chuan (1964) 'Chinese Studies and the Disciplines – the Twins Shall Meet', 112–114.

Chapter 6 Keeping Chinese for the Chinese

芬君（陆诒）：《鲁迅先生访问记》，1936 年5 月 30日《救亡日报》

Shen, Xiaolong (1988a) 貌合离神：中国现代语法学的困境 [Disparity between Form and Spirit: The Dilemma of Modern Chinese Grammatical Studies].

Shen, Xiaolong (1989a) 走出麻木与悲凉 [Making our Way out of Numbness and Depression].

Shen, Xiaolong (1989b) 《人文精神还是科学注意 ？：20世纪中国语言学思辩录》 [Humanistic Spirit or Scientism?: Reflections on 20th Century Chinese Linguistics].

Song, Qiang, Zhang Zangzang and Qiao Bian (1996) 中国可以说'不' [China Can Say 'No'].

Chapter 7 Construing 'metrosexual' in Chinese

Independent, 15 November 1994, Mark Simpson 'Here Come the Mirror Men', http://www.marksimpson.com/pages/journalism/mirror_men.html

Salon.com, 22 July 2002, Mark Simpson 'Meet the Metrosexual', http://dir.salon.com/ent/feature/2002/07/22/metrosexual/

Independent on Sunday, 22 June 2003, Mark Simpson 'Metrosexual? That Rings a Bell …', http://www.marksimpson.com/pages/journalism/metrosexual_ios.html

http://www.sina.com.cn 2003年08月08日10:13 国际先驱导报，《都市玉男》构建《第三性》 http://news.sina.com.cn/w/2003-08-08/10131503620.html (accessed 4 May 2006).

Men's Health, January 2003, 最后一张底，主编 / 瘦马 《时尚健康 • For Men》2003年1月号http://www.trends.com.cn 2002-12-27 14:57 http://www.trends.com.cn/article/a/0-21738.htm (accessed 8 May 2010).

Men's Health, April 2004, 做个花样男子：四月男子美容宝典 《时尚健康》4月号 pp.174–175.

MENBOX, May 2004, 魅力型男，文 / 陈哲民 《时尚君子》（《现代文明画报》总第168期) p.10.

MENBOX, June 2004, Be A Pretty Man 《时尚君子》 男人爱美无罪（《现代文明画报》总第169期) p.2.

China Daily Website 中国日报网站 (eastday.com) Updated: 2004-05-12 09:39 A new breed of man, the 'metrosexual' http://www.chinadaily.com.cn/english/doc/2004-05/12/content_330015.htm (accessed 8 February 2006).

MENBOX, July 2004, Editor's Note: Standard City 卷首语：瞄准城市新男人，文/ 杨林 （《现代文明画报》总第171期) p.8.

Men's Health, September 2004, Special Theme: Metrosexual 特别企划，花色一代男《时尚健康》9月号 pp.50–59.

Men's Health, September 2004, 男人的美丽新世界，文 / 丛二《时尚健康》9月号 p.66.

Men's Health, December 2004, Special Theme Men News 2004 特别企划： 男色新闻：[1] 男色：社会性别角色的一场革命教育 pp.54–69；[2] 男色工场 pp.70–71；[3] 最美丽的盛宴——女权主义视角下的男色消费，文 / 周筱赟 p.72.

Men's Style, January 2005, From Editor "闷士"更精彩，文 / 王一鹏 《魅力先生》2005年1月 p.10.

Men's Style, March 2005, From Editor 成为"傻瓜"的野心，文 / 王一鹏 《魅力先生》2005年3月 p.8.

Men's Style, October 2005, Metrosexual 裘德· 洛：爱与自我 《魅力先生》2005年10月 pp.56–58.

Men's Style, October 2006, Cover Show: Metrosexual 来了！ 《魅力先生》2006年10月，pp.40–55.

Men's Style, October 2006, 好男儿梦工厂： "加油，好男儿"节目细述台前幕后！p. 56 曹可凡："好男儿"的标准是宽乏的   p.57；秋林：我们在挖掘他们自身的潜质 p.58；陈辰：这个节目把几个人的命运放大了 p.59；徐威：长相肯定会增加'好男儿'的吸引力 p.59.

Men's Style, October 2006, 美少年生产力，   文 / KYRA pp.60–61.

Chapter 8   Reconstruction versus deconstruction

Saussure, F. de. (1916/1957) *Course in General Linguistics*.

Malinowski, Bronislaw (1923) 'The Problem of Meaning in Primitive Languages'.

Firth, J.R. (1956/1968) 'Linguistics and Translation'.

Hansen, Chad (1983) *Language and Logic in Ancient China*.

Green, Peter (1989) *Classical Bearings: Interpreting Ancient History and Culture*.

Lee, Guy (1990) *The Poems of Catullus*. Edited and translated with an Introduction and Notes by Guy Lee.

Hodge, Bob and Kam Louie (1998) *The Politics of Chinese Language and Culture: The Art of Reading Dragons*.

Barmé, Geremie R. (1999) *In the Red: On Contemporary Chinese Culture*.

LG S5000 – The handset for the metrosexual male. Source: Phonedaily (Chinese) http://www.phoneyworld.com/newspage.aspx?n=1765 (accessed 8 February 2006).

多智 moto 迷人 moto 手机壁纸赏析CNET中国 • PChome.net • 投稿 作者: Xphone 责编:李汝欣   时间:2007-06-07   http://new.product.pchome.net/article/content-374547.html (accessed 9 May 2010).

Barmé, Geremie R. (2005) 'On New Sinology'.

Fitzgerald, John (2005) 'The New Sinology and the End of History'.

Chapter 9   From 'Ed McDonald' to 'Ned McHorse'

Ang, Ien (2001) *On Not Speaking Chinese: Living between Asia and the West*.

Yang, William (1996) *Sadness*.

Ho, Ruth (1975) *Rainbow Round my Shoulder*.

SUGGESTIONS FOR FURTHER READING

The works given below, listed chronologically, are gleaned from a very long list, and in most cases represent recent or particularly influential works; in many cases they contain bibliographies that can be used to follow up the relevant issues. For certain chapters, works have been grouped under relevant subheadings.

Chapter 1   Arguing semantics with a Beijing taxi-driver

Clissold, Tim (2004) *Mr China*, London: Constable and Robinson.
Hessler, Peter (2006/2007) *Oracle Bones: A Journey between China and the West*, London: John Murray. Hardback edition, New York: HarperCollins, 2006.
Zhou, Raymond (2008) *X-Ray: Examining the China Enigma*, Beijing: China Intercontinental Press.
Coughlan, Chia-Mei Jane (2008) *The Study of China in Universities: A Comparative Case Study of Australia and the United Kingdom*, Amherst NY: Cambria.
Hessler, Peter (2010) *Country Driving: A Journey Through China from Farm to Factory*, New York: HarperCollins.

Chapter 2   Gateways to becoming sinophone

Language teaching

Chu, Madeline (ed.) (1999) *Mapping the Course of the Chinese Language Field*, Chinese Language Teachers Association Monograph Series, Vol. III, Kalamazoo MI: Chinese Language Teachers Association Inc.
Larsen-Freeman, Diane (2000) *Techniques and Principles in Language Teaching*, 2nd edition, Oxford: Oxford University Press.
McDonald, Edward (2008) 'Review of "Teaching and Learning Chinese as a Foreign Language. A Pedagogical Grammar" [Xing 2006]', *Electronic Journal of Foreign*

Language Teaching, 2008, Vol. 5, Suppl. 1, pp. 174–176, http://e-flt.nus.edu.sg/v5sp12008/rev_mcdonald.htm

陆俭明 (2010) 进一步以科学态度对待汉语教材编写 《第九届国际汉语教学研讨会论文选》高等教育出版社, 北京 2010年.

Modern versions of traditional readers

Simon, W. (1957) *1200 Basic Chinese Characters: An Elementary Text Book Adapted from the 'Thousand Character Lessons'*, 3rd revised edition, London: Lund Humphries. 《中英對照平民千字課》

[Beijing Municipal Women's Federation, Beijing Association of Marriage and Family Studies] (1995) *Trimetrical Verses on Family Relationships with Illustrations*. Dedicated to the Fourth World Conference on Women, Beijing, 1995, Beijing: Tongxin Press. 《家庭伦理漫画三字经》北京市妇女联合会北京市婚姻家庭研究会编，王复羊绘画，同心出版社，北京1994年

Descriptions of Modern Standard Chinese relevant for language learning

Kratochvíl, Paul (1968) *The Chinese Language Today: Features of an Emerging Standard*, London: Hutchinson.

Kane, Daniel (2006) *The Chinese Language: Its History and Current Usage*, Tokyo: Tuttle.

Pedagogical grammar of Chinese

Teng, Shou-hsin (1977) *A Basic Course in Chinese Grammar: A Graded Approach Through Conversational Chinese*, San Francisco: Chinese Materials Center.

Marney, John (1977) *A Handbook of Modern Chinese Grammar*, San Francisco: Chinese Materials Center.

McDonald, E. (1999) 'Teaching Grammar through Text: An Integrated Model for a Pedagogical Grammar of Chinese', *Journal of the Chinese Language Teachers Association*, 34.2, 91–120.

Chapter 3   Learning Chinese the Lee Kuan Yew way

Some reviews of Keeping My Mandarin Alive and other news reports

读《学语致用》想到的， 李清（中国）《人民日报》，2005年8月2日，第十六版 http://www.globalpublishing.com.sg/forumpl/020805x.html (accessed 13 July 2009).

老师谈新加坡资政李光耀：好学华文而不倦   http://news.xinhuanet.com/overseas/2005-05/08/content_2928903.htm (accessed 13 July 2009).

Insistence on bilingualism in early years of education policy was wrong: MM Lee by Hoe Yeen Nie, Channel NewsAsia | Posted: 17 November 2009 2142 hrs http://www.channelnewsasia.com/stories/singaporelocalnews/view/1018826/1/.html (accessed 22 November 2009).

Second language learning and multilingualism

Chao, Yuen Ren (1976) *Aspects of Chinese Socio-linguistics: Essays by Yuen Ren Chao*. Selected and introduced by Anwar S. Dil. Stanford: Stanford University Press.

Bialystock, Ellen and Kenji Hakuta (1994) *In Other Words: the Science and Psychology of Second-Language Acquisition*, New York: Basic Books.

Edward, John (1994/1995) *Multilingualism*, London: Routledge. Republished 1995, Harmondsworth: Penguin.

Cruz-Ferreira, M. (2010). *Multilinguals Are ...?* London: Battlebridge Publications.

Standard language and dialects

Kratochvíl, Paul (1973) 'The Norm and Divided Chinese', *Journal of the Chinese Language Teachers Association*, 8.2, 62–69.

Yan, Margaret Mian (2006) *Introduction to Chinese Dialectology*. LINCOM Studies in Asian Linguistics, Munich: Lincom Europa.

Spoken and written language

Li, Charles N. and Sandra A. Thompson (1982) 'The Gulf Between Spoken and Written Language: A Case Study in Chinese', in Deborah Tannen (ed.) *Spoken and Written Language: Exploring Orality and Literacy*, Norwood, NJ: Ablex.

Halliday, M.A.K. (1989) *Spoken and Written Language*, 2nd edition, Oxford: Oxford University Press.

Political background of Singapore

Chua, Beng-Huat (1995) *Communitarian Ideology and Democracy in Singapore*, London: Routledge.

Mauzy, Diane K. and R.S. Milne (2002) *Singapore Politics Under the People's Action Party*, London: Routledge.

Chapter 4   Character fetishisation and
Chapter 5   Ideolatry versus phonolatry?

Karlgren, Berhnard (1923) *Sound and Symbol in Chinese*, Oxford: Oxford University Press.

T'sou, Benjamin (1981) 'A Sociolinguistic Analysis of the Logographic Writing System of Chinese', *Journal of Chinese Linguistics*, 9.1, 1–19.

Mungello, David E. (1986) *Curious Land: Jesuit Accommodation and the Origins of Sinology*, Stuttgart: Franz Steiner.

Norman, Jerry (1988) *Chinese*, Cambridge: Cambridge University Press.

Tao, Hongyin (1996) *Units in Mandarin Conversation: Prosody, Discourse, and Grammar*, Amsterdam: Benjamins.

Saussy, Haun (2001) *Great Walls of Discourse and Other Adventures in Cultural China*, Harvard East Asian Monographs 212, Cambridge MA: Harvard University Asia Center.

Erbaugh, Mary S. (2002) *Difficult Characters: Interdisciplinary Studies of Chinese and Japanese Writing*. Volume 6 of Pathways to Advanced Skills series, Columbus OH: Ohio State University National East Asian Languages Resource Center.

Lurie, David B. (2006) 'Language, Writing and Disciplinarity in the Critique of the "Ideographic Myth": Some Proleptical Remarks', *Language and Communication*, 26, 250–269.

Hayot, Eric, Haun Saussy and Steven G. Yao (eds) (2008) *Sinographies: Writing China*, Minneapolis, MN: University of Minnesota Press.

McDonald, Edward (2009) 'Getting over the Walls of Discourse: "Character Fetishization" in Chinese Studies', *Journal of Asian Studies*, 68.4 (November), 1189–1213.

Chapter 6 Keeping Chinese for the Chinese

DeFrancis, John (1950/1972) *Nationalism and Language Reform in China*, Princeton, NJ: Princeton University Press. Reprinted New York: Octagon Books.

Seybolt, Peter J. and Gregory Kuei-ke Chiang (eds) (1979) *Language Reform in China – Documents and Commentary*, White Plains, NY: Sharpe.

DeFrancis, John (1984) *The Chinese Language: Fact and Fantasy*, Honolulu, HI: University of Hawaii Press.

Spence, Jonathan D. (1998) *The Chan's Great Continent: China in Western Minds*, New York: Norton.

《21世纪的华语和华文：周有光耄耋文存》周有光著，三联书店，北京2002年

McDonald, E. (2002) '"Humanistic Spirit or Scientism?": Conflicting Ideologies in Chinese Language Reform', *Histoire, Epistemologie, Langage*, 24/2. *Politiques linguistiques*, 1/2, 51–74.

Liu, Lydia H. (2004) *The Clash of Empires: The Invention of China in Modern World Making*, Cambridge, MA: Harvard University Press.

Mungello, David E. (2009) *The Great Encounter of China and the West, 1500–1800*, 3rd edition, Lanham, MD: Rowman & Littlefield.

Chapter 7 Construing 'metrosexual' in Chinese

Simpson, Mark (1994) *Male Impersonators: Men Performing Masculinity*, London: Cassell.

Louie, Kam (2002) *Theorising Chinese Masculinity: Society and Gender in China*, Oakleigh, Victoria: Cambridge University Press.

Louie, Kam and Morris Low (eds) (2003) *Asian Masculinities: The Meaning and Practice of Manhood in China and Japan*, London: Routledge.

Song, Geng (2004) *The Fragile Scholar: Power and Masculinity in Chinese Culture*, Hong Kong: Hong Kong University Press.

Louie, Kam (ed.) (2008) *The Cambridge Companion to Modern Chinese Culture*, Cambridge: Cambridge University Press.

Song, Geng and Tracy K. Lee (2010) 'Consumption, Class Formation and Sexuality: Reading Men's Lifestyle Magazines in China', *The China Journal*, 64 (July), 159–177.

Chapter 8 Reconstruction versus deconstruction

Halliday, M.A.K. and Ruqaiya Hasan (1985) *Language, Context and Text: Aspects of Language in a Social-Semiotic Perspective*, Geelong, Victoria: Deakin University Press.

Goody, Jack (1998) *Food and Love: A Cultural History of East and West*, London: Verso.

Honey, David. B. (2001) *Incense at the Altar: Pioneering Sinologists and the Development of Classical Chinese Philology*, New Haven, CT: American Oriental Society.

van Leeuwen, Theo (2005) *Introducing Social Semiotics*, London: Routledge.

Barmé, Geremie R. (2008) 'Worrying China & New Sinology', *China Heritage Quarterly*, No.14 http://www.chinaheritagequarterly.org/articles.php?searchterm=014_worryingChina.inc&issue=014 (accessed 10 May 2010).

Kress, Gunther (2009) *Multimodality: A Social Semiotic Approach to Communication*, London: RoutledgeFalmer.

Rudd, Kevin (2010) 'Australia and China in the World', 70th Morrison Lecture, Australian National University, Canberra, 23 April 2010. http://www.pm.gov.au/node/6700 (accessed 10 May 2010).

Chapter 9   From 'Ed McDonald' to 'Ned McHorse'

Identity, ethnicity, nationality

Smith, Anthony D. (1986) *The Ethnic Origins of Nations*. Oxford: Blackwell.

Anderson, Benedict (1991) *Imagined Communities: Reflections on the Origin and Spread of Nationalism*, revised edition, London: Verso.

O'Farrell, Patrick James (2000) *The Irish in Australia: 1788 to Present*, 3rd edition, Sydney: University of New South Wales Press.

Kildea, Jeff (2002) *Tearing the Fabric: Sectarianism in Australia 1910–1925*, Sydney: Citadel Books.

Kanno, Yasuko and Bonny Norton (2003) 'Imagined Communities and Educational Possibilities: Introduction', *Journal of Language, Identity, and Education*, 2.4, 241–249.

Lo Bianco, Joseph, Jane Orton and Gao Yihong (eds) (2009) *China and English: Globalisation and the Dilemmas of Identity*, Bristol: Multilingual Matters.

Family history: Australia, Ireland, Scotland

Windsor, Gerard (1991) *Family Lore*, Port Melbourne, Victoria: Minerva.

Allison, Hugh G. (2004) *Roots of Stone: The Story of Those Who Came Before*, Edinburgh: Mainstream.

REFERENCES

Ames, Roger T. and Henry Rosemont, Jr. (1999) *The Analects of Confucius: A Philosophical Translation*, New York: Ballantine Books.

Ang, Ien (2001) *On Not Speaking Chinese: Living between Asia and the West*, London: Routledge.

Bacon, Francis (1605/1998) *The Advancement of Learning*. Renascence Editions, an Online Repository of Works Printed in English between the Years 1477 and 1799 http://www.luminarium.org/renascence-editions/adv1.htm

Bai, Limin (2005) *Shaping the Ideal Child: Children and their Primers in Late Imperial China*, Hong Kong: The Chinese University Press.

Barmé, Geremie R. (1999) *In the Red: On Contemporary Chinese Culture*, New York: Columbia University Press.

—— (2005) 'On New Sinology', *Chinese Studies Association of Australia Newsletter*, No.3. May 2005; also at http://rspas.anu.edu.au/pah/chinaheritageproject/newsinology/index.php

Barmé, Geremie R. and Linda Jaivin (1992) *New Ghosts, Old Dreams: Chinese Rebel Voices*, New York: Times Books.

Barmé, Geremie R. and John Minford (1986) *Seeds of Fire: Chinese Voices of Conscience*, Hong Kong: Far Eastern Economic Review. Second edition 1988, New York: Hill & Wang.

Bauer, Robert S. (1988) 'Written Cantonese of Hong Kong', *Cahiers de Linguistique Asie Orientale*, 17.2, 245–293.

Bloomfield, Leonard (1933) *Language*, New York: Henry Holt.

Bo, Yang (1992) *The Ugly Chinaman and the Crisis of Chinese Culture*. Translated and edited by Don J. Cohn and Jing Qing, North Sydney, NSW: Allen & Unwin.

Boltz, William G. (1994) *The Origin and Early Development of the Chinese Writing System*, New Haven, CT: American Oriental Society.

Boodberg, Peter A. (1937) 'Some Proleptical Remarks on the Evolution of Archaic Chinese', *Harvard Journal of Asian Studies*, 2: 329–372.

Boodberg, Peter A. (1940) '"Ideography" or Iconolatry?', *T'oung Pao*, xxxv: 266–288.

Booth, Alan (1991) *Tuttle's Illustrated Guide to Japan*, Tokyo: Charles E. Tuttle.

Buruma, Ian and Avishai Margalit (2004) *Occidentalism: A Short History of Anti-Westernism*, London: Atlantic.

Catford, J.C. (1988) *A Practical Introduction to Phonetics*. Reprinted with corrections 1994, Oxford: Oxford University Press.

Chao, Yuen Ren (1948) *Mandarin Primer*, Cambridge, MA: Harvard University Press.

—— (1968) *A Grammar of Spoken Chinese*, Berkeley, CA: University of California Press.

—— (1976) 'My Linguistic Autobiography' in Anwar S. Dil (ed.) *Aspects of Chinese Sociolinguistics: Essays by Yuen Ren Chao*, Stanford, CA: Stanford University Press, pp.1–20.

Chappell, Hilary (ed.) (2004) *Sinitic Grammar: Synchronic and Diachronic Perspectives*, Oxford Linguistics, Oxford: Oxford University Press.

Chen, Ping (1999) *Modern Chinese: History and Sociolinguistics*, Cambridge: Cambridge University Press.

Chen, Wangdao (ed.) (1939/1987) *Zhōngguó wénfǎ géxīn lùncóng* 中国文法革新论丛 [Collection of Papers on Renewing Grammar], Beijing: Commercial Press.

Chomsky, Noam (1965) *Aspects of the Theory of Syntax*, Cambridge, MA: MIT Press.

Chou, Fa-Kao (1959–1962) *Zhōngguó gǔdài yǔfǎ* 中国古代语法 [The Grammar of Old Chinese], Taipei: Academia Sinica.

Chow, Rey (2001) 'How (the) Inscrutable Chinese Led to Globalized Theory', *Proceedings of the Modern Language Association of America*, Special Topic: Globalizing Literary Studies, 116.1, 69–74.

Chua, Chee Lay (ed.) (2005) *Keeping my Mandarin Alive: Lee Kuan Yew's Language Learning Experience*. Singapore: World Scientific & Global Publishing.

Clissold, Tim (2004) *Mr China*, London: Constable and Robinson.

Coe, Michael D. (1992) *Breaking the Maya Code*, New York: Thames and Hudson.

Cook, H.P. (tr.) (1938) *Aristotle: De Interpretatione*, London: Loeb Classical Library,

Creel, Herrlee Glessner (1936) 'On the Nature of Chinese Ideography', *T'oung Pao*, xxxii, 85–161.

—— (1938) 'On the Ideographic Element in Ancient Chinese', *T'oung Pao*, xxxiv, 265–294.

Creel, Herrlee Glessner, Chang Tsung-Ch'ien and Richard C. Rudolph (1938–1952) *Literary Chinese by the Inductive Method*, Chicago, IL: University of Chicago Press, Vols 1–3.

Davis, A.R. (1985) *In Search of Love and Truth*, Sydney, NSW: University of Sydney Centre for Asian Studies.

Deacon, T.W. (1997) *The Symbolic Species: Language and the Evolution of the Human Brain*, Harmondsworth: Penguin.

DeFrancis, John (1950/1972) *Nationalism and Language Reform in China*, Princeton, NJ: Princeton University Press. Reprinted New York: Octagon Books.

—— (1984) *The Chinese Language: Fact and Fantasy*, Honolulu, HI: University of Hawai'i Press.

—— (1989) *Visible Speech: The Diverse Oneness of Writing Systems*, Honolulu, HI: University of Hawai'i Press.

de Laclos, Choderlos. (1782/1961) *Les Liaisons dangereuses*. Translated and with an introduction by P.W.K. Stone, Harmondsworth: Penguin.

Derrida, Jacques (1974) *Of Grammatology*. Translated by Gayatri Chakravorty Spivak, Baltimore, MD: Johns Hopkins University Press.

Dunbar, Robin (1996) *Grooming, Gossip and the Evolution of Language*, London: Faber & Faber.

Du Ponceau, Peter S. (1838) 'A Dissertation on the Nature and Character of the Chinese System of Writing', *Transactions of the Historical and Literary Committee of the American Philosophical Society*, Vol. 2.

Ellis, John M. (1993) *Language, Thought and Logic*, Evanston, IL: Northwestern University Press.

Elman, Benjamin A. (1984) *From Philosophy to Philology: Intellectual and Social Aspects of Change in Late Imperial China*, Cambridge MA: Harvard University Press.

Erbaugh, Mary S. (2002) *Difficult Characters: Interdisciplinary Studies of Chinese and Japanese Writing*, Volume 6 of Pathways to Advanced Skills series, Columbus, OH: Ohio State University National East Asian Languages Resource Center.

Fairclough, Norman (1989) *Language and Power*, London: Longman.

—— (1992) *Discourse and Social Change*, Cambridge: Polity Press.

—— (1995) *Critical Discourse Analysis: The Critical Study of Language*, London: Longman.

Fei, Jinchang (ed.) (1997) *Zhōngguó yǔwén xiàndàihuà bǎinián jìshì* 中国语文现代化百年记事 [A Chronicle of a Century of Language Modernization in China], Beijing: Language Press.

Fenellosa, Ernest and Ezra Pound (1920/1936) *The Chinese Written Character As a Medium for Poetry*. Originally published in *Instigations*, 1920, London; reprinted 1936, San Francisco, CA: City Lights.

Finocchiaro, Mary and Christopher Brumfit (1983) *The Functional-Notional Approach: From Theory to Practice*, Oxford: Oxford University Press.

Firth, J.R. (1956/1968) 'Linguistics and Translation' in F.R. Palmer (ed.) *Selected Papers of J.R. Firth 1952–1959*. London: Longman, pp. 84–95.

Fitzgerald, John (2005) 'The New Sinology and the End of History', *Chinese Studies Association of Australia Newsletter* No. 32. November 2005; also at http://www.csaa.org.au/news11.05.html#TheNewSinologyandtheendofhistory

Fitzgerald, Stephen (1997) *Is Australia an Asian Country? Can Australia Survive in an East Asian Future?* St Leonards, NSW: Allen & Unwin.

Foucault, Michel (1969) *L'Archéologie du Savoir. The Archaeology of Knowledge*, translated by A.M. Sheridan Smith, London: Routledge, 2002.

Gabelentz, H.G. von der (1881) *Chinesische Grammatik* [Chinese Grammar], Leipzig: Wiegel.

Gao, Mingkai (1948) *Hànyǔ yǔfǎ lùn* 汉语语法论 [On Chinese Grammar]. Revised edition 1957, Shanghai: Kaiming Shudian.

Gao, Yihong (ed.) (1997) *Collected Essays of Shen Xiaolong on Chinese Cultural Linguistics*, Changchun: Northeast Normal University Press.

—— (2001) *Foreign Language Learning: "1+1>2"*, Beijing: Peking University Press.

George, T.J.S. (1973) *Lee Kuan Yew's Singapore*, London: Deutsch.

Gilbert, Rodney (1926) *What's Wrong with China*, London: John Murray.

Goodman, David S.G. (2000) 'Review of *The Politics of Chinese Language and Culture: The Art of Reading Dragons*', *Social Semiotics*, 10.1, 125–126.

Graham, A.C. (1989) 'The Relation of Chinese Thought to the Chinese Language', Appendix 2 in *Disputers of the Tao*, La Salle: Open Court Publishing, pp.389–428.

Green, Peter (1989) *Classical Bearings: Interpreting Ancient History and Culture*, London: Thames & Hudson.

Gregory, Michael (1967) 'Aspects of Varieties Differentiation', *Journal of Linguistics*, 3, 177–198.

Halliday, M.A.K. (1956) 'Grammatical Categories in Modern Chinese'. *Transactions of the Philological Society*, pp.421–492.

—— (1959) *The Language of the Chinese 'Secret History of the Mongols'*, Publications of the Philological Society XVII, Oxford: Basil Blackwell.

—— (1961) 'Categories of the Theory of Grammar', *Word* 17.3, 241–292. Reprinted in Jonathan J. Webster (ed.) *The Collected Works of M.A.K. Halliday, Vol. 1: On Grammar*, London: Continuum, pp.37–93.

—— (1967–1968) 'Notes on transitivity and theme in English', *Journal of Linguistics* 3.1, 3.2, 4.2.

—— (1973) 'Towards a Sociological Semantics' in *Explorations in the Functions of Language*, London: Arnold, pp.72–102. Reprinted in Jonathan Webster (ed.) (2003) *Collected Works of M.A.K. Halliday, Vol. 3, On Language and Linguistics,* London: Continuum, pp. 223–354.

—— (1977) 'Ideas about Language', *Aims and Perspectives in Linguistics*, Applied Linguistics Association of Australia, Occasional Papers 1, 32–39. Reprinted in Jonathan Webster (ed.) (2003) *Collected Works of M.A.K. Halliday, Vol. 3, On Language and Linguistics,* London: Continuum, pp. 92–115.

—— (1978) *Language as Social Semiotic: The Social Interpretation of Language and Meaning*, London: Edward Arnold.

—— (1985) 'Part A' in Halliday, M.A.K. and Ruqaiya Hasan (1985).

—— (1990) 'A Systemic Interpretation of Peking Syllable Finals' in Paul Tench (ed.) *Studies in Systemic Phonology*, London: Pinter, pp. 98–121. Reprinted in Jonathan J. Webster (ed.) (2006) *The Collected Works of M.A.K. Halliday, Vol. 8 Studies in Chinese Language*, London: Continuum, pp.294–323.

—— (1993) 'Systemic Grammar and the Concept of a Science of Language', in Zhu, Yongsheng (ed.) *Language, Text, Context: Papers from the Second Chinese Conference on Systemic Functional Grammar*, Beijing: Tsinghua University Press, pp.1–22. Reprinted in Jonathan J. Webster (ed.) (2003) *The Collected Works of M.A.K. Halliday, Vol. 3 On Language and Linguistics*, London: Continuum, pp. 199–212.

Halliday, M.A.K. and Ruqaiya Hasan (1985) *Language, Context and Text: Aspects of Language in a Social-Semiotic Perspective*, Geelong, Victoria: Deakin University Press.

Halliday, M.A.K. and Edward McDonald (2005) 'Metafunctional Profile of the Grammar of Chinese' in A. Caffarel, C.M.I.M. Mathiessen, and J.R. Martin (eds) *Language Typology: A Functional Perspective*, Amsterdam: Benjamins, pp. 305–396.

Halliday, M.A.K., A. McIntosh and P. Strevens (1964) *The Linguistic Sciences and Language Teaching*, London: Longmans.

Hannas, William. C. (1997) *Asia's Orthographic Dilemma* with a foreword by John DeFrancis, Honolulu, HI: University of Hawai'i Press.

—— (2003) *The Writing on the Wall: How Asian Orthography Curbs Creativity*, Philadelphia, PA: University of Pennsylvania Press.

Hansen, Chad (1983) *Language and Logic in Ancient China*, Ann Arbor, MI: University of Michigan Press.

Hasan, Ruqaiya (1985) 'Part B' in Halliday, M.A.K. and Ruqaiya Hasan (1985).

Hasan, Ruqaiya and Peter Fries (eds) (1995) *Subject and Theme: A Discourse Functional Perspective*, Amsterdam: Benjamins.

Ho, Ruth (1975) *Rainbow Round my Shoulder*, Singapore: Eastern Universities Press.

Hodge, Bob and Gunther Kress (1988) *Social Semiotics*, Cambridge: Polity.

Hodge, Bob and Kam Louie (1998) *The Politics of Chinese Language and Culture: The Art of Reading Dragons*, London: Routledge.

Honey, David. B. (2001) *Incense at the Altar: Pioneering Sinologists and the Development of Classical Chinese Philology*, New Haven, CT: American Oriental Society.

Hu, Zhuanglin, Zhu Yongsheng, Zhang Delu and Li Zhanzi (2005) *Xìtǒng gōngnéng yǔyánxué gàilùn* 系统功能语言学概论   [An Overview of Systemic Functional Linguistics], Beijing: Peking University Press.

Huang, Chichung (tr.) (1997) *The Analects of Confucius (Lun Yu)*. A literal translation with an Introduction and Notes by Chichung Huang, Oxford: Oxford University Press.

Hymes, D.H. (1971) *On Communicative Competence*, Philadelphia, PA: University of Pennsylvania Press.

International Phonetic Association (1999) *Handbook of the International Phonetic Association: A Guide to the Use of the International Phonetic Alphabet*, Cambridge: Cambridge University Press.

Jenner, William J.F. (1992) *The Tyranny of History: The Roots of China's Crisis*, London: Allen Lane.

Johnston, Trevor and Adam Schembri (2007) *Australian Sign Language: An Introduction to Sign Language Linguistics*, Cambridge: Cambridge University Press.

Karlgren, Bernhard (1926) *On the Nature and Authenticity of the Tso Chuan*, Goteborgs Hogskolas Arsskrift XXXII. Reprinted 1968, Taipei: Cheng-Wen.

Keane, Michael (1999) 'Review of *The Politics of Chinese Language and Culture: The Art of Reading Dragons*' , *Media International Australia, Incorporating Culture & Policy*, No. 91, May, 180–181.

Kennedy, George A. (1951) 'The Monosyllabic Myth', *Journal of the American Oriental Society*, 71.3. Reprinted in Kennedy (1964), pp.104–118.

—— (1953a) ZH Guide: *An Introduction to Sinology*, New Haven: Sinological Seminar, Yale University.

—— (1953b) 'Reviews of Books: *Literary Chinese by the Inductive Method*, Vol. III; *The Mencius*, Books I-III; *Talks on Chinese History* (Junggwo Lishr Jyanghwa); *Ch'ing Documents. An Introductory Syllabus*', *Journal of the American Oriental Society*, 73.1, 27–30.

—— (1958) 'Fenellosa, Pound and the Chinese Character', *Yale Literary Magazine* 126.5. Reprinted in Kennedy (1964), 443–462.

—— (1964) *Selected Works of George A. Kennedy*. Edited by Tien-yi Li, New Haven, CT: Far Eastern Publications Yale University.

Kildea, Jeff (2006) '"Where Crows Gather": The Sister Liguori Affair 1920–21', *Journal of the Australian Catholic Historical Society*, 27, 31-40. Also at http://findarticles.com/p/articles/mi_hb4815/is_27/ai_n29313550/

Kipling, Rudyard (1902) *Just So Stories for Little Children*, London: Macmillan.

Kress, Gunther and Bob Hodge (1979) *Language as Ideology*, London: Routledge. Second edition 1993.

Kress, Gunther and Theo van Leeuwen (1990) *Reading Images*, Geelong, Victoria: Deakin University Press.

Kress, Gunther and Theo Van Leeuwen (1996) *Reading Images – the Grammar of Visual Design*, London: Routledge.

Kuhn, Thomas (1962/1970) *The Structure of Scientific Revolutions*, International Encyclopedia of Unified Science, Vol.2 No.2, Chicago, IL: University of Chicago Press. Second edition 1970.

Ladefoged, Peter (2001) *Vowels and Consonants: An Introduction to the Sounds of Languages*, Malden MA: Blackwell.

Lee, Guy (1990) *The Poems of Catullus*. Edited and translated with an Introduction and Notes by Guy Lee. Oxford World's Classics, Oxford: Oxford University Press.

Lee, Philip Yung-Kin (1993) *You Can Speak Mandarin Vol. 1*, Sydney: Harcourt Brace.

Levenson, Joseph R. (1964) 'The Humanistic Disciplines: Will Sinology Do?', *Journal of Asian Studies*, 23.4, 507–512.

Li, Charles N. and Sandra A. Thompson (1976) 'Subject and Topic: A New Typology of Language' in C.N. Li (ed.) *Subject and Topic*, New York: Academic Press, pp.458–489.

Li, Jinxi (1924) *Xīnzhù Guóyǔ Wénfǎ* 新著国语文法 [A New Grammar of the National Language], Shanghai: Commercial Press.

Li, Rong (1952) *Běijīng Kǒuyǔ Yǔfǎ* 北京口语语法 [Grammar of Spoken Pekingese]. Translation of Chao (1948), Part One: Introduction, Beijing: Kaiming Shudian.

Liu, James J.Y. (1962) *The Art of Chinese Poetry*, Chicago, IL: University of Chicago Press.

—— (1988) *Language – Paradox – Poetics: A Chinese Perspective*, Princeton NJ: Princeton University Press.

Liu, Xun, Deng Enming and Liu Shehui (1981) *Practical Chinese Reader* 刘珣, 邓恩明, 刘社会编著; 李培元审订《实用汉语课本》北京语言学院 出版社, 北京2010年.

Logan, Robert K. (1986) *The Alphabet Effect: The Impact of the Phonetic Alphabet on the Development of Western Civilization*, New York: William Morrow.

—— (2004) *The Alphabet Effect: A Media Ecology Understanding of the Making of Western Civilization*, The Hampton Press Communication Series: Media Ecology, Cresskill, NJ: Hampton Press.

Loke, Kit-Ken (2002) 'Approaches to the Teaching and Learning of Chinese: A Critical Literature Review and a Proposal for a Semantic, Cognitive and Metacognitive Approach', *Journal of the Chinese Language Teachers Association*, 37.1, 65–112.

Louie, Kam (2002) *Theorising Chinese Masculinity: Society and Gender in China*, Oakleigh, Victoria: Cambridge University Press.

Lu, Jianming (2010) *Jìnyíbù yǐ kēxué tàidù duìdài hànyǔ jiàocái biānxiě* 进一步以科学态度对待汉语教材编写 [Take a More Scientific Attitude Towards the Writing of Chinese Textbooks]《第九届国际汉语教学研讨会论文选》高等教育出版社, 北京 2010年.

Lü, Shuxiang (1942/1990) *Zhōngguó wénfǎ yāolüè* 中国文法要略 [An Outline of Chinese Grammar] *Collected Works of Lü Shuxiang*, Vol. 1, Beijing: Commercial Press.

Lu, Xun in Fen Jun (Lu Yi) (1936) *Lǔ Xùn Xiānshēng fǎngwèn jì* [Notes on interviewing Mr Lu Xun], *Jiuwang Ribao*, 30 May.

Lurie, David B. (2006) 'Language, Writing and Disciplinarity in the Critique of the "Ideographic Myth": Some Proleptical Remarks', *Language and Communication*, 26, 250–269.

Ma, Jianzhong (1898/1953) *Mǎshì Wéntōng* 马氏文通 [Mr Ma's Compleat Grammar], Beijing: Commercial Press.

McDonald, Edward (1995) 'Zhōngguó wénhuà yǔyánxué yùndòng hé hànyǔ de běnzhì: guóqíng de xīn biǎoxiàn?' 中国文化语言学运动和汉语的本质：国情的新表现? [The Chinese Cultural Linguistics Movement and the Nature of Chinese: A New Manifestation of 'National Characteristics'?], *Northern Forum*, 4, 91–104.

—— (2000) 'Review of Hodge and Louie 1998', *Modern Chinese Literature and Culture*, 12.1, Spring, 209–217.

—— (2008) *Meaningful Arrangement: Exploring the Syntactic Description of Texts*, London: Equinox.

—— (2009) 'Getting over the Walls of Discourse: "Character Fetishization" in Chinese Studies', *Journal of Asian Studies*, 68.4, 1189–1213.

Mair, Victor (1991) 'What Is a Chinese 'Dialect/*Topolect*'? Reflections on Some Key Sino-English Linguistic Terms', *Sino-Platonic Papers*, 29, September 1991, 1–31.

—— (1997) 'Ma Jianzhong and the Invention of Chinese Grammar', *Studies on the History of Chinese Syntax*, *Journal of Chinese Linguistics*, Monograph Series No.10, 5–26.

Malinowski, Bronislaw (1923) 'The Problem of Meaning in Primitive Languages', Supplement I in C.K. Ogden and I.H. Richards *The Meaning of Meaning*, London: Routledge & Kegan Paul, pp.296–336.

Mathews, R.H. (1931) *A Chinese-English Dictionary Compiled for the China Inland Mission by R.H. Mathews*, Shanghai: China Inland Mission and Presbyterian Mission Press. Republished 1943, *Mathews' Chinese-English Dictionary*, Cambridge MA: Harvard University Press.

Menzies, Gavin (2002) *1421: The Year China Discovered the World*, London: Bantam.

Mitchell, T.F (1975) *Principles of Firthian Linguistics*, London: Longman.

Mote, Frederick W. (1964) 'The Case for the Integrity of Sinology', *Journal of Asian Studies*, 23.4, 531–534.

Mullie, J. (1932) *The Structural Principles of the Chinese Language: An Introduction to the Spoken Language (Northern Pekingese Dialect)*, Vol. 1, Peiping: The Bureau of Engraving and Printing.

Mungello, David E. (1986) *Curious Land: Jesuit Accommodation and the Origins of Sinology*, Stuttgart: Franz Steiner.

Parker, Dorothy (1931/1973) 'Review of Theodore Dreiser: *Dawn*', originally published in 'The Constant Reader' column in *The New Yorker*, 30 May 1931. Reprinted in *The Penguin Dorothy Parker*, Harmondsworth: Penguin, pp. 540–544.

Pierce, C.S. (1931–1958) *Collected Writings*. Charles Harthorne, Paul Weiss and Arthur W. Burks (eds), Cambridge MA: Harvard University Press.

Pound, Ezra (1934/1951) *ABC of Reading*, London: Faber.

Reischauer, Edwin O. and John K. Fairbank (1948) 'Understanding the Far East through Area Study', *Far Eastern Survey*, 17.10, 121–123.

Robins, R.H. (1951) *Ancient and Mediaeval Grammatical Theory in Europe*, London: G. Bell & Sons.

—— (1997) *A Short History of Linguistics*, Fourth edition, Longman Linguistics Library, London: Longman.

Said, Edward (1978) *Orientalism: Western Conceptions of the Orient*, New York: Pantheon. Revised edition 1995, London: Penguin.

Sampson, Geoffrey (1985) *Writing Systems: A Linguistic Introduction*. Stanford, CA: Stanford University Press.

Sapir, Edward (1921) *Language: An Introduction to the Study of Speech*, New York: Harcourt, Brace & Co.

Saussure, F. de. (1916/1957) *Course in General Linguistics*. Translated by Wade Baskin, New York: McGraw-Hill.

Saussy, Haun (2001) *Great Walls of Discourse and Other Adventures in Cultural China*, Harvard East Asian Monographs 212, Cambridge MA: Harvard University Asia Center.

Shen, Xiaolong (1984) 'Hànyǔ yǔyán lèixíng de xīn tànsuǒ: lùn zhǔtíjù yánjiū de yǔyán lèixíngxué yìyì' 汉语语言类型的新探索：论主题句研究的语言类型学意义 [A New Investigation into the Typology of Chinese: Topic-Comment Sentences and their Typological Significance], *Journal of Fudan University*, 6, 143–164. English translation in Gao (ed.) (1997).

—— (1988a) 'Mào-hé-lí-shén: Zhōngguó xiàndài yǔfǎxué de kùnjìng' 貌合离神：中国现代语法学的困境 [Disparity between Form and Spirit: The Dilemma of Modern

Chinese Grammatical Studies], *Yuwen Xuexi* 语文学习1988.1, 40–42. English translation in Gao (ed.) (1997), 1–11.

—— (1988b) *Zhōngguó jùxíng wénhuà* 中国句型文化 [Chinese Sentence Patterns and their Cultural Explanations], Changchun: Northeast Normal University Press.

—— (1989a) *Zǒuchū mámù yǔ bēiliàng* 走出麻木与悲凉 [Making our Way out of Numbness and Depression], *Shulin* 书林1989.2, 14–17. English translation in Gao (ed.) (1997), 347–362.

—— (1989b) *Rénwén jīngshén háishi kēxué zhǔyì?: 20 shìjì Zhōngguó yǔyánxué sībiànlù* 《人文精神还是科学注意?: 20 世纪中国语言学思辩录 》 [Humanistic Spirit or Scientism? Reflections on 20th Century Chinese Linguistics], Shanghai: Xuelin.

—— (2001) *Hànyǔ yǔfǎxué: xiě gěi 21 shìjì de dìyībù 'Hànyǔ yǔfǎxué'* 《汉语语法学: 写21世纪的第一部"汉语语法学"》 [Chinese Grammar: The First 'Chinese Grammar' Written for the 21st Century], Nanjing: Jiangsu Education Press.

Shlain, Leonard (1998) *The Alphabet Versus the Goddess: The Conflict between Word and Image*, New York: Viking Penguin.

Simpson, Mark (2003) 'Metrosexual? That Rings a Bell …', *Independent on Sunday*, 22 June 2003. http://www.marksimpson.com/pages/journalism/metrosexual_ios.html

Skinner, G. William (1964) 'What the Study of China Can Do for Social Science', *The Journal of Asian Studies*, 23.4, 517–522.

Slingerland, Edward (tr.) (2003) *Confucius: Analects. With Selections from Traditional Commentaries*, Indianapolis, IN: Hackett.

Song, Qiang, Zhang Zangzang and Qiao Bian (1996) *Zhōngguó kěyǐ shuō 'bù'* 中国可以说'不' [China Can Say 'No'], Beijing: Chinese Industry and Commercial Joint Press.

Song, Xiaojun, Wang Xiaodong, Huang Jisu, Song Qiang and Liu Yang (2009) *Zhōngguó bù gaoxìng* 中国不高兴 [Unhappy China – lit. China isn't Happy], Nanjing: Jiangsu People's Press.

Stern, H.H. (1983) *Fundamental Concepts of Language Teaching*, Oxford: Oxford University Press.

Sun, L.-K. (2001) 'Review of *The Politics of Chinese Language and Culture: The Art of Reading Dragons*, by Bob Hodge and Kam Louie', *China Journal*, 45/46, 216–217.

Sweet, Henry (1899/1972) *The Practical Study of Languages*, London: Oxford University Press.

Ting, Yen Ren (1987) 'Foreign Language Teaching in China: Problems and Perspectives' Special issue: Chinese Educators on Chinese Education, edited by Ruth Hayhoe, *Canadian and International Education*, 16.1, 48–61.

Titone, Renzo (1968) *Teaching Foreign Languages: An Historical Sketch*, Washington, DC: Georgetown University Press.

Twitchett, Denis (1964) 'A Lone Cheer for Sinology', *The Journal of Asian Studies*, 24.1, 109–112.

Unger, J. Marshall (2004) *Ideogram: Chinese Characters and the Myth of Disembodied Meaning*, Honolulu, HI: University of Hawai'i Press.

Ure, J. (1971) 'Lexical Density and Register Differentiation' in G. Perren and J.L.M. Trim (eds) *Applications of Linguistics: Selected Papers of the Second International Congress of Applied Linguistics, Cambridge, 1969*. Cambridge: Cambridge University Press, 443–452.

van Leeuwen, Theo (1999) *Speech, Music, Sound*, London: Macmillan.

von Däniken, Erich (1971) *Chariots of the Gods? Unsolved Mysteries of the Past*. Translated by Michael Heron, New York: Bantam Books.

von Wilamovitz-Moellendorf, U. (1921/1982) *History of Classical Scholarship*. Translated by Alan Harris, edited by Hugh Lloyd-Jones, London: Duckworth.

Waley, Arthur (tr.) (1938) *The Analects of Confucius*. Translated and annotated by Arthur Waley, London: Allen & Unwin.

Walton, A. Ronald (1989) 'Chinese Language Instruction in the United States: Some Reflections on the State of the Art', *Journal of the Chinese Language Teachers Association*, Vol. X, May 1989, 1–42.

Wang, Li (1944/1985) *Zhōngguó xiàndài yǔfǎ* 中国现代语法 [Modern Chinese Grammar], Beijing: Commercial Press.

Watters, T. (1889) *Essays on the Chinese Language*, Shanghai: Presbyterian Mission Press.

Whitney, William Dwight (1875) *The Life and Growth of Language*, London: King.

Wright, Mary C. (1964) 'Chinese History and the Historical Vocation', *Journal of Asian Studies*, 23.4, 513–516.

Xing, Janet Zhiqun (2006) *Teaching and Learning Chinese as a Foreign Language: A Pedagogical Grammar*, Aberdeen, Hong Kong: Hong Kong University Press.

Yang, William (1996) *Sadness*, St Leonards, NSW: Allen & Unwin.

Zhan, Xuzuo and Zhu Liangzhi (1995) *Zuòwéi wénhuà quèzhèng de hànzì* 作为文化确证 的汉字 [Graphology and Culture: How Chinese Characters Verify Beliefs and Ideologies], *Journal of Oriental Studies*, XXXIII.1, 76–94.

Zhou, Youguang (2001) 'Language Planning of China: Accomplishments and Failures' Special Issue: Language Management and Language Problems: Part II, *Journal of Asian Pacific Communication*, 11.1, 9–16.

INDEX